GOD'S MAN
FOR THE GILDED AGE

BRUCE J. EVENSEN

GOD'S MAN
for the GILDED AGE

D. L. Moody and the Rise
of Modern Mass Evangelism

UNIVERSITY PRESS

2003

OXFORD
UNIVERSITY PRESS

Oxford   New York
Auckland   Bangkok   Buenos Aires   Cape Town   Chennai
Dar es Salaam   Delhi   Hong Kong   Istanbul   Karachi   Kolkata
Kuala Lumpur   Madrid   Melbourne   Mexico City   Mumbai   Nairobi
São Paulo   Shanghai   Taipei   Tokyo   Toronto

Copyright © 2003 by Bruce J. Evensen

Published by Oxford University Press, Inc.
198 Madison Avenue, New York, New York 10016

www.oup.com

Oxford is a registered trademark of Oxford University Press

Library of Congress Cataloging-in-Publication Data

Evensen, Bruce J.
God's man for the Gilded Age : D.L. Moody and the rise of modern mass evangelism /
Bruce J. Evensen.
p. cm.
Includes bibliographical references and index.
ISBN 0-19-516244-7
1. Moody, Dwight Lyman, 1837–1899. 2. Evangelistic work—United
States—History—19th century. 3. Mass media—Religious
aspects—Christianity—History—19th century. I. Title.
BV3785.M7E94 2003
269'.2'092—dc21   2003042041

All figures are courtesy the Moody Bible Institute, Chicago.

2 4 6 8 9 7 5 3 1

Printed in the United States of America
on acid-free paper

For Uncle Rudy,

who walked beside me

when Christ came calling

CONTENTS

GOD'S MAN

FOR THE GILDED AGE

"Some day you will read in the papers that D. L. Moody of East Northfield is dead," Moody often said, anticipating his own epitaph. "Don't you believe a word of it! At that moment I shall be more alive than I am right now." The passing of the 62-year-old lay evangelist on the eve of the twentieth century was as big a news story as the Gilded Age campaigns he successfully waged across urban America.

The End

ONE

MOODY IN NORTHFIELD, DECEMBER 1899

T he end was apocalyptic and variously reported. "The world is receding and heaven opening," the dying man was supposed to have said, although accounts differed. "I see earth receding; Heaven is opening; God is calling me," other newspapers reported to their readers. D. L. Moody had always been greatly annoyed whenever he was misquoted. Perhaps that was why he wrote his own epitaph before the press in his sixty-second year wrote one for him. "Some day you will read in the papers that D. L. Moody of East Northfield is dead," he had long been famous for saying. "Don't you believe a word of it! At that moment I shall be more alive than I am now." His son would use the statement on the eve of a new century to begin his biography of one of the most beloved men of the previous century. "I shall have gone up higher," Moody wanted his readers to know, "that is all, out of this old clay tenement into a house that is immortal—a body that death cannot touch; that sin cannot taint; a body fashioned like unto His glorious body." Moody spoke to an estimated one hundred million souls in little more than a quarter century's ministry on both sides of the Atlantic, reportedly reducing the population of hell by a million in doing so. At his death, he was one of the best-known and most widely quoted men of the Gilded Age. He had fashioned a news release he gave to all the papers in all the cities where he went to work. It amounted to this: "I was born of the flesh in 1837. I was born of the

Spirit in 1856. That which is born of the flesh may die. That which is born of the Spirit will live forever."[1]

The 62-year-old Massachusetts-born shoe salesman with a fourth-grade education had been in the midst of revival work in Kansas City when congestive heart failure forced him to reluctantly give up his pulpit. "I have had trouble with my heart for a good many years," he confided to the press, as a special car was outfitted for his comfort along the Wabash Railroad. Moody's failure to preach "with the old-time energy and power" had led to speculation in the press that he might be gravely ill, but he wouldn't hear of it. "There is nothing alarming about my condition," he said reassuringly, despite published reports that trains east of Chicago were being rerouted "to hurry his car homeward in the shortest possible time."[2] The press appeared at every stop along the way. In Detroit, as Moody's train awaited a car ferry to carry it across to Windsor and the end of the Grand Trunk Line, Moody's personal physician told reporters and well-wishers that his famous patient was "tired and nervous" but was "resting nicely now, stretched out in an invalid's chair in the smoking compartment." The doctor gave orders there were to be no interviews with reporters or anyone else. That had not stopped the press from spreading the sad news nationwide that Moody might not recover. Readers everywhere were alarmed. William Jennings Bryan, the Democratic Party's former and future presidential nominee, wrote Moody that he had "read with sorrow of your sickness" and prayed that the great revivalist's "recovery may be speedy and permanent." Booker T. Washington thought "Moody's work is of lasting value to all races." That was why nine-year-old Lenore B. Anthony of El Dorado Springs, Missouri, spoke for many when she said she "couldn't bear picking up the paper and reading that you are very sick" and would pray for Moody's complete recovery.[3] Moody's secretary was under orders not to excite the evangelist with news from well-wishers. A nationwide vigil began, the press soon reported, on behalf of "God's man for the Gilded Age." It led many to hope that Moody might still recover for a nation that desperately needed him.[4] Moody was quoted as saying that he would recover if the Lord willed it, but his many admirers couldn't bear the uncertainty. Charles Blanchard, the president of Wheaton College, went so far as to say that Moody was "a little mistaken in his view" if he didn't agree with those eager to see him stay. Blanchard had no doubt "Satan is seeking to destroy" the servant God had lifted up. Walter Douglas, general secretary of Philadelphia's Young Men's Christian Association (YMCA), an organization long championed by Moody, believed there was "no man living in the United States" who could be taken away at greater cost than Moody. Frederick del Booth Tucker, the U.S. commander of the Salvation Army, thought that was why "the Lord will spare your life for many years of increased usefulness." The Yoke Beavers Bible Class of Syracuse was among the many that felt the same way. M. B. Williams of Shenandoah, Iowa, thought it inconceivable that the Lord would take a man such as Moody before he finished his "earthly pilgrimage." That was why Arthur Long of West Philadelphia, Pennsylvania, "searched the paper this morning and every morning to catch a glimpse of some word from you."[5]

Moody feared that reports in the press had frightened his family and friends. He cabled home on November 17 saying that "the doctor thinks I need rest" and a day later that he was "improving rapidly" and "hadn't felt so well for a week." He wired home from Montpelier, Ohio, later that day insisting that he had "had a splendid day." He had "no fever, no pain," and his heart was "growing stronger all the time." Moody told his wife "I am taking good care of myself, not only for loved ones, but for the work that I think God has for me to do on this earth."[6] The press shared this sentiment. The *New York Times* was exclusively reporting that "Moody had eaten a hearty breakfast" and "is improving." Editorial writers, however, feared Moody's "phenomenal career" might be over. The *Chicago Tribune* thought "no one is better known in this country and more highly esteemed." Moody had become "a household name" as a "simple earnest man" who for more than a quarter of a century had "placed his hand upon the shoulder of his audience and talked to it as one friend talks to another." The paper had long championed Moody's crusade work, his schools for needy boys and girls, and his training centers for men and women preparing to follow him into ministry. That was why its editors could think of no man since John Wesley "who has exercised a more potent moral influence" or been "a greater power for good."[7]

As Moody's train neared his boyhood home of East Northfield, Massachusetts, church leaders across the nation led their congregations in prayer that their hero would live to see the twentieth century, even if there was some uncertainty when it began. "The church of the Twentieth Century will take its stand more firmly than ever on the great, soul-comforting truth of a supernatural book," said one. The Higher Criticism had had its day, said another. Moody's "pure and undefiled" ministry had powerfully demonstrated "the masses need for pardon" and their restless search "to find a cleansing fountain." For 40 years Moody had shown that way in his work as a revivalist, and later as an evangelical publisher and educator. "Now the hope is universally felt," the secular press was reporting, that God would again raise up His prophet "to this generation."[8] The nationally syndicated *Christian Herald* had "stopped the presses and changed the electrotypes," hoping to give "the earliest and widest circulation" to Moody's request that "Christian people pray for him." John Wanamaker, the Philadelphia department store king and former postmaster general, wired his lifelong friend: "anxious how you are and if I can do anything." A quarter century earlier, the two men had been central to the great Philadelphia campaign of America's centennial year. Now, a Wanamaker family–owned newspaper, the *Philadelphia North American*, cabled the gravely ill evangelist that "Mr. Wanamaker will regard it as a favor if you will wire to the *North American* a statement concerning your condition." Ira D. Sankey, the gospel singer who teamed with Moody in staging their great evangelistic campaigns of the 1870s, well knew Moody's power in publicity and didn't know what to believe about the true state of his health. He sent Moody a clipping from a New York newspaper whose November 22 headline claimed: "Moody Improves Fast." He wrote from New York City, hoping it was true, while wondering whether "it would be too much for you to see an old friend."[9]

By the first week of December, Moody was still not seeing any visitors, leading friends and the press on both sides of the Atlantic to fear the worst. Britain's leading evangelical weekly, the *Christian*, which had been more responsible than any journal in building Moody's reputation when he came to England in the summer of 1873 as a relative unknown, begged Moody's family for "a word of information" that would serve "some consolation for our many readers."[10] J. Wilbur Chapman had become a "hero worshipper" of Moody as a young man after reading "exciting accounts" of Moody's big-city spectacles in the Gilded Age press. The two men had worked together at the Chicago World's Fair of 1893 and in building the educational institutions that marked Moody's emphasis in later years. Chapman told Moody that "the whole Christian world waited anxiously for favorable news from Northfield." Chapman thought Moody "a master in moving men." In one of two dozen book-length appreciations that appeared in the months after Moody's death, Chapman would argue that Moody "reached more people during his lifetime than any other man, possibly in the world's history."[11] That this was so owed much to Moody's mastery of the press and his exquisite use of the twin powers of prayer and publicity. Moody's press aide Will C. Howland had seen each at work. "Moody realized the power of the press as few men do," Howland told the *Congregationalist*. It became central "to the work of spreading the gospel. He never ran to the press with personals. The papers ran after him." Press tables were always front row center at Moody's many meetings with his evangelistic team, who were well aware of the deadline pressures reporters always faced. Moody made certain that their wishes were always gratified "so long as he could use them for the good of the cause." He drew the line only at posing for artists. "No, I can't let you take my picture," he would tell them. "That would be preaching Moody and not Jesus Christ."[12] It was a distinction lost on many in the press, whose stories saw Moody and not the Spirit at the center of the civic spectacles that filled seats and sold newspapers across the Gilded Age.

Daily medical bulletins were reporting by mid-December that Moody's health had deteriorated and his condition was now considered critical. The family's physician, P. N. Wood, confided to reporters that Moody's "extremities are swelling" and "albuminuria has appeared." On the basis of that report, some in the press speculated that Moody was suffering from Bright's disease and had "little hope of recovery," although Wood never said so. Frederick C. Shattuck, professor of clinical medicine at Harvard, consulted on the case and was reported "quite hopeful of ultimate recovery," even as many in the press were predicting that "Mr. Moody is likely to die within a few days." The *Broadway Tabernacle Tidings*, remembering the evangelist's unparalleled success at bringing Gotham to its spiritual senses a quarter century earlier, spoke for many when it said: "When we consider the size and number of the audiences that Mr. Moody addressed, the marvel is, not that his heart broke down at the age of sixty-two, but that it did not collapse many years ago. Had there been less blood in his veins," it reported, "there would have been less fire in his sermons."[13] It was difficult, however, for many to imagine a world without Moody. He seemed "such a primitive and elemental man" with "a tremendous capacity for work," a "general so full of life and hope" with "a genius for bringing things to pass," that it seemed impossible that he would not again be in his pulpit. The neighboring *Springfield* (Mass.) *Republican* remembered him there: "Standing before his audiences, a stout man, with no physical grace, a large head, abundant hair, that well-trimmed brown beard, growing grayer year by year; his eyes bright, though not large, his swaying motion as he spoke, like a bird springing to flight, a light, high-pitched voice, given to earnest and downright talk, when his moment had come."[14]

In the week that remained of his life, D. L. Moody staged one last, highly publicized fight to live. Doctors reported "a little improvement" and then "steady gains," leading friends and family to hope he would recover. Fans were heartened to hear Moody tell his family: "If God has more work for me to do, I'll not die." It was difficult for many to imagine that God hadn't more work for the man who Scottish religious leader and lecturer Henry Drummond had said had exceeded every other man "in uniting man to God and in restoring men to their true center." That achievement made Moody in Drummond's view "the greatest man I have ever met."[15] The press was reporting that Moody's family had been told he "soon might be out and about." But in the early morning hours of December 22, his energies ebbing, Moody came to realize "the end was near." He told his doctors to stop treatment, "for it is only prolonging the suffering of those who are dear to me." He called his wife, two sons, and a daughter to his bedside for what one later described as his "triumphant march into heaven."[16]

The press, particularly in those communities that Moody had evangelized in his big-city sweep of the 1870s, were quick to record that celestial procession. "The death of Brother Moody," the *Chicago Tribune* lamented, was "a great grief in this great, bustling, worldly city," which he had long called home. As head of the infant YMCA in the 1860s, Moody had greatly annoyed the paper's Presbyterian publisher, Joseph Medill, by his frequent visits to *Tribune* offices in behalf of Christian causes. The city's leading daily thought Moody an overly aggressive "self-seeker" then, but his success and sincerity eventually changed all that. Medill was now dead—preceding Moody to the pearly gates by nine months—so his surviving editors could now enlarge on this history, claiming that the paper had "discovered" Moody and "shared him with the world." Although he had not seen "the whole of the truth" that presumably the paper and its class of business readers saw, Moody did champion a truth that was "the corner-stone of salvation" by "an earnestness so great and a personal appeal so forcible that everyone felt Moody was talking to him alone."[17]

The strictly Sabbatarian *Chicago Daily News*, published by Victor Lawson, a devout Norwegian Lutheran, got Moody's age wrong but his reputation right in celebrating "the greatest lay preacher and evangelist of this or any other time." Lawson had reportedly rededicated his life to Christian service at a Moody meeting in the city 23 years earlier, and had "the closest personal knowledge of the man and his work." Moody had come to Chicago in 1856 as a 19-year-old New England farm boy who hoped to make a lot of money in the boot business in the fastest-growing city in America. Within three years he became a leader among laymen in the city's YMCA and organized a mission school to the city's poorest children. He stopped selling shoes, slept in church basements, and dined on cheese and crackers. Lawson thought that "energy" and "zeal" set Moody apart for Christian service and later gave him "a strange power the press called magnetism" that was "absolutely unique in the modern religious world."[18]

Thousands of mourners converged on the tiny hamlet of East Northfield, Massachusetts, the day after Christmas in 1899 to pay their final respects to Moody. Press coverage suggested the funeral of a head of state. Thirty-two students from the evangelist's Mount Hermon School carried the body, on an oblong ebony-colored bier 30 feet long and 12 feet wide, from the modest frame home where he lived and died to a local Congregational Church. There those long associated with the life of "the lion of the age" offered their tributes. Among them was Moody's veteran coworker the singer Ira Sankey, who had been an anonymous and ill-paid Internal Revenue Service agent, living in New Castle, Pennsylvania, when he had first met Moody at a YMCA convention in Indianapolis in the summer of 1870. Three years later the two men and their young wives, with barely a cent in their pockets, sailed to England for the start of revival work that would make both men household names on both sides of the Atlantic.[19]

It had been an amazing adventure that was now being commemorated in memorial services across America. In Boston, the site of the highly publicized New England revival of 1877, Moody was likened to Lincoln. "American boys in the next century," listeners were assured, "should study the lives of a model patriot and its preacher of righteousness." Chicago was certain that even Emerson would admit that "here lies a Christian!"[20] The *New York Sun*, a reluctant convert to Moody's cause, now praised the dead revivalist as "a master of men. His strong, bearded face, round head, thick neck and big burly body with short fat hands and feet all went with the type of the gladiator of trade or politics, who neither asked nor gave quarter." He was Tennyson's man who "made by force his merit known."[21] Philadelphia found the "irrepressible" evangelist "the dominant personality of the English-speaking religious world." December 22 may have been the shortest day of the year, but "to Dwight L. Moody its dawn ushered in that day that knows no night." Thousands who gathered in Association Hall were told "though he made no inventions and had no discoveries, though he wrote no poems, painted no pictures and led no triumphant armies, the unlettered son of a poor widow in New England who has been carried to his grave made an impression on the world that this dying century has seldom seen."[22]

Mountain ivy and holly covered every inch of the evangelist's simple grave atop Round Top, a spot with a commanding view across the foothills of the Connecticut River valley. In the days that followed, scores of visitors came to the site, leaving flowers in their wake. It was becoming apparent, reported the *New York Times*, that "the death of no man now living could so greatly stir the hearts and minds of so great a multitude on both sides of the ocean." The paper had puffed Moody when he staged his famous crusade in America's centennial year in P. T. Barnum's old Hippodrome. "No man in modern times," it thought, "had come nearer the standard" set by Christ in proclaiming the gospel. The *Herald* shared the sentiment. "No man living," it felt certain, "has made more friends."[23] In Brooklyn, where Moody and Sankey began their Gilded Age campaign across America, even the Plymouth Church now sang Moody's praises. Twenty-four years before, its sin-stained celebrant Henry Ward Beecher had taken Moody's measure and not been sure what all the excitement was about. His successor, Newell Dwight Hillis, thought Beecher's preaching "an orchestra of many instruments" and Moody "a trumpet of narrow range." But it was a rush of brass, when heralded in the press of the period, "that sounded the advance." In those days Moody admittedly was "the leader of a flying band, who went everywhere in the enemy's country," as "a friend of the common people" and as "an advocate for reaching the country's great unchurched masses."[24]

It had been in another country, however, that Moody's name first became widely known. There, the London *Telegraph* spoke for many when it lamented Moody's loss. "Our bishops have back of them a state income, great cathedrals and a small army of paid helpers and musicians," it reported. "But where our bishops have reached tens, this man has reached thousands." London's *Evening News* thought it impossible "to exaggerate Moody's phenomenal success" in moving masses.[25] The *Manchester Guardian* well remembered Moody's "remarkable" mission to Britain, starting in the summer of 1873, although his Yankee pertinacity had greatly irked the paper then. It now admitted that "the secret of his magnetic charm was not apparent on the surface." His "educational deficiencies seemed so great," it had once thought, that "he appeared unlikely to be of much service in propagandistic work." To have made that cursory assessment, the paper now admitted, was to miss that Moody was "deeply in earnest" and able to surround himself with workers who were equally so. As a result, Moody "addressed more people and spoke to larger audiences than any man of the nineteenth century."[26]

Twenty-six years earlier, only six souls had come out to see the 36-year-old evangelist when he arrived in Britain. The press that had ignored him then acknowledged now that he "had been a powerful force for good" even if his "denunciations sometimes seemed extreme." He had "done his best" to leave the century "better than he found it" and had succeeded beyond everyone's early estimation other than his own. Moody appeared to put the lie to "the wise men who are telling us that Christianity is played out." Moody's methods of evangelism, including his citywide spectacles of faith and men in action seemed to show that "the old-fashioned gospel message" had "lost none of its power" and in the hands of a cooperative press had gained even greater reach.[27] As Moody's reputation began to grow in Britain, old-timers recalled, publicity preceded his appearance in succeeding cities. That press release told a personal story that became widely reported and well known. It began with his birth on February 5, 1837, "in the lovely little valley of Northfield in New England." Then followed the early death of his father, a stonemason, and the continuing efforts of his proud mother, "a woman of singular capacity to rein him and his siblings in."[28] The narrative of his life had Moody "carving out his own career in the world" through his own energy and intuition, first as a clerk in his uncle's Boston shoe store and later as a dogged recruiter for the YMCA in

Chicago. The same insistence that Moody had shown in selling shoes, obituary writers would say, explained his ability to persuade Britain's evangelical leaders to join him in a holy crusade to save their island from its sins. He "worked heroically," as Belfast's Protestant press saw it, "with a genius for organization." Moody lived to see "his method of evangelism become a system," the *Glasgow Herald* said. The city became the site of perhaps Moody's greatest triumph. There was something "intensely American" in the man, the paper found, in his optimism and in his "gospel of hope that quaintly influenced large masses of men for the better" while inspiring them to a better life." The "Pool of Bethesda," the paper preached, was stirred "by a Yankee whose faithful following and influence" approached that of Wesley and George Whitefield.[29]

Moody's success was not without its critics. Queen Victoria heartily disapproved of Moody's methods of stirring up the populace through the press to religious excitement. Some editorial offices were equally antagonized. "Moody was not a mission adapted to every taste," the self-consciously snobbish *London Daily News* had found in 1875 and insisted even at his death. His capacity to nightly pack London's large Agricultural Hall had admittedly been a "sensation." More than one million heard him there. "A rural ignorance and roughness," the paper sniffed at the time, was behind his "bumptious conceit," which may have entertained the masses but made him "totally unfit for cultivated society."[30] Moody did, indeed, seem the least likely of men to move the masses. His early inability to articulate his faith had led Congregational elders in Boston to reject his petition for membership. His initial efforts at evangelization in Chicago were met with chagrin. Church fathers there asked him to remain silent and to take his unfettered enthusiasm to street children. He did. The outcome was a congregation of street urchins so large that even Abraham Lincoln came to have a look. Once he was on the revival trail, not a single stenographer on either side of the Atlantic could keep up with him. As his fame and following grew, secretarial staffs would work in relays, picking up gaps in syntax and grammar that required the blue pencil of more than an occasional co-pyeditor. He admitted he was the least of all laymen likely to command such crowds. It made the careful chronicling of his journey through the Gilded Age one of the great stories of the century and the century of celebrity evangelism that would come.

R. A. Torrey would live to follow Moody's footsteps without capturing his following. Billy Sunday and Billy Graham would do that. As head of the Chicago Bible Institute, founded by Moody and soon to bear Moody's name, Torrey told mourners at Moody's graveside that the great man's death had made "life on earth a little less real" and "the life of heaven more real." It was a sentiment widely shared in the North American cities that marked the start of his unrelenting campaign to use something old and something quite new—the power of prayer and the power of publicity—in bringing the continent to its spiritual senses. "Thousands in Philadelphia are poorer for his going," the *Ledger* reported, remembering the time he came to the centennial city. "They are richer for his life and will bless him in all eternity for the message that they heard here," it announced. The modern world required "re-civilizing," the city's *Evening Bulletin* had observed at the close of Moody's meetings in that city a quarter century earlier. New times required "new methods," and Moody's success had given many the hope that the "uncertain and onward sweep of progress" might yet continue through Christianity. "The immense force of Moody's zeal," the *North American* noted, in an age of religious indifference, had strangely "kindled cooler men to sympathetic action."[31] "The greatness in the man," the Boston press found at his funeral, was "a conviction that never halted" and was ever needed. "I would rather be D. L. Moody dead and in his grave," they acknowledged in a widely quoted remark, "than any man now living."[32]

Wendell Phillips has written "how cautiously men sink into nameless graves, while now and then one forgets himself into immortality." That view would have applied well to D. L. Moody, the unexpected evangelist. What follows is the story of how an ordinary man of modest gifts and Old-World inclinations helped revolutionize religion in America. By building on the foundations set by Whitefield and by Charles Grandison Finney in colonial and rural America, Moody helped harness the power and reach of modern mass media to serve the cause of mass evangelism in the first days of the modern era. As a child of revival, I am a descendent of this revolution. In the spring of 1962, I was one of the 704,900 individuals to attend Billy Graham's evangelistic campaign in Chicago's old McCormick Place and was one of the 16,597 who came forward to express a personal need for a savior.[33] My personal pilgrimage followed weeks of press accounts of Graham's meetings that magnified their outreach and seized the attention of my family. We came out of curiosity just as thousands of others did. It was part of the preevent planning and organization of the Billy Graham Evangelistic Society that was patterned on the late Gilded Age work of D. L. Moody. In 1954, as Graham was beginning to build his reputation by retracing Moody's steps in Britain, he admitted to "standing on the foundations that Moody had laid" that were "everywhere apparent." Moody's work had "changed the entire religious structure of a nation," Graham observed, and with it the future of big-city evangelism.[34]

By millennium's end, technology had evolved so that Graham could preach to the wired world via satellite from a single small studio. Moody would have greatly admired this outcome. In his day, the sense that something significant was happening had to be built brick by brick in preevent planning, preparation, prayer, and publicity. This book is an account of how revival became a mass media campaign, begun anonymously and innocuously in the summer of 1873 an ocean away, and how it created a space and set a standard for revival work on this side of the Atlantic ever since. In Moody's world and since, the sacred and the profane have been mixed to serve mighty purposes and each others' interests. Moody needed the publicity, and the press needed a good story. Their transaction, however, was not without cost, as Moody reluctantly came to understand. Religion would be played in the nation's press as civic spectacle, commodifying belief and making Moody a spiritual celebrity, something he both resisted and resented. Moody's campaign machinery sought to use the press in publicizing spiritual activity. However, it had the inadvertent effect of making Moody the star of the show. The spectacle drew rave reviews from circulation managers in search of a good story at a time of acute economic panic and from readers and worshippers who in city after city had never seen anything like it. In chronicling Moody's use of the press and their use of him, the historical intersection of mass media and popular religion comes into view, and with it a glimpse of modern America.

"*Expecting a Blessing of Unusual Magnitude*"

TWO

MOODY IN BRITAIN, JUNE 1873–AUGUST 1875

When the little-known Chicago evangelist D. L. Moody arrived in Liverpool, England, on June 17, 1873, the local press considered it less significant than the story of a ship's captain who had been fired for assaulting a steward "over pastry improperly cooked." When he left the same city two years and two months later after preaching all over England, Scotland, and Ireland, Moody was celebrated as God's man for the Gilded Age, the greatest evangelist in the English-speaking world.[1] When "arousing preachers" of other times had to be content "with apathy where they did not meet approbrium," the circuit of Moody and his colaborers in the United Kingdom resembled "a triumphant tour." Although the "round-shouldered, beetle-browed" former shoe salesman appeared "very much like other men," editorial writers in city after city were constrained to admit that there was "no parallel in the religious history of Britain" to what Moody had done.[2] Everywhere the press reported "a great anxiety to be present" at Moody's overflow meetings, a widespread understanding that "we are passing through a marvelous experience"—one that in sheer numbers seemed to swamp the outpouring of religious conversion that had marked the Reformation.[3]

The adulation was not entirely hyperbolic. When Billy Graham launched his crusade in the British Isles 81 years later, he met "everywhere" people eager to tell him that they had been converted in

D. L. Moody and Ira Sankey arrived in Britain in June 1873 as anonymous American evangelists. When they left two years later, the press portrayed Moody as "God's man for the Gilded Age."

Moody's meetings. Bible schools and missions founded by Moody still stood. Christian leaders continued to mark their evangelical calendars "before" and "after" Moody. To their minds and his many converts in the press, Moody would be remembered as the man who "changed the entire religious structure" of a nation.[4] Such success was hardly anticipated by the handful of people who attended Moody's meetings in Britain in 1867 and 1870. Moody's eagerness to stir the spiritual sentiments of Britons initially failed to find a following. The poorly organized exercises were haphazard and underpublicized and were all but ignored in the press. A speaking tour in Manchester in 1872 fared even worse. Only six people came to see one of Moody's midday services. Twenty-two came that evening. On the return trip home, Moody clung to his berth, desperately seasick, and wondered whether God wanted him to be a full-time revivalist.[5]

AN OSTENTATIOUS SELF-SEEKER

For more than a decade D. L. Moody's ministry with Chicago's YMCA and the city's poor had won him space and increasing respect from a press corps skeptical of what they initially saw as "Crazy Moody's self-promotion." The tendency of the young evangelist to burst into the offices of Chicago's newspapers and insist that they publicize his work among the orphans and destitute of the city pegged him as "an ostentatious self-seeker" determined to disturb the status quo. Moody grist received scant attention in the city's press in the years before the Civil War, when he was a man in his early twenties just starting out in life. Moody's nuisance stories were sure to head the sacrificial list of pieces never appearing in print on a heavy news day.[6] Moody's work among the poor, however, received national attention when John Farwell, a politically connected merchant whom Moody knew through the YMCA, arranged to have President-elect Abraham Lincoln visit Moody's 1,500-member Sunday School in Chicago's North Market Hall Mission.[7]

The National Week of Prayer and Fasting at the close of the war prompted a revival to break out at the noon prayer meetings of Chicago's YMCA. Local newspapers found it a difficult story to cover. They wondered whether the overflow crowds were Moody's doing or that of the Holy Spirit. The compromise course was to report Moody's "hastening of a movement believed begun by influences above human agency." As the excitement deepened through January 1866, Moody's meetings jumped off the "Religious Intelligence" sections of the Chicago press and into "City News." The *Chicago Tribune* justified the leap by acknowledging that "on all ordinary occasions" religious activity merited modest attention in the secular press. But the current excitement, it wrote, rivaled the religious passion of the "Great Awakening" and "could no longer be properly ignored."[8]

The following year Moody met evangelical leaders in Britain, setting the stage for the success of his 1873–75 campaign there. He visited the office of R. C. Morgan, editor and publisher of the *Revivalist*, a leading evangelical weekly. He sat at the feet of George Williams, a London wholesale draper and founder of the YMCA, and he traveled to Bristol to shake the hand of George Muller, the man who ran the largest orphanage in England. At Exeter Hall on the Strand he spoke before an audience that included Lord Shaftesbury, a man known for his support of evangelical causes. In South London, he met Charles Spurgeon, England's great preacher, and attended a service at the 5,000-seat Metropolitan Tabernacle. In West London he prayed on the floor of a carriage with a wholesale butcher named Henry Varley, whose preaching as a Plymouth Brother packed a local mission hall. In Dublin he reluctantly extended an invitation to a pimply-faced Lancashire lad to "come to Chicago and preach for me." The man was Harry Moorhouse, a converted pickpocket and "gutter snipe," who would soon make headlines as England's powerful "boy preacher."[9]

Returning home, Moody experimented with techniques and texts learned from Moorhouse and some of his own invention, seeking always to "unlock the power that lies buried in the church" and to bring men and women to it. A public appeal to fund a missionary to serve prisoners in the County Jail drew positive publicity and a large subscription, as did editorial support for the right of the YMCA to conduct open-air meetings after "a gang of local toughs" stoned a speaker and closed the organization down.[10] The destruction of the YMCA's meeting rooms by fire, first in 1867 and then in the Great Fire of 1871, launched Moody's campaign to attract investors in a rebuilding project that would include, for the first time, the largest lending library in the city. The effort solidified his relationship with philanthropists like Farwell, George Armour, the meat-packing king, and Cyrus McCormick of reaper fame and strengthened his ties with Joseph Medill and the Chicago newspaper establishment. The continued publication of his own paper, *Heavenly Tidings*, a weekly adapted to Sunday School and mission work, seemed to symbolize the certainty that the city would survive its fiery ordeal and furthered Moody's reputation as "an up and comer" who "gets things done."[11]

By the spring of 1873 Moody had finally wearied of endless fund raising in behalf of the YMCA and related evangelical outreaches. Farwell implored him to stay, but Moody admitted "my heart is no longer in the begging."[12] His experience in Britain the year before, however, had been anything but encouraging. Uncharacteristically, he equivocated. The joy had gone out of administration and social service work. He felt called to preach but feared he lacked the power a revivalist needed "to move men and women." A March meeting in New Orleans and an April crusade in Mobile, Alabama, which enjoyed the strong support of local churches, appeared to make up his mind. Moody's reports to the Chicago press on those campaigns preceded his decision, announced abruptly at Chicago's Second Presbyterian Church, to "get back to Great Britain and win ten thousand souls there." The decision seemed well meaning but ill timed. In the same editions that reported his plan to leave for Europe were accounts of Moody's 2,500-seat tabernacle, resembling Spurgeon's, that was to be built on Chicago's near North Side. Newspapers considered it an edifice "as capacious as Mr. Moody's energy in the great cause he serves."[13] But that was only half the story. Moody thought his work in Chicago was ending. He longed to be back in Britain. And he was convinced that God wanted him to give it another try.

OFF TO A FALSE START

Moody's momentous march to save Britain from itself did not begin propitiously. His delay in deciding to make the voyage stripped him of his primary strength, his ability to bring people together in a concerted organizational effort that prepared the soil for the positive press his crusades cultivated and desperately needed. Moody told the *Chicago Tribune* that he was going to Europe "not to sight-see but to preach." But his announced crusade path—York, Manchester, Liverpool, Birmingham, Sheffield, Leeds, Bristol, Scotland, and Ireland—had one problem: no one in those cities had been alerted to his coming. If it had not been for a last-minute gift of $500 from Farwell, Moody would never have been able to pay for his passage. Moody's first and second choice for a singer refused his invitation, and his reluctant third choice, Ira Sankey, nearly accepted an offer from another evangelist. Sankey had been an Internal Revenue Service agent in New Castle, Pennsylvania, when the two men had met at the YMCA convention in Indianapolis in 1870. Sankey was promised $100 a month to make this voyage and was under the impression that he and Moody would be gone at most three or four months.[14]

When Moody and Sankey and their families left for Liverpool on June 7, 1873, it rated only a small item in the Chicago press and went unreported in Britain. The two men Moody expected would help him most in coordinating his early meetings in the north of England—a London vicar and a Newcastle merchant—died before Moody's ship landed. As the party wearily made their way to the Northwestern Hotel, the unusually optimistic Moody considered going home. Moorhouse agreed to take Sankey and his family to his home in Manchester, while Moody went to London. There, Moody persuaded Morgan to run an ad in the *Christian* asking "any friends who desire his help" to write Moody in care of the YMCA in York.[15] George Bennett, a Yorkshire druggist and YMCA organizer, was so chagrined by Moody's obstinacy that he first mentioned Moody's visit to a doctor of a local lunatic asylum. Moody, seeing his host's discomfort, felt like an unwanted "white elephant." In a latter to Farwell, Moody was more upbeat. He enclosed the advertisement that Morgan had printed and sent to several hundred pastors in the north of England and Scotland. Moody was certain that soon "invitations will be coming in from all over the country. I think we shall have all we can do here."[16] Moody toyed with the idea of joining Moorhouse in Manchester, but over dinner with Bennett he hastily pored over a map of York and decided to canvass the town with posters promising "a memorable evening" of evangelistic services to all those attending. Fewer than fifty did, and they sat so far away that Sankey could barely hear them sing. The following noonday prayer meeting in a small upper room of the local YMCA, reached through a long, dark passageway, drew only six.[17]

If Moody was discouraged, he gave little outward indication of it. He intensified his poster and advertising campaign and met with pastors and—when they'd see him—the press to improve his numbers. Bennett's own glowing reports of Moody's meetings appeared unedited in Morgan's weekly, giving the crusade national visibility. Admitting that the campaign had gotten off to a sluggish start because of poor planning, Bennett reported by July 10 that "the congregations from the first have become increasingly larger," with "the Lord greatly blessing our brother's labours." Any mention of crowd numbers was scrupulously avoided. Moody's meetings were utterly avoided by the local press, which did find space for the Oriental Circus of his fellow American Sam Hague and the recent arrival of 16-shilling trousers for summer wear.[18] Moody's decision, however, to bring a singer to the meetings was making them a bit of a local curiosity. Tradesmen, washerwomen, railwaymen, and a few sailors from local barracks began attending. The York press gave the meetings their first mention, attributing "improving crowds" to "Sankey's fine singing." The crowds and the favorable publicity appear to have legitimized the meetings in the minds of several York ministers, who also began coming out. A Sunday school teacher at a local Baptist assembly reported that her students had cried when they heard Moody's sad story of a dying Sunday school teacher in Chicago who feared that none of his students knew Jesus. The church's popular pastor, F. B.

Meyer, opened his pulpit to Moody. Crowds increased. The *Yorkshire Gazette* published the story and praised Moody's direct and energetic preaching style.[19]

Bennett was given more space in Morgan's weekly to report Moody's meetings. The attention undoubtedly helped Moody make his way in the days after York but did less to whet York's appetite for more of Moody. York was a conservative town and a tough sell for an American lay evangelist. The publicity Moody sought to help sustain and intensify the effect of his campaign never developed. The Established Church largely ignored his meetings. The archbishop had not heard of Moody even after five weeks, when his meetings ended. The local press, which had long done battle against Nonconformists, was not eager to embrace a little-known American layman, even if he had been "taken to the bosom of the dissenters." Moody competed unsuccessfully for newspaper space with grouse hunting and a prize of bacon to a local couple who had demonstrated "conjugal felicity." Nor did his meetings eclipse the perceived newsworthiness of a 20-inch-long snake that was found wrapped around the ankle of a celebrant at St. James Church who otherwise sat happily asleep.[20]

Both at York and then Sunderland, Moody continued to feel his way. He built on his alliances, listened to friends, and interrogated reporters and newspaper editors, when they gave him the time, to understand better what he was up against. Moorhouse and Morgan accompanied Moody to Sunderland to strengthen his showing in this northern shipbuilding town known for its suspicion of music in worship. Here Sankey, a star in York, was of little assistance. Moorhouse's meeting got off to a good start, and the endorsement of Arthur Rees, a seaman turned popular preacher, seemed to assure Moody a hearing in the Nonconformist press. Morgan, writing under the pen name "Omega," was doing all he could to promote Moody in the pages of the *Christian*. A long profile introduced Moody to Britain's evangelical readership. Moody was a "beloved brother" who "had left home for the sole purpose of saving souls." He and Sankey "nobly depended on the Lord for the supply of all their temporal wants" and were sworn enemies of the forces of evil, who held captive "the seething and lawless masses" of the city. Morgan commended this "blessed work" to the "earnest attention of God's saints everywhere."[21] Morgan's plea, however, fell on deaf ears within Sunderland's pastoral community. Local rectors had leaned on Rees, arguing that Moody's meetings cut down on their collections. Even members of the local YMCA were reluctant to be seen publicly with Moody for fear of alienating the local churches. The Sunderland press sided with local ministers, mistakenly deploring "Moody's singing style" when they really meant Sankey.[22] Their limited coverage decried Moody's presentational style of "stray Americanisms." Moody and Sankey took to the streets, leading marchers in songs of praise as a way of "advertising our meetings" and in the hope that "outsiders would be swept up in the exhortation." But the local press stood mute, and opposing churches failed to support the spectacle. When Moody escaped Sunderland three weeks into the campaign, he wearily remarked, "God save me from the devil and ministers."[23]

THE BREAKTHROUGH

M oody observed that common problems at York and Sunderland had been lack of support from evangelical assemblies in those cities. Without local legitimacy the press remained skeptical or, even worse, indifferent. In agreeing to go to Newcastle, a coal seaport a dozen miles up the Tyne, he insisted and received assurances that the city's Nonconformist community would endorse him and the city's most powerful publisher would watch with interest as the campaign proceeded. Richard Hoyle, a layman, the city's leading Presbyterian pastor, David Lowe, and William Skerry, Newcastle's most prominent Baptist, had been introduced to Moody's work through Morgan's articles, and after meeting with Moody suggested that Joseph Cowen, a Liberal member of Parliament and widely respected publisher of the *Newcastle Chronicle*, might agree to support the work.[24]

The strength of Newcastle's opposition to the state church played to Moody's advantage. A petition by more than 400 clergymen in the Church of England to establish confession as a sacrament of the church had struck many inside and outside the church as a repudiation of the Reformation and a symbol of how far the church had slipped from a previous position of honor in British society. The *Newcastle Courant* put it bluntly when it urged the archbishop to "save the life of the church by cutting this cancer out." Cowen's own paper was frankly discouraged by the archbishop's failure to heed a petition signed by 60,000 lay members of the church to censure the protesters. This flight from responsibility, it argued, had "accelerated the winnowing away of the moral and religious qualities which are the highest glory and the chief source of eminence of the people of Great Britain."[25]

This sense of danger had animated evangelical solidarity in Britain, particularly in the north of England, Scotland, and Ulster, from the awakening of 1859–60 onward. Sometimes the enemy was Darwinism, popery, or rationalism. In each case, what separated Nonconformist congregations seemed less crucial than what united them.[26] The Reform Act of 1867 and the Ballot Act of 1873 had doubled Britain's electorate and enabled them to vote by secret ballot. Cowen had come to Parliament through the reform, and although the earl of Shaftesbury had opposed it, each understood that the public would be a full participant in the conduct of national life, and that included the operation of its church.[27] Moody began to build a coalition of evangelical congregations, drawn from interested Methodists, Baptists, Congregationalists, and Presbyterians. John Wesley's belief in the possibility of universal salvation had motivated revival movements in his generation and was no less a force in Moody's day.[28] Furthermore, Moody would not be the first itinerant preacher around whom laymen and ministers alike had mobilized in the Nonconformist community. The *Christian* had been launched in the excitement of the 1859 revival, and the annual convention of Christian workers in Mildmay, begun by Moody backer William Pennefather, as well as quarterly assemblies held in London, Perth, Dublin, and Aberdeen, spoke to the determination of evangelicals to further the spirit of 1859. Their clarion call came from the earl of Shaftesbury in July 1873 when he told an Exeter Hall crowd that "believers everywhere would stand to the last" in resisting the corruption of spiritual devotion and religious worship in Britain.[29]

Moody helped mobilize this sentiment around him when he called for an all-day meeting in Newcastle on September 10. The unprecedented action was a risk. If it failed to generate large numbers, the campaign might easily stall out and suffocate for lack of public airing in the press. If it succeeded it would probably solidify his growing base in the North and might easily galvanize Nonconformist elements across the border in Scotland. Morgan gave Moody's dramatic gesture unprecedented coverage—4 full pages in the *Christian*. Moody made the better-known Skerry and Moorhouse partners in the all-day event. This drew Rev. William Moreley Punshun up from London to strengthen participation of area Methodists and involved lay leaders from Bristol and Yarrow to strengthen Moody's claim that these meetings "are to be open and free, a celebration of what the Lord is doing in our midst." Cowen's account of the meeting emphasizes how audiences were "caught up in the spirit and intention of these words," resulting in "a holy and pleasing exercise." As the campaign deepened, he noted that "in ordinary circumstances it is difficult to fill chapels on Sundays," but Moody's meetings were "filled to overflowing" each night. People sit for hours "and like it."[30]

For seven consecutive weeks, Cowen and the *Newcastle Daily Chronicle* devoted increasing, daily coverage to Moody's campaign. The paper praised Moody's ability to bring denominations together. "Almost impassable barriers seem to be disappearing," the *Chronicle* claimed. Moody's proclamation of "no new gospel" but "eternal truths of the old one" created common ground for the region's many ministers. The Church of England might remain aloof, but that only magnified Moody's growing reputation among evangelicals. One thousand celebrants a night testified to the certainty that "something extraordinary is happening." Moody's meetings were moved to a larger hall, and tickets were required to "control the crowds unable to gain attendance."[31] That announcement intensified interest in the meetings even further. In the afternoons Moody met with factory workers, Quakers, and housewives. His wife wondered how he could keep his concentration with "all the babies squealing."[32] Some were "disgusted" by the mixing of social classes at Moody's meetings. Others chaffed at Sankey's songs. Some considered it "impertinent" to ask a man about his sin. These critics, however, only made Moody's defenders more passionate. Men who came to Moody's meetings "curious" and left "convinced" testified in print. Cowen joined them. Moody was a "businessman" who conducted his meetings as ministers ought. "He never talks twaddle. His earnestness is intense, his energy untiring."[33]

Cowen's crusade in Moody's behalf was an important turning point in Moody's ministry in Britain. It followed Moody's ability to weld together a coalition of evangelical forces and led to a flurry of speaking invitations throughout Scotland and Ulster. Morgan printed 10,000 extra copies of the *Christian* to further Moody's message and published a book of hymns sung at Moody's meetings that quickly went through multiple printings. At Moody's suggestion, area ministers and churches raised enough money to send a three-month subscription of the *Christian* to every one of the 40,000 ministers in the United Kingdom. Moody reasoned that "ministers everywhere should be alive" to what God had done in Newcastle. It would raise "a spirit of expectation among the people."[34]

The pattern of Moody's successful campaigns in Scotland, Ireland, and the south of England was set in Newcastle. He insisted on and received the commitment of evangelical pastors to participate in his meetings and to get their congregations to come. The curious followed to get in on the excitement. The secular press, seeing a good story, both followed and led. They helped move the Moody story from religious sideshow to page one city spectacle. Cowen's stories were reprinted in Carlisle, Moody's next stop. Friendly stories in Carlisle found their way to Edinburgh, where he went after that. And so the pattern continued in the 18 months that remained of his time in Britain. Morgan's publicity machine gave Moody a nationwide following. Soon some clergy in the Established Church joined in. For the secular press that made Moody's meetings an even bigger story.

Moody was becoming a personality that readers were becoming interested in. So he helped prepare a press release to introduce himself and his coworker Ira Sankey to British readers.[35] It recounted Moody's

Moody as a 17-year-old. He had just arrived in Boston to work as
a salesman in an uncle's shoe store on condition that he regularly
attended church. He reluctantly agreed. The following year he prayed
to become a Christian.

birth in East Northfield, Massachusetts, on February 3, 1837, the sixth of nine children of Edwin and Betsey Holton Moody, who were poor but dedicated Unitarians. The death of his father when Dwight was four years later, the press release read, forced him to look for a living at a young age, leaving him little formal education. At 17 Moody moved to Boston and became a shoe salesman in his uncle's store. As a condition of his employment, he attended Samuel Holton's church, Mount Vernon Congregational, and there received Christ as his personal savior on April 21, 1855.

British readers learned that Moody went west, arriving in Chicago in September 1856, where he hoped to make a small fortune as a shoe and boot salesman, only to find himself drawn to religious activity. Moody's work among street orphans led to his long association with the YMCA. During the Civil War, Moody, now married, served the nation's war wounded through the Christian Commission. After the war, Moody's ties to the YMCA led to his teaming with Ira Sankey and their evangelistic campaigns across the nation. The Great Chicago Fire in October 1871 devastated the evangelist's work and hastened his fundraising tour throughout Britain's YMCA network during the summer of 1872. That, the press release read, laid the foundation for the pair's return in 1873. What the release did not explore was Moody's genius at organization, publicity, and marketing. The outlines of this revival machine first became apparent in what historians would record as the Great Scottish Revival of 1873–74.

Moody's marketing strategy

Moody believed that encouraging people to "expect a blessing of unusual magnitude" helped to create "a spirit of excitement among the people." He worked to create that climate by organizing the churches behind him and advertising his message. "It seems to me a good deal better to advertise and have a full house," he told fellow ministers, "than to preach to empty pews."[36] The church could learn something about selling from the world, he argued. "They advertise very extensively," he told his detractors. "This is the age of advertisement and you have to take your chance." Moody did not think it "beneath a man's dignity to go out and ask people to come in." This meant preceding his British campaigns with a saturation handbill, placard, and newspaper advertising campaign. Those who deplored his merchandising the gospel in this way needed to understand the reality of modern living. Sacred institutions and religious work now competed against theaters and places of amusement for people's time and attention.

Moody at 22. He was drawn to Chicago, the nation's
fasting growing city, hoping to make a lot of money in the
boot business. Instead, he became involved in the Young
Men's Christian Association and gave himself entirely to
Christian work.

And newspapers, in his view, were one of the places where the battle lines were drawn.[37]

Revivalism was Moody's business, and he saw to it with a businessman's attention to detail. No task was too insignificant if it encouraged attendance at his meetings and their positive publicity in the press. Henry Drummond, a leading Scottish preacher who greatly aided Moody's campaign in Britain, thought the evangelist had no peer as an organizer. "His expertise and management of men," Drummond observed, "was worthy of a field general."[38] Advertisements signed by sympathetic ministers in Carlisle, and then Edinburgh and Glasgow, promised "a blessing of unusual magnitude" for those attending Moody's campaigns in their cities. These ministers were in conspicuous attendance at Moody's meetings, where he urged converts and anxious inquirers to affiliate with friendly churches.[39] Press accounts of Moody's success in Carlisle were republished in cities next on Moody's schedule. This meant that capacity crowds and full pews could be organized prior to Moody's coming. In Carlisle, additional churches had to be opened to handle the overflow. The press reported that clergy not affiliated with the state church had begun "flocking" to Moody's cause "with one northern town after another catching the spirit of the enthusiasm."[40] Emma Moody began tracking her husband's success in the local press and sending the clippings home. He did the same, encouraging prayer partners on both sides of the Atlantic to continue supporting his work.[41]

William G. Blaikie, a professor of apologetics at New College, was among those organizing Moody's work in Edinburgh. He saw Moody as the man who could bring the warring factions of the Scottish church together through the centrality of "God's word." The six-week buildup to Moody's meetings emphasized prayer and publicity. Blaikie shared Moody's passion for the public proclamation of the gospel and the use of the press as a weapon in reaching "the sunken masses." Blaikie believed that a quarter of the city's 200,000 souls remained unreached because of petty differences over creeds that many in the public no longer took seriously. In the pages of *Sunday Magazine*, which Blaikie edited, the professor made much of the prophecy by the late Scottish churchman R. S. Candish that a "great blessing" from a "strange source" would soon win Edinburgh. Moody, Blaikie told the press, was that blessing. Moody stayed at Blaikie's home during the Edinburgh campaign and Blaikie facilitated Moody's contacts with local clergy and the press. An observer of Moody's mission noted that the two men worked well together because Moody was "practical." That meant he knew how to listen as well as lead "the men who gathered to help him."[42]

That organization proved to be a powerful tool in creating conditions that promoted success. "A spirit of excitement and expectation has been built up in many," the *Daily Review* of Edinburgh reported, even

The four poses of D. L. and his young wife, Emma, were taken in 1864 and 1869. She was a faithful chronicler of her husband's evangelistic campaigns as they appeared in the press and eagerly mailed home his clippings from Britain.

on a day when Moody was too sick to speak. It was not uncommon for anxious inquirers attending Moody's meetings to refuse to talk to anyone but Moody himself.[43] The crusade as civic spectacle with Moody at the center of the stage increasingly became the theme of press coverage. As Moody and Sankey rotated each evening among three churches and Edinburgh's Music Hall, the press reported that "the desire to see and hear him became more widespread and earnest." Many lined up outside the doors early, carefully reading reports of the campaign that were appearing in the broadsheets of the Edinburgh press.[44] Even some reporters fell prey to the excitement. One of them, W. Robertson Nicoll, editor of the *British Weekly*, made his own profession of faith following a Moody meeting, finding its impact "difficult to ignore." Sankey's own account of the campaign received nationwide circulation through the *Christian*. Letters were printed from those who testified: "Christ has come to Edinburgh."[45] The local press, in turn, embraced the language of Moody's organizing committee in referring to Edinburgh's "awakening" as "a democratic movement." The committee reported that "all denominational and social distinctions are entirely merged." The old and the young, soldiers and students, "the backslidden, the intemperate, the skeptical, the rich and the poor, the educated and the uneducated, the wounded and the burdened" were reportedly drawn to Moody's meetings. Special assemblies were called for shopmen, millworkers, dressmakers, and tailors. Moody's committee emphasized the unity of participating churches and quoted Moody's view that "if we're going to live in heaven together, why shouldn't we be united here." It did little good, Moody observed, "to work for a denomination, if one wasn't working first for Christ." The *Daily Review* reiterated that logic when it editorialized that Moody had united the nation's churches in a frontal assault against "spiritual slothfulness" and for "the revival of the spiritually dead."[46] Even the vanity press was picking up on the story. *Family Treasury* magazine thought Moody uniquely qualified for the task of reawakening Edinburgh because "he is on fire himself and kindles those he comes in contact with." Those contributing even a shilling to publish word of the awakening through the *Christian* received letters of appreciation from Moody's coordinating committee. Readers reported culling clergy lists and Nonconformist yearbooks in their districts to make sure that "every minister gets on the mailing list." Committee members deluged the daily press with accounts of the hundreds "who have had their prejudices vanquished and their hearts impressed."[47] Sometimes the accounts were exaggerated, like the time 600 men reportedly "fell on their knees" in a hall where Moody was speaking, "willing to give themselves to Christ." The reality was 400 Christian workers had merely been seen in prayer. Moody "disliked nothing

A somewhat austere Moody, at age 25, was taking himself seriously long before others did. The Chicago press initially treated "Crazy Moody" with indifference if not disdain, seeing him as a tireless self-promoter when he burst into newspaper offices seeking publicity for Christian outreach in the city.

more" than such inaccuracies. "Romancing about numbers," he warned, hurt the campaign's credibility in the press.[48]

Moody's sense of the dramatic generated extensive coverage in Edinburgh's most widely read dailies. A "Week of Prayer" was launched through an urgent appeal to Scotland's 2,600 pastors. Simultaneous daily prayer meetings across the city undergirded Moody's outreach to the poor. His services near the Grassmarket slum reportedly saved more than 1,000 people.[49] When Margaret Lindsay, a teenaged convert at Moody's meetings, was critically injured in a train wreck following a watch-night service, the press made much of her determination to sing the words of her favorite hymn, "The Gate Ajar for Me," until her death two days later. It was reported that efforts were being made to keep Moody and Sankey in Edinburgh "as long as possible" for the tens of thousands still eager to attend. At the year's end, as Moody prepared to take his campaign to industrial Glasgow, Edinburgh's ticket committee found itself "unable utterly to meet the demand" with Moody's meetings "packed to the fainting point."[50] Nor was Moody any longer able to pray over individual requests at his meetings. Instead, prayers were offered in behalf of 14 brothers for their unsaved sisters, 18 sisters for their worldly brothers, those "fallen under the influence of drink," the covetous, the cruel, the doubter, the sick, the lame, and the halt. Each day the press reported answers to prayer, "whole families coming to Christ," of "blessings of unusual magnitude," with "all Scotland stirred" by a winter without parallel in its history. On the first Sunday of the New Year Moody launched six meetings in as many hours in three area churches, with a waiting carriage racing him from one site to the next. The 6,000-seat Corn Exchange was finally rented and filled to overflowing each night.[51] Reluctantly, Edinburgh would soon have to give up its adopted son to neighboring Glasgow.

THE FIRE SPREADS TO GLASGOW

The organization that Moody had fashioned in Newcastle and Edinburgh helped to assure him a smooth start in Glasgow. This included daily advertising in the city's press with running accounts of his success in other cities being reported weeks before his arrival. Moody was praised for recreating the religious fervor of the Reformation and for outdoing George Whitefield in the number of souls saved. Syndicated press reports claimed that all Scotland was getting "into the spirit of hope" and "earnestly desired Moody." Glasgow's 70,000 young men between the ages of 15 and 25 were particularly targeted. Those who could not gain entrance to Moody's meetings were reported to be listening eagerly outside for "sounds of praise inside." Sometimes the temptation became too much and they crashed through the auditorium's doors. Many simply wanted "counsel and communication with Mr. Moody." It showed only too clearly that Scotland was surrendering "to a breadth of blessedness that hems us in and forbids unbelief." The press was reporting Moody's Scottish tour as "a spreading fire, an unusual day in the Lord's power." It seemed certain "the business of heaven is being carried on." Communities receiving the news sent widely publicized petitions to Moody pleading with him to come to their cities. At prayer meetings, Moody thanked God for reporters who had "communicated throughout Scotland" the power they had witnessed, and he "besought Providence to put into their hearts the faithful chronicling of how Scotland had been blessed."[52]

Moody shared letters from desperate readers overjoyed by accounts of his campaign that they had seen in the press. He observed that there was no way of estimating "how much good these reports are doing" and reiterated the importance of an advertising strategy that combined posters, handbills, and the daily press to saturate the city with news of the campaign, street by street and house by house. Moody endorsed a plan to subsidize "communicating the glad tidings of the Lord's work" by placing copies of the *Christian* in every Scottish home. He could think of no better way "to go to the people and seek them out." Moody was "sick and tired of aristocratic notions." Christianity was dying from respectability. From Saltcoats to London, Moody's coordinating committee made certain the word went out that a spiritual revival was sweeping Scotland. Placards of the *Christian* that were placed in the lobbies of more than 8,000 Scottish churches advertised that fact.[53]

Moody's newly won celebrity was not without its risks. Glasgow's leading paper, the *Herald*, known for its delight in bursting bubbles, castigated city clergy for falling for "Yankee tomfooleries," while the competing *Glasgow News* published glowing reports from Moody's organizing committee "of the many mercies of God" now seen in the city. The establishment *Herald* decried Moody's "theatricality" and the new "star system" in evangelism, but the *News* asked readers to see "with their own eyes what God is doing in Glasgow."[54] The *Herald's* accounts of the money Moody was supposedly making in selling hymnals disturbed him greatly. The *News* gave great play to his denial that he "was in it for the money," and Moody read that denial at his Glasgow crusade. Moody was urged to go to the press directly and deny the allegations. He publicly claimed "the Lord will take care of my reputation," while he privately wrote John Farwell suggesting he launch a letter-writing campaign commending his character that could be "widely circulated." It was important, he told Farwell, that it not appear "I have asked anyone to defend me." An enthusiastic testimonial, signed by 35 prominent ministers and business leaders, received wide play in the Scottish press and encouraged the momentum of Moody's campaign.[55]

Moody's knack for positive publicity extended to a group of local atheists and the chairman of its Infidel Club. When the man received Christ at a Moody meeting, Moody had him stand and give his testimony. The press loved this and similar stories and played it large. Moody had an instinctive sense of the dramatic and knew how to package news the Scottish press could not do without. He also understood the significance of symbolism. When he spoke in Glasgow, where Whitefield had preached 121 years before, he knew the comparison would not be lost on celebrants or the press. The excitement was making him a celebrity. Moody's private quarters were awash in fan mail "reaching chairs and shelves in every corner." Moody's own letters began appearing regularly in the city's secular press, including his call for Christian care of orphaned children. When a Scottish newspaper published a biography of Moody it quickly sold out, and another press run was needed. One disaffected cleric was clearly puzzled. He thought "there is no proportion between Moody's abilities and his results."[56] What the analysis missed was Moody's capacities as an organizer and his ability to draw evangelical leaders to his cause. As an outsider he avoided doctrinal taint and served as a symbolic rallying point opposed to the sterility of the state church. Moody legitimized evangelical opposition to the Established Church, and their support magnified Moody's cause in the pages of the Scottish press.

The meaning of that symbolism to the individual convert was the ultimate triumph of Moody's meetings. No one profile fits the estimated 3,000 men and women who received Christ in Glasgow under Moody's ministry, but one is suggestive. Family friend Jane MacKinnon described in her diary how Moody brought to her a middle-aged woman at the end of a Monday night meeting. The woman said that she had first heard of Moody from a newspaper. When she read that that night's service was "for those who desired personal conversation about their souls" she decided to come. She had grown up in the church, married a man indifferent to religion, had five children, and now found herself painfully ambivalent too. She "never went to church anymore," but a friend who had been to a Moody meeting urged her to go. The great many who stood at the end of the meeting for prayer and conversation about their souls impressed her. She "desperately needed comforting," and the magnitude of Moody's meetings seemed to sanction her hope. The two women later met at the woman's home in a fashionable part of the city. Mrs. MacKinnon read Matthew 11:23, "Come unto me, and I will give you rest." The woman received Christ and "went away glad," and her name was turned over for followup to a local churchman who had been involved in the Moody meetings.[57]

The testimony demonstrates the power of publicity and the importance of organization in sustaining the momentum of Moody's meetings. Salvation as civic spectacle legitimized personal conversion, particularly for the doubter seeking certainty. The distribution of clergy across Scotland's denominations who supported Moody's campaign appeared to amplify "the one true hope" represented by Moody's preaching. The magnitude of the meetings created an incentive for churchmen to forget their differences and for many in the daily press to suspend their skepticism. Something appeared to be happening. And whether or not the spectacle was one part spiritual and one part secular, who could say? Critics might carp that not men's plans but God alone brought revival, but the reality was that Moody's meetings in sheer size had taken on a curiosity as well as a weight of their own. No one in Glasgow had ever seen anything like it. The desire grew to get in on it. The washerwoman who left her wash to another day because she simply "had to go" to Moody's meetings symbolized the strength of the Scottish awakening and hinted at the power of publicity in helping to make it happen.

Moody was careful to use the press to steer clear of doctrinal issues that might otherwise have splintered his support and sapped the strength of his campaign. This was not always so simple. A controversy over predestination erupted within the committee coordinating Moody's ministry in Glasgow. When headlines asked whether men holding opposing views could serve on the same committee, Moody told reporters he was just "passing through" Scotland, that he "had never been embroiled in a newspaper controversy and didn't want to start now."[58] To the ongoing rancor of members of the state church and those decrying the "crusty formalism" of that church and its "alienation from the masses," Moody attempted to avoid taking sides. He simply urged opposing ministers "to come to my meetings and see for yourselves." His support within the Established Church was growing, as the civic spectacle launched by evangelical forces and a sympathetic press encouraged a tide that raised all boats. Moody was anxious to expand this base, not diminish it. For this reason he told reporters that he had "nothing more to do" with the dispute between the Established and the Free churches than he did with "the laws of China."[59] To those opposed to his careful cultivation of the press in publicizing revival work he suggested that "new means must be found to spread the gospel" and "there is no more effective way of doing so" than the print press.[60]

Moody was an inveterate newspaper reader and eagerly sent home reports of his campaigns that he had clipped from the daily press. Now that he was being recorded verbatim, with stenographic transcripts of his pulpit preaching often appearing in the next day's news, he worked more direct quotation from the Bible into his messages. Even though audiences might not suspect it, he was nervous on such occasions, aware of his lack of education and concerned that his eagerness for souls made him talk too fast, which made him "no friend to shorthand reporters."[61] There were newspapers that noted Moody's mixed metaphors—like the time he asserted "God gave Moses a blank check and all he had to do was fill it up, and then water gushed forth from the rock." But it was also apparent to reporters that crowds "enjoyed these peculiar turns of thought" and it was "pointless to be hypercritical" of a manner "eminently calculated to win over an audience."[62] Moody did not hesitate to privately and publicly thank reporters for "minimizing my mistakes" and for helping him to reach through their pages those who would otherwise have been unreachable. In letters home Moody cited the circulation of the British press that had been friendly to the progress of his campaigns and acknowledged their central role in "helping to stir the dry bones of the United Kingdom."[63]

Glasgow would be one of the high points of Moody's more than two-year mission to Great Britain. On the afternoon of his final service in the city, the meeting place filled with 5,000 souls hours before his arrival. Milling crowds surrounded the building and packed in against one another along the Great Western Road. Reports characterize many of them as "unusually unsettled." When Moody arrived he could not get in the meeting hall. Standing atop a coachman's box, he began to preach. The Crystal Palace emptied, its occupants pushing against the crowd for a sight of the man. An estimated 30,000 heard Moody that night, the largest gathering in municipal history. Two thousand reportedly received Christ within the hour. "Blemishes might cleave" to Moody's ministry, Glasgow's press observed the following day, but there was no denying "his shrewdness and common sense." His earnestness had a way of making others earnest and expectant and encouraged them to work for results. His "inner vitality made men and churches fresh," stirring even those "who thought themselves Christians because they were born in Scotland." As a result "currents mingled" and "an ocean emerged." Even the uncertain admitted that "thousands have been deeply stirred" in the city and thousands more outside it. Hardly anyone could dispute the district's awakening was "a genuine Christian work" distinguished by "the Catholic consent of the churches." The early crowds and sustained success of the movement had encouraged ecumenism. Press puffing sometimes led, but always followed, the excitement. R. C. Morgan, on hand at the Crystal Hall, was moved to tears as he watched "a vast multitude slowly disperse." Their "stillness" spoke of "a strange and solemn night," a civic spectacle of unparalleled proportion.[64] It also spoke of the matchless success of Moody and his organizing committee in creating conditions that encouraged early crowds and a positive press. That Scotland was ready, even eager, for revival there can be little doubt. What was required was a man with a message

Crowds clogged the Great Western Road on May 24, 1874, Moody's final day in Glasgow. Unable to make his meeting, Moody stopped the carriage, stood on a coachman's box and began preaching. The Scottish press loved it.

and a means of amplifying that message across an anxious city. The result was a citywide shaking unlike anything in living memory. At its beginning and end Moody led the way in understanding that "the lapsed masses can be reached only if we find the means to take the gospel to them." Nine months earlier, Moody admitted, he had come to Scotland "a perfect stranger." He had felt "powerless" then, but "ministers, the press, and the whole people of Scotland" had seen to his success.[65] In turn, that success had created unexpected celebrity, which both furthered and complicated Moody's mission to Ireland.

MOODY AS SUPERSTAR

By the time D. L. Moody left Scotland for Ireland on September 4, 1874, he was on his way to becoming a Christian superstar whose exploits would be chronicled in the publishing world on both sides of the Atlantic. A narrative of Moody's "marvelous work" in Edinburgh was being prepared by Partridge and Company days after Moody departed the city. More than a dozen accounts of Moody's British campaign would follow within three years.[66] Various forms of Moody's sermons began appearing in print. Some were edited by Henry Drummond. Others were published by companies unabashedly out to make a fast buck off a suddenly hot prospect.[67] Moody publicist John MacPherson, who had written accounts of the Edinburgh awakening for the *Christian* and other publications, observed that Moody's new notoriety seemed to "disarm" his critics in the press and obligated "every newspaper" to cover Moody's coming. "On the train and in the busy mart," MacPherson noted, "no place was too secular, no business so pressing, no company too indifferent, to exclude all reference to the topic of the day." The status made Moody a target of those unsettled by his success, a vulnerability made all the greater when his organizing committees failed to operate in the "cordial cooperation" that had marked his triumphs in Edinburgh and Glasgow.[68] Those cities had been divided into precincts, and volunteers had gone from home to home and church to church, alerting the crowds to Moody's coming. When this network broke down or its members were divided, as was the case in Ireland, initial crowds were down, and the press pounced on the possibility that Moody's star was sinking. It gave a fresh angle to the Moody story, while complicating his work in Belfast and Dublin.

Moody knew that Scotland would be a tough act to follow and hesitated to preach in Ireland. Mrs. MacKinnon's narrative suggests Moody's uncertainty in following up his enormous success in the major cities of Scotland. He considered a campaign in London, where his work had been heavily reported in the daily press, but decided that divisions among the churches were too great an obstacle.[69] He had never been to Ireland, felt "a perfect stranger" there, and felt "utterly powerless" without the full support of participating churches. His almost reluctant switch to touring Ireland gave his organizing committee less time to advertise and unify local congregations. This made Moody vulnerable to press criticism. The character issue that Moody had so artfully diffused in Scotland greeted him in Ireland. When one member of the congregation noisily interrupted a September 7 meeting in Belfast, charging that Moody "had no business being in the pulpit," the protester was arrested. The local press had a field day. The fine imposed on the man struck editorial writers as "small price to pay for telling our American guests off."[70]

Moody used his early difficulties in Ireland in a publicized campaign to rally many of the English to his side and to prepare the way for his London campaign. Moody's open letter, published in the *Christian* and sympathetic secular dailies, appealed for nationwide noontime prayer to help him sanctify believers and save sinners in Ireland. Moody advertised a week in advance what he would be preaching on and asked ministers and congregations to join hands across the United Kingdom so that Ireland's "heathen might know where is their God." His London organizing committee urged readers "who want to see God do great things in London" to "heed Mr. Moody's call" and "make such a fire as shall not easily be extinguished."[71]

Moody maximized what benefits were to be found in his slow start in Ulster. His publicity proclaimed that Ireland had "sat so long in the shadow of death" that Belfast would prove whether God's work or the devil's would be done. "All Christian readers" were urged to set aside doctrinal differences and work to magnify Moody's message in their neighborhoods and congregations. The "glorious" success of Scotland would be repeated in Belfast only if the "visibility" of Moody's mission visited each household. The secular press might sniff at "strangers" who "preach for money," but the "eyes of faith" saw great crowds where empty seats remained.[72]

Within weeks, Belfast's daily press could not deny the "overflowing attendance" at Moody's meetings. It was apparent that the American revivalist was "deeply in earnest," and for that reason some in the press were prepared to forgive the "curious manner" in which he went about his work.[73] In an open letter that was published in friendly newspapers, Moody associated the awakening in Belfast with the Ulster Revival of 1859. He urged all Britain to pray for unprecedented results. He moved his meetings outdoors, and as was the case in Edinburgh and Glasgow, the curious and incredulous came, padding the civic spectacle and raising crowd estimates to 10,000, 20,000, and 30,000, depending on who was doing the estimating. Belfast's "higher classes" might be unmoved, but the city's shopkeepers, mechanics, and mill and warehouse workers could not get enough. Backsliders, sinners, and skeptics were reported "blasted as by an east wind." And every night "fine young men" were seen among the anxious inquirers who stayed after service "to know more from Moody." Moody, perfectly capturing the hyperbole of the occasion, said he would like to see 100,000 assembled "at the grandest gathering ever seen in the town of Belfast." Although crowds never reached that level, Moody seemed satisfied that he had overcome forces that might have gutted his mission to Ireland just as it was beginning.[74]

Moody reported to Irish readers that Belfast had produced "the most remarkable meetings we have yet had in Europe" as he made ready his descent on Catholic Dublin. There danger lurked. The Irish were "not as gullible as the Scots," the city's leading Catholic newspaper, the *Nation*, reported. The Irish were said to have little use for "preachers of the roaring type." What attendance Moody managed, the paper insisted, came from free admission and the fact that Dublin "has but few attractions at present for sensation-loving people."[75] Moody courted Catholic cooperation with his mission by minimizing sectarian dispute in his advance work. Friendly papers like the *Dublin Daily Express* released long lists of Catholics, Presbyterians, Episcopalians, and Wesleyans who were participating in the preparation. Moody advertised himself as a "lay preacher" who was "disinterested" in doctrinal differences. In an open letter to Irish newspapers, Moody promised there would be no "political Protestantism" at his meetings. The Exhibition Palace was rented to send an appropriate secular signal. Its seating capacity was 20,000, and that sent another signal. W. B. Kirkpatrick, editor of the ecumenical *Witness*, and W. Marrable, of the Church of Ireland, were invited to Belfast and left impressed with Moody's "energetic" evangelism, the cross-section of the church that supported it, and the "immense audiences" it produced. Kirkpatrick characterized Moody's "gospel message of forbearance and sympathy" as just the "medicine" Protestants and Catholics needed.[76]

Moody's scrupulous care to avoid offending Catholics hardly converted Dublin's oppositional press but at least won their neutrality. The *Nation* had no quarrel with curious Catholics who came to Moody's meetings. The "deadly danger" of the age was secularism, not Moody and Sankey. Irish Catholics preferred their Protestants "deeply imbued with religious feeling" rather than "tinged with rationalism," and Moody's meetings seemed to genuinely offer that. A sister paper, the *Freeman's Journal*, took the same line. When one comedian at a Dublin theater remarked "I am rather Moody tonight," the other said he felt rather "Sankey-monious." Some in attendance laughed. Others reportedly sang a hymn. Better publicity followed when the reporter for the *Nation* was found in an inquiry room "asking about the state of his own soul."[77] This unexpected ecumenism and civic spectacle struck the Dublin correspondent for the *Times* of London as a sure story. In November 1874 he reported that Moody's meetings in Dublin were "the most remarkable ever witnessed in Ireland." Few preachers, he wrote, had ever been followed "by so many eager reporters." Moody sent the clipping and several others to Farwell in Chicago, urging his benefactor to meet him in London the following spring for the culmination of his British campaign.[78]

THE ROAD TO LONDON

By the end of 1874 Moody had all but formulated a campaign structure that he would follow successfully for a quarter century on both sides of the Atlantic. The plan was conceived in the trial and error of hundreds of campaigns in as many cities and was forever added to and subtracted from as Moody polished and perfected his techniques of mass evangelism. It was guided by his growing understanding that "every means is good that works to good," and that included advertising and manly planning. "The progress of the work, under God, depends upon the state of mind manifested by God's people," Moody observed. While they continued "hungry" and "hopeful" they would look to Moody's meetings and missions like it for solace and certainty. Their excitement would create the kind of crowds and civic spectacle that encouraged the simply curious to come. That was what made the careful cultivation of the secular press such a crucial strand in campaign planning. Through it, the realm of the unreached was opened to Moody and his event organizers. Anxious Christians, "hoping for a time of refreshing," would be joined in long inquiry lines by simple scoffers. A "divine arrest" would be upon them all. A new kind of Christian community could be created as people "in tram cars and omnibuses, on the street, and in every social circle" heard and read "of God's great blessing." People were attracted "like iron filings to a magnet" under those conditions. The key was to "advance in solid column upon a common enemy" and to make sure potential allies and enemies would hear of it. Summarizing Moody's success, the *Daily Mail* of Dublin observed that Moody's message might be old, but the merchandising of that message through organization and advertisements decidedly was not.[79]

Between December 1874 and mid-March 1875, Moody's entourage, which now included a personal secretary to answer all the fan letters he was receiving, put its organizational acumen to work in Manchester, Sheffield, Birmingham, and Liverpool as final preparations were launched for his finishing four-month campaign in the heart of London. These comings and goings were carefully chronicled in the religious and secular press, along with Moody's "reluctant" admission that he was "unable to undertake any further engagements." The press made much of Liverpool's decision to build a tabernacle seating 7,000 to house Moody's meetings. A house-to-house canvass there and in the residential districts of Manchester meant positive publicity for Moody's organizing committee weeks before his arrival. Heartwrenching testimonies ran as sidebars to these accounts: for example, the young factory girl who "saw the savior" at a Moody meeting and later caught her hand in a machine only to "sing His praises" as one by one her fingers were cut off; or the 11- and 12-year-old boys who had forsaken corrupted lives as pickpockets for places in the choir following the dictates of 1 John 5.[80]

Moody's every move made good reading, and for each newspaper that remained unimpressed, there were three others anxious to get in on the act. When the upper-crust *Manchester Guardian* couldn't be bothered with Moody's meetings in that city, the one- and two-penny *Manchester Evening News* and the *Alliance* filled column inch after column inch with Moody's exploits. If the Moody phenomenon struck some editors as old news, the systematic scattering of circulars by Moody's men signaled to the hopeful that there might well be "a mighty work in our midst." And even when Moody met opposition he was often able to turn it to his advantage. In Sheffield, as had been the pattern elsewhere, Moody welcomed clergy from the Church of England, as well as the opposing Ecumenical Unionists, to join in the precampaign planning. On the eve of the crusade's opening, the press publicized the reluctant withdrawal of a Church of England clergyman from the 21-member executive committee that was planning Moody's visit. The resignation was treated in the local press as another instance of the Established Church's resistance to a revival movement not under its authority. Further investigation showed that the clergyman had been "threatened with ecclesiastical prosecution" by a local incumbent whom the press saw as "an opponent of revival."[81] The local press seized on this "lamentable" incident to excoriate the partisanship of the church, while embracing the ecumenism of Moody's meetings. "Crowds of eager, anxious people" were reportedly packing the city's largest hall "awaiting Moody's message." Moody did not disappoint. His "wonderfully simple and winning style" struck the Sheffield press as an overdue antidote to the pretenses of the state church. Critics charged that his success sprang from "vulgar curiosity, sensational advertising and press exaggeration," but supporters saw the supernatural at work wherever Moody spoke. They argued that ministers standing in pulpits could never get at the masses as Moody did.[82]

One unexpected and unwelcome artifact of Moody's success as campaign organizer and patron saint of the press was the new celebrity status he now inherited. The determination of the daily press to focus more on the man than his message during Moody's final five months in England was more curse than blessing for a man who had always understood revival to be the sovereign work of the Holy Spirit and not the result of any single person's ingenuity. There were personal risks in newly acquired fame, like the time an escapee from a local lunatic asylum stalked Moody in Liverpool on a "commission from God" to kill him. Moody's reputation now required bigger buildings to be built to hold him and his fan following. In Liverpool, his organizing committee collected $17,000 to win a bidding war for Moody's and Sankey's services. The construction of the 7,000-seat Victoria Hall, complete with inquirers' room and state-of-the-art acoustics, assured headlines leading up to and through Moody's "mighty work" in Liverpool. Costs to bring Moody to London would be 10 times more.[83]

When 2,000 ministers and Christian workers met on February 5, 1875, at London's Freemason's Hall, it was to plan Moody's final meetings in that city and to generate publicity for those meetings. After initial failure and then astonishing success, the mechanics of Moody's media campaign moved from notes scribbled on the backs of envelopes to coordinating committees led by prominent bankers and supportive pastors who could assure the financing and staffing of citywide campaigns unlike anything ever attempted in the Gilded Age. Moody multiplied the Farwells around him by publicizing his appeal to "well known Christian men of means."[84] Workers who had learned their stuff in Manchester and Liverpool divided London into quarters with a house-to-house handbill campaign designed to reach "every square, street and lane" of this "Great Babylon" and its far-reaching suburbs. Moody's central committee equipped district superintendents with two maps apiece. One was to be used as reference and the other cut into pieces for volunteers who took on a block. They would be sent out in twos, after the apostolic example, carrying a leaflet written by Moody himself, urging everyone to attend his meetings and to follow their chronicling in the daily press. All team members kept a log of all contacts and turned them in to their supervisors. The result was an intensely publicized attack on the "one million Londoners indifferent to public worship," many of whom were targeted by "the most gigantic religious undertaking of its kind in the world."[85]

CELEBRITY STATUS

The machinery of mass evangelism that Moody brought to London inevitably situated its leader at the center of the civic spectacle. "Pulpit photographs" appeared in the local press profiling his "history, character, the secret of his power, and the nature of his influence." The adulation was an outgrowth of Moody's celebrity status, and it had a curious press asking "Who is Moody? No man who moves multitudes as he does can hope to remain in the background. Who is this man? What is behind his success?"[86]"The circuit of Moody and Sankey," one paper reported, "resembles a triumphant march" of Roman conquerors, with an attendance "never witnessed under one roof in the history of our cities."[87] The London campaign was widely seen as "a masterpiece of administrative care and skill." On opening night, a "great sea of humanity that seemed to stretch as far as vision could go" was escorted to seats by ushers who did their work "with quiet and effective energy." Thousands of gas burners in the city's mammoth Agricultural Hall blazed, and well-known ministers from every participating denomination took their seats on the stage. A handful of titled gentlemen joined them. Reporters covering the spectacle found "no screw loose anywhere."[88]

Moody's Greater London campaign began on March 9, 1875. When the crusade ended 285 meetings later, 2,530,000 had attended, and Moody's status as a celebrity evangelist was assured. "Men of distinguished evangelistic gifts" were reported to be coming from America and Asia to assist in the movement Moody had launched in the British Isles. Some within the London press remained skeptical regarding "glowing reports from the provinces" and the descent on the city of "this new soldier of the cross." However, the several thousand energetic souls who attempted to crash the hall in the middle of Moody's message, the *Times* reported, put the lie to critics who predicted that London would prove to be "indifferent" to Moody's menagerie.[89] In the days that followed, several papers conceded that the stoutly built American "with the strange sounding twang" was "no ordinary ranter." Educated listeners might have no use for Moody's massacre of the King's English, the *Morning Post* noted, but nightly crowds of 21,000 didn't seem to mind. "The appearance of vast throngs was, in itself, a sight worth going many miles to see," the press observed. And Moody's continued ability to attract capacity crowds made some see in him "another Spurgeon," a man "with an obvious desire to do good," someone whose genuine gifts would likely do the city much good. Even the oppositional *Vanity Fair* admitted that the "greatest multitudes gathered in this generation" came nightly to Moody's meetings in London, demonstrating that "there is in mankind a strong desire and yearning for something more than a mere material existence." Moody's methods of marketing religion were of "universal application," and "he is not afraid of them."[90]

Even the aristocracy got in on the act. When Moody would not take his meetings to the Opera House, the titled came to him, insisting, however, that special seats set them apart from the great unwashed. When Moody later spoke at the West End Opera House, some season ticket holders refused to allow their boxes to be used. In a crowded hall these were the only empty seats. The spectacle seemed to assure Moody's symbolic association with the faithful over the professionally religious. His meetings in Agricultural Hall, scene of cattle and horse shows, gave a whiff of Moody's marketing appeal. Here no high church was to be found. Moody was, instead, a simple man who offered a simple message to the masses. The metaphor was sustained when Queen Victoria declined to be present. She had no doubt that Moody was "sincere" but did wonder whether "this sensational style of excitement can last."[91]

Figurines of Moody and Sankey were hawked on London street corners, as were replicas of Moody's curious American cap. Doggerel sang their praises. "The rich and the poor," it went, "the good and the bad, have gone mad over Moody and Sankey."[92] Moody's printed sermons were widely circulated through booksellers. Later reports would emphasize what contemporary accounts saw only too clearly. Moody's ability to sustain audiences of 150,000 a week over four months by gaslight and simple sounding board had no parallel in the civic history of London.[93] Summaries of what the meetings meant to those present were freely reported and stirred sentiment further in Moody's favor. R. W. Dale, a churchman who was reluctant at first to join in the civic spectacle, thought Moody ordinary in every respect except results. He could see "no real relation between Moody and what he had done." Those coming hopefully to his meetings "carried their new joy with them to their homes and workshops. It could not be hid."[94]

As Moody prepared in midsummer to close his two-and-a-half-year campaign in Britain and return to the United States, the *Christian Standard* lamented that "we do not have a thousand preachers in our land such as Mr. Moody." Moody reiterated his certainty that if a great work had been done in London, it had been the Lord's doing. Although God's ways weren't man's ways, or necessarily those of evangelists, Moody admitted, that had not stopped him from "marking out channels where the Holy Spirit might work." Critical to this effort in Moody's mind were reporters who had "muted" his failures while communicating to an unsaved world his campaign's many successes. If secular men and women now lived in an "enlightened age," it took an enlightened church to reach them. That meant a body of believers prepared to go where the church had not gone before, to reach the previously remote with the gospel through every available means.[95] One hundred eighty-eight clerics from the much-maligned Church of England were among the 700 pastors who met with Moody on the eve of his departure for New York. They were urged to embrace his strategy "of going out to all the people with the good news of Jesus Christ. What London wanted, and what the whole world wanted, was not eloquence, but Christ, and Him crucified."[96] For Moody that would mean using the daily press as a key instrument in mass mobilization with techniques he would con-

More than two and a half million people attended Moody's meetings in Greater London during the spring of 1875. This pen and ink drawing captures the opening of those meetings on March 9 at the Agricultural Hall in Islington.

tinue to hone in a series of record-shattering campaigns in Brooklyn, Philadelphia, New York, Chicago, and Boston.

A SECOND REFORMATION

When D. L. Moody left the United States in the spring of 1873 to embark on his British campaign, it was in relative anonymity. But when he returned in the summer of 1875 he was celebrated as the greatest evangelist in the English-speaking world. Moody resisted this sudden celebrity, claiming that God's sovereignty, not organization and publicity alone, made for successful revivals. The *Christian* suggested that the "absence of excitement" that pervaded Moody's meetings demonstrated that "the Spirit of God has done more, and man less, in this work than any similar awakening since the days of the Reformation."[97] That did not mean, however, that Moody saw any inconsistency in urging "every man and woman, who loves the Lord Jesus, to publish the glad tidings of salvation." It might not be the message the world wanted preached, but it was, in Moody's view, just what the modern world most needed. Industrialization and urbanization had helped produce a democratic marketplace on both sides of the Atlantic with a daily press at its center, newly capable of taking the day's news into every home and hamlet. The Christians of London had "lifted high the standard of Christ," and now Americans would have their chance.[98]

Salvation in the context of civic spectacle would become the pattern of Moody's ministry, and those of many of the evangelists who would follow him. Moody's meetings were a businessman's Bible camp for believers and those anxious over the condition of their souls. And what the machinery of big city evangelism now sacrificed in spontaneity, it gained in predictability. Organization and careful marketing might not assure success, but it certainly didn't hinder the work of evangelism either. Moody would always link the power of publicity to the pre-eminence of prayer in revival work. His contribution to the primer on evangelism he was about to write introduced the element of civic spectacle as a means of rationalizing the process by which unbelievers could be encouraged to believe. Even Moody seemed surprised at the magnitude of the plan's success. He had "never met so many infidels" as he had in the largest cities of the British Isles. That was because his operation had never been quite so successful in drawing the unchurched and backslidden to him.

Moody's Great Britain campaign of 1873–75 demonstrated that God's purposes and man's plans could now create conditions that let whole communities in on a public extravaganza larger than anyone had ever seen. The growth and ubiquity of the Gilded Age press helped make that possible. Those uncomfortable with using secular means for spiritual purposes warned that "only that which the Lord made, and not man, will stand."[99] Moody, as a practical man, found this marriage of secular means and spiritual purposes was not without its personal consequences. Celebrity was the unexpected price Moody paid for being among the first to understand the power of the press in reaching the realm of the unreached with the gospel message. What George Whitefield had succeeded in doing in colonial America and Charles Finney had achieved in upstate New York and across rural America, Moody would now attempt in urban America, with its engines of mass communication poised in each of the nation's big cities. Revivalists might continue to claim that quickening a slumbering spirit was God's job and not man's, but after Moody they could no longer dispute that modern crusade work required mass media and organization, and lots of it, to arrest the attention of and compete for customers in an age of indifference and leisure. Moody knew that sleepers awake when God got on the front page. And it was on that page that American readers followed his progress across the Atlantic and editorial writers wondered whether what had worked in the Old World would work in the New.

"Sidewalks and Rooftops Are Black for Blocks Around"

THREE

MOODY IN BROOKLYN, OCTOBER–NOVEMBER 1875

At five in the morning on Saturday, August 14, 1875, the *New York Herald* received word that the Steamship *Spain*, which had left Liverpool 10 days earlier, had been seen off Sandy Hook near New York harbor. An hour later a *Herald* reporter saw the ship drop anchor opposite the Upper Quarantine Landing, her flag at half-mast. The reporter at first feared that D. L. Moody "worn out by hard work might have given up the ghost." Despite a more than two-year absence, he was "more the center of religious thought and expectation than any man in America."[1] That was why the reporter was so relieved to finally find the famed evangelist, under a great beaver hat, leaning out over the starboard side of the ship.

"Good morning, Mr. Moody," the young man abruptly said, while awkwardly reaching for his notebook.

"Where did you come from?" Moody, weary from the rough sea voyage, wanted to know.

The reporter gave him his business card and explained that "all the English papers" were showing Moody in his fur hat. Now it was his turn "to pen a picture of the great exhorter." Moody, however, seemed unmoved. He was "uninterested" in answering questions about his voyage or health. Newspapers on both sides of the Atlantic had made much of the revival he and Sankey had led across Britain, but they were not the story, God was. Moody insisted he was not "a revivalist" who "led

A confident D. L. Moody, at 38, returns to the United States after his success in Great Britain and Ireland made him the best known revivalist in the English-speaking world. The press was so anxious to see him they sent boats out into New York harbor to get a quote from the great man for the morning editions.

revivals." He told his interviewer "the Holy Ghost alone has the power to revive," and it was "very erroneous" to report otherwise.[2] A reporter from the rival *New York Tribune* had positioned himself with other members of a welcoming party at Pier 42 in the North River. When the "great man" came into view he was eager to ask where Moody and Sankey would be ministering next. Many of America's largest cities, the press was reporting, wanted the honor of being first to host God's man for the Gilded Age. A kind of competition was underway. He'd heard from Boston, Brooklyn, Chicago, New York, and Philadelphia, Moody admitted, but no decision had yet been made.[3]

An entourage of reporters, pastors, and hangers-on accompanied Moody and his trunks, filled with suggested sample sermons sent by fans, to the Grand Union Hotel. This Manhattan mecca, known for entertaining royalty, served dinner to Moody and his honored guests. The press had reported that Moody would be spending the night at the home of D. W. McWilliams, the Sunday School superintendent of Theodore L. Cuyler's Presbyterian church on Lafayette Avenue in Brooklyn. Sankey was staying with E. L. Kalbfleisch, a trustee in the same church. The Brooklyn church had hosted the two men when they were little known. Now rumors were rife that Moody and Sankey would repay the favor by beginning their North American revival work in the nation's third-largest city. For the record, Cuyler neither confirmed nor denied the reports, and when Moody announced he would be leaving New York on the three o'clock train for Northfield, it stimulated speculation the "city of churches" was no longer the front runner.[4]

The guessing game made good copy. The press reported Moody meeting delegations from several cities, when word was received that Charles Finney, the 82-year-old evangelist, had died. The *New York Times* eulogized the ex-president of Oberlin College as "the Moody of his day." The *Herald* was certain his passing had made Moody "the lion of the hour."[5] Finney was celebrated as the transitional figure between the Great Awakening of Jonathan Edwards and George Whitefield and a growing nineteenth-century reliance on using man-made means to spiritually excite the slothful. Where Edwards and Whitefield and their contemporaries would have expected God's leading in stirring the dry bones of indifferent congregations, Finney's work in the Oneida region of upstate New York and in the upper Mohawk Valley, beginning in 1824–25, set the standard for human agency in revivalism.[6] Moody shared Finney's certainty that God was always interested in reviving his people. For Finney that had meant "the wise use of constituted means" that would awaken sinners to "a sense of guilt and danger." By "taking advantage of man's excitability," Finney hoped to create a community-wide wave that would "rise so high as to sweep away every obstacle."[7]

Finney's ideas for promoting revivals were widely employed by Methodist and Baptist itinerants in Moody's day. Eastern seminaries and the powerful pastors they produced opposed these "new measures," complaining that "getting up" a revival was invariably a noisy affair that improperly competed with established churches legitimately engaged in Christ's work. New converts disrupted church society, and when their enthusiasm receded, they languished or left the church.[8] As Moody considered his next step, some ministers saw his work as a potentially disruptive force. George W. Porteous of the All Souls Independent Episcopal Church on Brooklyn Heights refused to sign a petition urging Moody to come to Brooklyn, saying: "I do not believe in the trashy, canting way" of professional revivalists. Their "peculiar methods" did "a good deal of injury and mischief to the cause." George Houghton, known for his charitable work at New York's Little Church Around the Corner, had a distinctly uncharitable view of Moody's methods. He told the *Herald* there was no point in Moody coming to Manhattan because "we have about enough to take care of as it is." Moody would not repeat his success in America, he predicted, because "the people on this side of the Atlantic are much more used to that style of thing than the English."[9] The *Herald*, which competed with the *Tribune* for the title of Moody's biggest booster, urged the evangelist to come to the city. "The pulpit," it observed, "has never equaled its idea of excellence." Too many preachers had become "timid and eloquent in their glittering use of generalities." They were too busy securing salaries by defending the rich. There was "no compromise" with Moody. He "hit hard"; that was the reason "the great body of people respect his work." Moody's coming would "wake up the ministry," and that was "the equivalent of waking up everybody."[10]

Moody made news while remaining in Northfield, the papers pointing out that Christ hadn't been welcomed in his hometown but Moody had. When the *Greenfield Recorder Gazette* reported that Moody would be speaking on Sunday, September 5, at the local Congregational church, so many came that he had to speak outside to accommodate them. By September 12 the sabbath sessions had become daily rituals with 2,000 people in attendance. New York, Boston, and the Associated Press sent reporters to see what was happening.[11] Moody told reporters he hadn't had a break in two and a half years and was planning to take time off, but D. W. Whittle, a friend of Moody's since their Chicago YMCA days, observed that "Moody's idea of rest and seclusion included dozens of meetings and hordes of people." This was never more true than the fall of 1875 when, flushed with his success in Britain, Moody was impatient to get going.[12] "Water runs down," Moody explained to supporters, "and the highest hills in America are the great cities. If we can stir them we shall stir the whole country."[13]

Britain had taught him the importance of organizing the churches and unleashing the power of publicity in revival work. He had begun badly in Liverpool when his eagerness to evangelize had initially overwhelmed his instincts at organization. Now, back home, he was again growing weary of waiting. It led to an exclusive report in the *New York Tribune* that he would begin his revival work in Brooklyn on the same day the Associated Press was reporting he was ready to go in Philadelphia.[14] Moody later admitted to reporters that the "very unfortunate mistake" was his doing. He had traveled by train to Brooklyn on October 5 to be told by campaign organizers that they weren't yet ready to start his campaign in that city. The following day he heard firsthand in Philadelphia that event planners "were not quite ready" either but "would be soon." They set October 31 as the starting date. Returning to Brooklyn October 7 he was greeted by the happy news that "every arrangement had been completed" for his coming. Doubting that Philadelphia would really be ready and "impressed with Brooklyn's preparations," he told the *Tribune* he would begin in Brooklyn October 31.[15] The simple statement put civic pride on the line and sparked a widely publicized competition between organizing committees in Philadelphia and Brooklyn, the nation's second- and third-largest cities, for the right to host Moody first. The press captured, to Moody's great embarrassment, every delicious detail.

Moody's "Philadelphia friends," Brooklyn's readers were told, were asking Brooklyn to release Moody from his pledge because he'd promised Philadelphia first. But Moody's "friends in Brooklyn" were refusing. The *Brooklyn Daily Times* couldn't believe that "a gentleman of such natural firmness of character and long experience in public life would so far forget himself" in getting into this mess. The competing *Daily Eagle* argued that "were it not that these evangelists claimed to be influenced in their movements by a higher power than human reason, they would be open to a charge of infirmity of purpose."[16] It was the *Eagle's* view that "the Quaker City" needed reviving a good deal more than Brooklyn. Revivalists were "less needed in the city of churches," it proclaimed, than anywhere else. "A large body of able men minister here," it maintained, and the city's experienced churchgoers were skeptical of "noisy camp meetings" designed to "cause a stir." The civic strutting struck the *New York Graphic* as conceit. "The people of Brooklyn seem to have more churches than religion," the paper editorialized. They suffered from "a surfeit of gospel gush" and "a plentiful lack of piety."[17]

Reporting rumors about Moody's closed-door meetings encouraged public curiosity about Moody's work but did little to organize it. The *Brooklyn Times* reported "on good authority" that Moody had finally decided on Philadelphia for October 31, barely two weeks away. The

Herald said the same. Moody had surrendered, it disclosed, after seeing a telegram, signed by 200 Philadelphia ministers, arguing that he had to come now or wait until after the city's centennial celebration.[18] The reports mobilized Brooklyn's ministers. Cuyler, accompanied by William Ives Budington, a 20-year veteran of the Clinton Avenue Congregational church, and Thomas De Witt Talmage, Presbyterian pastor of the Brooklyn Tabernacle, held an emergency meeting for four hours with Philadelphia's evangelical leaders at the Broad Street Methodist church in Philadelphia on October 12. The press was kept out, but word of the "spirited exchange" leaked out. Cuyler commented that Moody was ready and so was Brooklyn. Money had been raised, a building secured, and "the wide fame of the evangelists" had "set the city aglow with fervor." The 14 Philadelphians present were no less insistent. They had invited Moody first and he had accepted their offer first. They admitted, however, that they wouldn't be ready until the end of the month and that Moody "wanted to begin his work at once." A press release followed. Moody would open in Brooklyn on October 24 for four weeks only and then would visit Philadelphia. All "misunderstandings" had been "adjusted." Brooklyn's delegates reportedly came away "rejoicing."[19]

A CITY BUILT ON RUBBLE

In a land of opportunity, Brooklyn's earliest boosters proved to be among the most opportunistic. Anxious to encourage development, they advertised Long Island as another Eden. From the beginning, however, it was a paradise built on rubble. The city rests on 300 feet of feldspar, sandstone, mica, and basalt that drifted down from the Adirondacks and New England. Competing Indian tribes had followed deer, wild turkeys, and heath hens into the salt meadow only to encounter bears, wolves, foxes, and more than an occasional skunk amid tall oaks and cedar groves threatened by the sea. The region was rich in wampum. Its beaches were littered with shells the Canarsie used in paying tribute to the Pequods in the east and the Iroquois in the west. Long before Moody came, the Pawwaws, or high priests, of the Nyacks and Jamecos held revivals of their own. They'd yell and thrash about, aligning themselves with gods who assured a happy afterlife for the brave in a land to the west, where there was no end to the feast, hunt, or dance.[20]

Breucklin's municipal affairs were contentious from the outset. The *Half Moon*'s Dutch and English crew quarreled on the trip over, and one of Henry Hudson's sailors took an arrow from an Indian eager to send them on their way. Hudson failed to find a passage to the Pacific and would later be set adrift for his trouble.[21] Ministers of the gospel were similarly received. The village's 31 families refused to pay the Reverend Johannes Theodore Polhemus a guilder in 1657. They argued that he had "intruded himself upon us against our will" and told the local leader Peter Stuyvesant the minister was "of no use to us." Only when Stuyvesant forbade harvesting until the tithe was paid was it paid. Lutherans did even worse. Stuyvesant turned down their request for a meeting place, urging the Dutch church on them. The colony's economic overseers favored "moderation" of all parties so as to better turn a profit.[22]

The seventeenth century saw Brooklyn change hands three times; the British finally forced the Dutch to give up title to the land by 1674. By that time the Marechawicks and their allies had been forced out, and Lady Deborah Moody and her English dissenters had settled in Gravesend. King James deposed the royal governor and put a Catholic in his place. Long Islanders under Jacob Leisler deposed the magistrate in 1689 and elected their own. Street riots followed. Leisler, who had made his money in fur, tobacco, and wine, proved a poor politician. On the order of William and Mary he was hanged and beheaded, the first a sentence, the second a symbol.[23] Blacks brought in from the West Indies fared little better. A 1698 census shows that more than half of the community's 90 households had forced labor. Slave auctions began in 1711. Thereafter, blacks were not allowed to meet together or hold property. They could appear in city streets at night only while holding a lit lantern. Lawbreakers were arrested and treated to 39 lashes. Those slaves who murdered their masters were burned alive and hanged from trees. On the eve of the Revolution, 60 percent of the city's residents owned slaves.[24]

Brooklyn stayed small and remained purely parochial up to the Revolution. Contemporary accounts suggest the city's 3,000 residents were seized by "a great lukewarmness" on the eve of the Battle of Long Island. War "injured prospects," which was why locals "did not greatly lament the British victory" or the loss of 2,000 colonials killed, wounded, or taken prisoner. The British used the North Dutch Church at Fulton and William Streets to pen their prisoners. Each morning rebels were commanded to "bring out your dead." The bones of 1,000 soldiers were added to the bodies of 10,000 more removed from prisoner ships moored in Wallabout Bay. On the eve of Moody's ministry in Brooklyn, nearly 100 years later, city fathers finally, to settle a public nuisance, excavated a shallow trench off Canal Street that grave robbers knew well and interred what remained of those rebels in a burial vault at Fort Greene.[25]

Brooklyn liked to see itself as "the city of churches," but during the first third of the nineteenth century it developed a reputation as a city of taverns. There was one bar for every 69 inhabitants of Brooklyn in 1834, the year it officially became a city. Brooklyn's 24,310 residents crowded into only 13 churches, one for every 1,807 people. A decade later, the numbers were barely better—52 churches served a city of 75,000. They soon competed in satisfying the local thirst with 35 breweries that annually produced one million barrels of beer worth $8 a barrel.[26] A cholera epidemic in 1832 and a devastating fire in 1848 did little to diminish the promotion of Brooklyn as a bucolic suburb for New York City businessmen. Real estate developers began cashing in on a developing residential ideal that included the homes of the virtuous who had escaped the moral and physical miasma of the metropolis. Brooklyn was advertised as New York's "nearest country retreat and perfectly healthy in all seasons." The first sidewalk had yet to be built, yet readers were told that Brooklyn offered "all of the advantages of the country with most of the conveniences of the city." Ferry service across the East River and affordable housing were offered to "gentlemen eager to secure the health and comfort of their families."[27]

As late as 1845 Brooklyn enjoyed a splendid isolation at the edge of the urban frontier. Locals cracked that crossing the East River was "more formidable than a voyage to Europe," although steamboats would soon settle that. Dutch farmers had clung to their land "as a cripple his cane," but the prices that speculators offered proved too tempting. In the 1850s "the loveliest landscape ever mortal vision was permitted to gaze upon" was cut up into building sites, swelling the city's population to 200,000, half of whom were ferried daily to work in Manhattan.[28] On the eve of the Civil War, Brooklyn was the nation's fastest-growing city, surpassing Cincinnati, Boston, Baltimore, and New Orleans and trailing only New York and Philadelphia. City fathers sought "only the better classes" but often got "lawless pleasure seekers" who had fled the cheap shanties of New York's Lower East Side in search of "a brownstone box that had gas, water and a sewer." Old-timers who remembered the settlement's pastoral past griped that they "desecrated the Sabbath by ball-playing and profanity."[29]

James Fenimore Cooper observed that in a few years Brooklyn had grown from "next to nothing" to a "flourishing city." Charles Dickens was less impressed. He took a stroll out of New York one day and couldn't remember if he wound up on Long Island or Rhode Island.[30] Walt Whitman, a Brooklyn native, was a town booster by day in the editorial offices of the *Brooklyn Daily Eagle* and *Brooklyn Daily Times* but spent his evenings in Manhattan where the real action was. New Yorkers boasted their city was three times larger than Brooklyn and offered the cultural life that a backwoods like Brooklyn so obviously lacked. The impertinence was not appreciated. Brooklyn had its rope works and wheelwrights, its coach makers and glass manufacturers, food processors, watch makers, and sugar refiners, but Manhattan was where men made their money. Some saw Brooklyn as Manhattan's vegetable stand and occasional landlord, but Brooklynites preferred to see their city as a republican enclave in a country ruled by small property holders.[31]

Not all segments of the city participated in Brooklyn's republican promise. The wealthiest 1 percent of the population owned a quarter of the city's wealth in the early Republican period and nearly half in the age of Jackson. Irish and German immigrants became a third of Brooklyn's antebellum population but had to fight for their share of the profits. The Irish were crammed into tenements near the Navy Yard and Red Hook. The Germans were crowded into Dutchtown, where they brewed, baked, and made hats and machinery. The Germans arrived in Brooklyn "with a few dollars and a plan of action," their biographer writes. "The Irish had neither."[32] The Irish liked to think that Saint Brendan or some other Irish seafarer had visited Brooklyn between the sixth and ninth centuries, a sentiment not shared by Brooklyn's Protestant majority. Henry Ward Beecher spoke for many when he said the Catholic reluctance to support abolition was because they were "slaves themselves."[33]

A CIVIL UNREST

On the eve of the Civil War, Brooklyn's major daily paper diagnosed a civil unrest beneath the city's self-satisfied surface. "We are called the city of churches," it said, mocking the municipal motto, "because we have nothing but churches." Those churches were central to the city's sense of gentility and self-identity but were also Brooklyn's bane. They stimulated the social and intellectual sentiment of the city, while avoiding its awkward political life, leaving that to the shrewd and the belligerent.[34] The city's Democratic machine often groused that the party's newspaper, the independent-minded *Brooklyn Daily Eagle*, "owed" the party its life, but its editors pointed out the only thing party hacks had ever given it were "police items." The city suffered from an inferiority complex, the paper said, that Moody's meetings might help to erase. Since revolutionary days the joke had been that General Howe captured Brooklyn first so that his troops would have somewhere to sleep before taking New York. The town had quickly tired of being Manhattan's laughing stock or anyone else's. On the eve of Moody's meetings, civic boosters advertised it as a $60 million industrial center that wore the face "of a man with serious work to do."[35]

The *Eagle* had grown up with Brooklyn and claimed to be its conscience. It began life on October 26, 1841, in a tiny walkup at 39 Fulton Street, with a good view of the ferry, when Brooklyn was little more than a destination for New Yorkers trying to escape New York. The paper promoted the political fortunes of its founder, Henry C. Murphy, who became Brooklyn's mayor the next year at the age of 31. The day-to-day operation was handled by Richard Adams Locke, whose principal fame had been won six years earlier when he persuaded readers of the *New York Sun* he had seen batmen and blue unicorns on the moon.[36] In six months both men were out. Isaac Van Anden, a small, taciturn, 33-year-old printer with a passion for order, bought the paper for $1,500 and made it pay through job printing. Six stagecoach lines connected Brooklyn to Long Island, and the reserved bachelor could be seen on any one of them, making connections and marketing the paper.[37]

When William Marsh, the *Eagle*'s editor, died on February 26, 1846, of a "congested liver," reportedly brought on by "an unflagging attention to his duties," he was replaced by Walt Whitman, a local youth who had been in newspaper work since becoming an apprentice printer when he was 13. Whitman wrote that Americans were "a newspaper-ruled people" and that meant editors needed to discriminate between "the good" and "the unreal."[38] He attacked the often long-winded writing of his day as "unworthy of the American reader" and attempted to elevate the "spiritual sentiment" of his readers with stenographic accounts of the city's best Sunday sermons.[39] Whitman was not a member of any church and disdained the "prostitution of religious sentiment" and "sectarian controversies" initiated by "obsessive trinitarians." However, he saw biblical Christianity as a means of remoralizing his city while awakening it from "spiritual complacence." Whitman editorially urged Brooklynites to "do the work of the Father rather than dispute who had the most authentic religion."[40]

Whitman liked his time at the *Eagle*, particularly the "good pay, easy work and hours." The sentiment, however, was not altogether reciprocal. In January 1848, after 22 months on the job, Whitman was sacked. Van Anden had tired of Whitman's "indolence." The editor's long communes with nature and not infrequent naps on the shaded grass of Greenwood Cemetery had become "a clog on our success." Whitman, the paper charged, "lacked steady principles." Whitman's tendency to target members of the business community and the professionally prominent had become an embarrassment to the paper's self-identity as civic booster. His antislavery crusade had been the last straw.[41] Life in Brooklyn, the paper liked to claim, while remaining light on specifics, was "rationally agreeable" because "we make business a pleasure." Brooklyn's "sky, its immeasurable vault of air," and "the sweep of its waters" had made it a paradise. It had "green robes about its shoulders" and "its skirts are wet with dew when it walks out in the morning." The city's lyceums, lit gatherings, municipal music, choral groups, cricket clubs, lodges, and benevolent societies made it a "middle class utopia." Brooklynites had an appetite for moral living and the "moral life" even if the "Gomorrah" on the other side of the East River did not.[42]

Henry McCloskey, a states' rights Democrat, succeeded Whitman but was forced to resign at the start of the Civil War because of his overly eager opposition to Lincoln. His city editor, Joseph Howard, was arrested at his desk for publishing a proclamation from the president that proved to be phony. Van Anden brought the Irish immigrant Thomas Kinsella in as editor in September 1861 to quiet the fears of those who "questioned the *Eagle's* commitment to the union."[43] Van Anden claimed his paper sought only to serve "the smallest large city in America," but opponents were not so certain. Republicans claimed he took his marching orders from Hugh McLaughlin, a machine politician who had fought his way up through Brooklyn's fish market and Navy Yard. On the eve of Moody's meetings in Brooklyn, 60 of McLaughlin's men had been indicted for election fraud, and the city's reform comptroller claimed his predecessor had embezzled nearly $200,000 in taxpayers' money. The president of the Brooklyn Trust Company committed suicide rather than face criminal charges that he had privately invested $150,000 of the city's money. Kinsella made news of his own when the city's school superintendent charged him with adultery. McLaughlin told reporters from his comfortable accommodations in the coroner's office that "pure politics" were behind the allegations.[44]

The *Brooklyn Daily Times*, long locked in a rhetorical war of words with the competing *Eagle* for the mantle of Brooklyn's most progressive paper, was eager to endorse Moody's mission. Only "a new crusade against religious indifference," it claimed, could save the city from itself. Bernard Peters, the paper's German-born editor, argued that "a city that won't obey the word of God will soon go to pieces."[45] Peters had planned a career in law before reverses in the family's fortunes made him a clerk in a dry goods store in Marietta, Ohio. By night he studied the speeches of famous Americans and began studying the scriptures. He graduated from New York's Clinton Liberal Institute in 1852 and pastored the Second Universalist Church in Cincinnati for four years before his call to All Souls' Church of Brooklyn. Peters's preaching generously combined the sacred and the profane, faith and politics, and never more so than during the war, when his letters in behalf of unionism became a staple in the pages of the *Times*. His health broke under the stress, and in 1864 he took a pastorate in Hartford, Connecticut, determined to do "the Lord's work" first.[46]

Peters's penitence didn't last long. Republicans persuaded him to edit the *Hartford Post*, a job he so enjoyed that he abandoned the pulpit for a bully one. The paper prospered and was sold for a tidy profit. He tried pastoring for a final time in Reading, Pennsylvania, before buying a half interest in the *Times* in 1868 and returning permanently to Brooklyn. Six years later he was in sole possession of the paper. His mission of "guarding the interests of this city" necessarily meant attacking special interests with an evangelical zeal. This approach broadened the paper's appeal beyond the German district. The city's common council, he wrote, was composed of "saloon keepers" and "illiterate party hacks" who had turned Brooklyn's firehouses into "assignation rooms and distilleries." The "accumulated filth of a long winter," its "rotting meat, fishheads, fins, and leaves from stunted and drooping trees, its pools of mud and cabbage leaves, its heads of beets, and dead cats and dogs" were all "ground down by passing wheels" along city streets.[47] The city seemed suspended in permanent municipal debt, he wrote, while "corruption remains endemic to the way Brooklyn does business." Party chiefs eager to discredit the wrongdoing of opponents were eager to hide their own misconduct. Each would claim "to the victor belongs the spoils." It had left the city in desperate need of a revival that only Moody could bring. Peters promised to do all he could "to arouse public anticipation to the very highest pitch" on behalf of "evangelists raised up by God in this generation to do His work."[48]

BEECHER AND BROOKLYN'S DIVIDED CHURCHES

Divisions in Brooklyn's municipal life were paralleled in its Christian community on the eve of Moody's mission in the city. The trial of Henry Ward Beecher, Brooklyn's best-known minister, in the spring and summer of 1875 on adultery charges had become a citywide spectacle and made him a national laughingstock. The case was brought by Theodore Tilton, erstwhile editor of the *Brooklyn Daily Union* and the evangelical *Independent*. Tilton and Elizabeth Richards had been married in Beecher's Plymouth Congregational Church on October 2, 1855, eight years after "Beecher the Screecher," as Mark Twain later called him, had arrived in Brooklyn. Dickens and Lincoln, Whittier and Grant, Charles Sumner and Horace Greeley had all sat under the spell of the great landscape painter of positive Christianity. Sightseers arriving on the Fulton Street ferry were simply told to follow the crowds to Beecher's 3,000-seat tabernacle near the corner of Cranberry and Orange Streets and to feign that they were hard of hearing if they wanted to get a good look at him.[49]

Beecher's annual salary of $100,000 bought a home on Brooklyn Heights overlooking the harbor, which he decorated with silk scarves and stuffed hummingbirds. He was not above advertising watches, trusses, and soap and was the master of the dramatic gesture. He held an auction at Plymouth Church that bought the freedom of a mulatto slave girl named Sarah. His church sent so many Bibles and rifles to the antislavery faction in Bloody Kansas that those sharpshooters came to be known as "Beecher Bibles." When South Carolina's Senator Preston Smith Brooks nearly killed Charles Sumner with a caning in the U.S. Senate chamber, Beecher preached from the steps of city hall that southern secessionists risked war. When war came, Beecher preached in London, Liverpool, and Manchester, urging British opposition to the cause of slavery. His widely publicized speeches made him in the minds of many "the most popular man of the North."[50]

Beecher was at the height of his powers and influence, a combination of Saint Augustine, Barnum, and John Barrymore, Sinclair Lewis would later write, when reports of his affair with a married parishioner first appeared in print in November 1872. Some papers played it for farce. "Beecher, Beecher is my name," the doggerel went. "Beecher till I die. I never kissed Mrs. Tilton. I never told a lie." Richard Salter Storrs, veteran pastor of Brooklyn's Church of the Pilgrims, was not amused. He pressed congregational authorities to investigate the charges, even after Beecher's own congregation found in his favor. Generationally, Beecher's flock was young, new to church life and trusting. They had been drawn to Beecher's side by the power of his personality. The professionals who lived in Brooklyn's wealthy wards tended to make the Church of the Pilgrims their home. Like Storrs, many of them came from New England. They shared the view of their spokesman that Beecher's gospel of love was a rationalization for self-indulgence.[51]

Moody's eagerness to get going in his campaign to evangelize America, and his long absence from the country, insulated him from the seriousness of the sex scandal and the degree to which it had divided Brooklyn's Christian community. Nor did he grasp the impact these divisions might make in his effort to take Brooklyn by storm. His success in Britain had hinged, in part, on the cooperation of evangelical churches in getting the word out and in organizing the opening of Moody's meetings, thereby creating the momentum he needed in bringing the sin-stained to those meetings. In the city of churches, Richard Storrs and William Ives Budington, two of Beecher's most ardent accusers, steadfastly supported Moody and brought their evangelical allies with them. Beecher, however, was conspicuously absent from planning meetings, a detail not overlooked by Beecher's friends at the *Brooklyn Eagle*. John T. Howard was one of Beecher's biggest backers at Plymouth, and his son Joseph had been city editor at the paper. The Republican *Times*, however, chided Beecher on "enjoying the pleasures of this life a little too much." That was all Thomas Kinsella needed to hear. Any enemy of his enemy was his friend. He had the *Eagle* puff Beecher and deride his opponents as "knaves and dogs." The organizing committee's failure to include Beecher in preevent planning only meant, in the eyes of the *Eagle*, that "the Christians of Brooklyn are not very well satisfied" in Moody's coming mission to the city.[52]

Beecher's defenders stood by their man. The *Eagle* published his vehement denial that he had been intimate with the attractive Mrs. Tilton and attacked his accusers, who promptly sued the *Eagle*. Beecher countersued Tilton and his supporters. Plymouth's 1,500 members caught the spirit of the litigious times. They brought charges against Theodore Tilton for his "slander" and voted to excommunicate the church's Sunday School superintendent, Henry C. Bowen, and longtime member Henry Moulton for corroborating Tilton's charges. Evidence that Beecher had attempted to buy Tilton's silence was ignored. Bowen, who had helped found the Christian *Independent*, which had given Beecher a national platform for his antislavery views, had long been appalled at Beecher's reckless disregard of moral probity. When Storrs, an editor on the *Independent*, asked the Congregational Council to probe the case, Plymouth's members protested "any action taken by this council on any issue relating to Plymouth Church." Storrs was deeply distressed at the personality cult that now surrounded Beecher and its effort to immunize him from the consequences of conduct the church had an obligation to punish.[53]

Days before Moody's arrival in Brooklyn, Beecher would win his case when a hung jury failed to convict him on adultery charges. A delegation from Plymouth hurried to his summer home in Peekskill with the good news. The *Eagle* took the occasion to condemn the "cadaverous, malignant and malicious" forces that had brought disrepute on Brooklyn's most beloved public servant. The *Times* argued that Tilton had emerged the defender of public virtue. The national press widely condemned "the whole Plymouth Church crowd" for reflecting the "passionate egotism" of their founding father. It was ridiculed as "a half-civilized tribe worshipping strange gods."[54] To Storrs, the whole "sad spectacle" reflected the central threat to the Gilded Age church. The liberal churches had abandoned biblical inerrancy and substitutionary atonement as a diagnosis of the human condition and its cure. Now their message was joined by that of Darwinists who seemed to challenge the Genesis account of man's origin and his final destiny. Beecher, in Storrs's view, showed how clearly the corruption had invaded the believing church, when Storrs observed that he and his generation were suspended "in judgment between two devils—but and if." Storrs, whose systematic theology had been developed at Andover Seminary, thought Beecher's "loose and uncertain mind," combined with his "need to secure assured support," led to a "personal religion" that "trusted the inspiration of the moment," whether that truth flowed from Emerson or Ecclesiastes.[55]

The *Eagle* had heartily approved when Beecher eliminated from Plymouth's ecclesiastical code the principle that "the scriptures are the only infallible guide in matters of church order and discipline" and the long-held Congregational certainty that the Bible was "given by inspiration of God." This struck the *Eagle* as "a less rugged path" for those who flocked to Beecher's meetings. When finally Beecher dropped the requirement that new members subscribe to any article of faith, the *Eagle* eagerly applauded a newly opened door "to men and women who only want to become Christians." Beecher may have seen this step as an antidote to his father's "hyper-Calvinism," but Storrs and his supporters in Brooklyn's business community and established merchant class saw it as precisely what had gone terribly wrong with "the Plymouth machine." A theology that abandoned "church history, precedent and tradition" in responding to the challenges of modernism had "already gone to pieces."[56] That was what they earnestly prayed Mr. Moody would come to mend.

MOODY IN BROOKLYN

Some of Moody's biggest boosters were chagrined that he should have chosen Brooklyn to begin his American campaign. The *New York Sun* spoke for many when it feared the "stony soil" of "the wickedest city in America" had hardly been properly prepared for his coming. Barely two weeks before he began his work at the Brooklyn Rink, preparations at the site were still in the planning stage. The organizing committee had raised only half of the estimated $7,000 it would cost to stage the month-long meetings. It was enough money to order 4,300 seats at 27 cents a chair, reserving 40 seats for reporters who would occupy 20 tables. Storrs and Cuyler, Talmage and Budington could be called on to find 150 singers for the choir, and the local YMCA would provide the 100 ushers. Cooperating papers would report "a busy, pleasant uproar" at the rink and that "a united community" awaited Moody.[57] Those familiar with the fragmentation of Brooklyn's churches knew better. "Behind its spotless cloak," the *Sun* reported, "lies the deep depravity of a city that has abandoned the glory of God for the glory of men." Brooklyn was "a blot which rests on professed religion" because "it thinks itself good enough already." Only "a concerted assault" could shake the city's smug self-confidence, editorial writers noted, and Moody seemed to lack the resources he needed in "seeking Brooklyn's repentance first."[58]

The Organizing Committee went out of its way to publicize the "cooperation" and "zeal" of Brooklyn's many ministers. Reporters were told that organizers didn't have enough room on the stage to seat all the

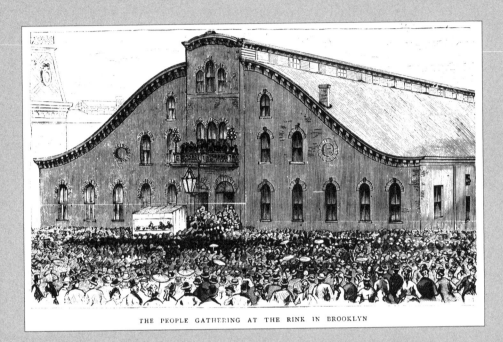

THE PEOPLE GATHERING AT THE RINK IN BROOKLYN

Opening night outside the Brooklyn Rink—October 24, 1875. Crowds came to see Moody and singer Ira Sankey. Police kept the overflow out, posting guards at the doors. The excitement made for good publicity in the morning press.

pastors who planned to be present. Moody put the best face on the preparations. Arriving in town the afternoon before the start of the services, he toured the rink and pronounced it "the best building for religious services" he had yet seen. He was "eager" to again "be at work," a sentiment he was sure was shared by Brooklyn's many ministers. Their "enthusiasm" seemed to suggest "the complete success of the revival movement in Brooklyn."[59] To professing Christians who stood aside while others prepared the way for revival, Moody had another message. He urged the reluctant to "ask yourselves this question. Are you standing in God's way? Are you opposed to God's work? The time will come when you will regret it." In Moody's mind there was "no neutral ground. You are either opposing the cause of Christ or helping it." While American Christians slept, he warned, others "wander over the precipice of sin. What a picture!"[60]

The "vast emptiness" of the Brooklyn Rink on Clermont Avenue struck many as a perfect metaphor for what Moody faced in his efforts at evangelizing America's city of churches. Built a generation before at the height of the ice skating craze, it soon stood abandoned, "cold and lifeless," when the excitement over skating receded. Having failed in its original purpose, it opened its doors to the Kings County Industrial Exhibition and an occasional German band. Its size, however, made it "unfit for ordinary use," leaving it almost always closed, a monument to a costly failure of municipal planning. John French, a sympathetic Brooklyn city alderman, had the City Railroad Company construct a branch from their main track along Myrtle Avenue and Greenpoint to the door of the Rink at Clermont and Willoughby Avenues. The Vanderbilt Avenue line did the same at the rear of the Rink.[61] It was a good thing too, because on the Sunday morning that Moody started his mission to America, 36 cars leaving every four minutes from those locations brought 5,385 interested spectators to the steps of the Rink, where they squeezed among the throngs who came on foot. The scene was likened by the great crowd of reporters present to wave after wave being "swallowed by an already swollen sea."[62]

There was "a great anxiety to see and hear him," the *New York Sun* reported, something that G. W. Smith would learn only too well. Smith, a rubber goods manufacturer, was about 40, barely five feet six, with a full beard, strong shoulders, and purposeful walk. He wore a double-breasted Prince Albert coat, like the one the papers said Moody liked to wear, and for those on their way to the Rink that was all they needed to know. "Hundreds of people began following me down Fulton Street," he told reporters. "They were whispering but I could not imagine what they meant." Only later did he learn that they had taken him for Dwight Moody.[63] As early as six, two and a half hours before the scheduled start of morning services, streetcars on all the avenues passing the Rink had hoisted the names of Moody and Sankey in "blazing letters." Even the earliest cars were all filled. In an 11-deck headline the *New York Herald* compared the multitudes to "one large river of life" following through "a promised land," creating a scene "never before witnessed in any city on this continent." The *Tribune* correspondent heartily concurred. "The sidewalks and housetops were black for blocks around," he reported. Four times as many people were turned away as admitted. Thousands couldn't get near the building, a pattern that would be repeated that afternoon and before the evening service. They lingered, intrigued at the size of the spectacle, hoping to get in. Those who had come so far and been so near, when told the rink was full, stayed, blocking the entrance, determined to get a glimpse of the man they'd come to see. Neighboring churches were throwing open their doors, but the dense throngs refused to budge. They began shouting for Moody by name, and when they heard the choir practicing inside, the *Sun* reported, the crowd "grew wild with excitement."[64]

This was not an excitement that Moody had made, the *New York Evening Post* noted, but one that had been made for him, and not by his Organizing Committee alone. "Mr. Moody has not created the fervor, he found it awaiting him," the paper editorially observed. The "excitable temperament of Americans" had been aroused by the press, the *Herald* reported, and it "had prepared the popular heart for a great outpouring of the divine power." The public was showing how utterly "nauseated" it had become by the Beecher scandal, the *Eagle* reported, "and all its obscene offspring." Their eagerness to be present at Moody's meetings suggested a determination to "bury the scandal story once and forever." For once the *Brooklyn Times* agreed. The press was always out to aid an ally in "quickening the religious fervor of a community," and Moody was just such a soldier. That was why, the *Post* replied, the press had generally heralded Moody's coming "and multiplied his influence a thousandfold."[65]

Inside the Brooklyn Rink, police held the doors shut, preventing anyone else from entering. The overflow of those who had made it inside quickly filled every seat, including what had been the auditorium's large center aisle. They could look up and see children who had climbed into window wells to get a better look. Just before 8:30 the stage was filled with more than 300 largely familiar faces of local politicians and municipal ministers, but the crowd could see that Beecher was not among them. A choir of 250 volunteers, hastily trained the night before by Ira Sankey, stood patiently, waiting. Sankey, tall and elegant, strode out on stage just before 8:30, took his position beside his cabinet organ, and opened a hymnbook that had been especially prepared for the Brooklyn campaign. Copies would go on sale the following day—25 cents for a book of 130 hymns with music and a nickel without. He found the hymn he wanted and looked hopefully at his choir and briefly to galleries on three sides of the great hall, where anxious crowds awaited Moody's arrival.[66]

Reporters portrayed Moody's appearance as that of "a businessman coming to work." His manner of arrival was compared to that of a man entering his office. He removed his heavy dark blue overcoat and black felt hat first, showing a double-breasted Prince Albert coat of dark plum color and dark trousers, carefully pressed. To reporters, eager to make much of little, he appeared "dressed for the occasion and eager to get on with it." At 8:30 Moody turned to greet some of the clergy seated on stage. Reporters could hear gasps and whispers coming from the crowd. "There he is," some were saying hesitatingly. "Is that him?" said the unsure. "A sea of upturned faces" watched as the "electrical evangelist" bowed his massive head in silent prayer, the right hand and wrist becoming briefly buried in the dark brown beard. Then his keen eyes opened, and his voice, loud and strong, but higher than expected, asked Sankey to lead in the first chorus and Reverend Budington to take the first prayer.[67]

Moody raised his left arm over the railing of his plain pine pulpit and began by reading from Numbers 13, at verse 25, of Israel's reluctance to take the Promised Land because some feared "the giants in the land. Now can we cross the Jordan and take the land?" he asked his listeners as they sat in uncertain silence. "Can we take the land?" he repeated, nearly yelling this time. "We can," reporters heard someone in the crowd shouting. "We can," shouted another. "Then we are able to go up and possess it," he said, amid many amens. "Let the question be settled this morning in every heart that loves the Lord Jesus that we will cross the Jordan, that we will go up and possess the land!" The shorthand writers were struggling unsuccessfully to keep up. Moody's simple spoken English would be likened in the Brooklyn press to "a mountain torrent—rushing, leaping and carrying all before it." Moody was depicted "standing on his toes" and "striking with the force of a sledge hammer the railing in front of him." Before coming to Brooklyn he had been told "there are giants in the land." Those giants, like the ones Israel faced, looked down on doubters as if they were grasshoppers. "I tell you when unbelief comes in we are like grasshoppers in the sight of the world," he said, turning a three-quarter circle, "but when we are filled with faith those men look like grasshoppers to us. Then instead of our being eaten up, they are bread to us. Then we are able to go up and take the land." Reporters wrote that he "sends a volley of sentences to the right and left." It struck one writer like "the discharge of a whole battery" firing at once. "What do the ministers of Brooklyn say," Moody said, pivoting to face them. "Shall we go up and take the land?" he asked, as they sat silently. "Shall we go up, Dr. Budington," he repeated, and the old man nodded his head. "Shall we go up at once, Dr. Cuyler?" Moody asked, and the minister nodded his head also. "All ready then!" Moody said, turning to his audience. "Let us go up and take the land. Let us go up and take this land in the name of God."[68]

It was an arresting performance. Word got around. Fully 15,000 persons massed at the Rink hours in advance of the afternoon service. Decorum quickly gave way to "a fearful rush." Such "pushing, jostling and scrambling" of "curiosity-seekers" had seldom been seen in the city. The press reported that the crush was "perfectly terrific." Police were called out after "women fainted, children screamed, hats were lost and shirts torn off." Families became separated, and police "were lifted off their legs" across "perilous human jams and gorges." Signboards on the Clermont Avenue side of the Rink with Moody's name on them were carried away as souvenirs, with ushers sensing they were "chaff before a mighty wind." In 40 years the *Herald* had never seen anything like it. "Clermont Avenue is wide," it told its Monday morning readers, "but its whole width and beyond it, away up the stoops of the houses and as high as the third stories, one living throng of human beings, packed as close as they could be, stood immovable long after the doors were closed."[69]

The *Brooklyn Eagle*, which had been cool to Moody's coming, admitted that the crowds that turned out were "a sight to see." Since the city was "the center of religious activity in the country," it concluded that it was not altogether surprising that Moody should create some excitement. The paper admitted that "the air itself is full of them and their work." However, the paper did not expect that spiritual revival would suddenly sweep over the nation from the East River onward. Moody "entertains and amuses," much like a circus act, the paper observed, and his success in stimulating onlookers showed the power of publicity but little else. God's cause could use a little publicity, the *Brooklyn Daily Times* retorted, since Satan's had quite a lot. It was necessary "to arouse public anticipation to the very highest pitch." Big crowds carried the message that something extraordinary was happening. Given the division in Brooklyn's believing community, it was hoped the early momentum would overcome the obvious obstacles that event organizers faced. The paper wondered what Moody could do to sustain the early interest in his campaign to evangelize America.[70]

"GOD COMMANDETH MAN EVERYWHERE TO REPENT"

By the end of its first week, D. L. Moody's ministry to North America was either faltering or gaining strength, depending on which Brooklyn newspaper one read. The *Eagle* acknowledged that Moody's "supreme self-confidence" continued to claim the attention of the community but said that "the froth of excitement seems to be washing off." The competing *Times*, not unexpectedly, reported that "Moody's earnest self-forgetting zeal" had created a revival spirit unparalleled in national history.[71] The judgment of many others, however, seemed suspended between these two opposing convictions. Whether the crowds came "seeking a blessing of unusual magnitude" or "to get in on the excitement," it was apparent to all that Moody was at the center of the storm. Some decried his organizing acumen and use of "extraordinary means" in moving the masses, while others defended his common-sense "businessman's approach" of uniting the churches and bringing sinners to repentance.[72] Others, like Beecher himself, simply withheld judgment while watching from a distance.

Moody had chosen as his text Acts 17:30, "But now God commandeth man everywhere to repent," the night that Beecher was first sighted sitting at the rear of the Rink. The verse in context teaches that God will judge the world by an immutable standard of righteousness and that on that day all men will be without excuse. Beecher, of course, was not so sure. He long had preached that there was much that man could do on his own to get to God, and if he was not morally perfectable he was at least capable of reconstruction. But Beecher told reporters he was in too forgiving a mood to quibble over doctrine. He had just dropped his countersuit against two former members of the Plymouth Church whom he had prosecuted for slander and told reporters that what Brooklyn now needed was "a real cleansing movement" that revival might bring. It was clear to him that Moody's ability "to bring a message home" had made the revival, thus far, "a grand work and a great success." Beecher defended Moody from critics who claimed that manmade means of "getting up a revival" left little room for God to do his work in awakening the spiritually dead. "We may have too much legislation," he told interviewers, "but we can't have too much religion." The farmer "uses machines to produce abundance," he observed. So he didn't see how "Moody's machinery of revival" took the production of spiritual abundance "out of God's hands."[73]

Beecher sightings became a preoccupation of Brooklyn's press as Moody's Brooklyn campaign entered its second and third weeks. He chose not to sit with Storrs and his other accusers on stage and would often arrive after the opening prayers had been uttered and leave before the benediction was pronounced. This was not altogether welcomed by those who had waited for hours to get into the rink, only to find the security gate opened by police and ushers eager to make the late-arriving Beecher a special exception. Their "severe strictures" reportedly reached Beecher's ears more than once.[74] Beecher's prayers would finally reach the ears of his fellow pastors at a special minister's meeting, set by Moody for the morning of November 11. Moody had just finished reading from Daniel 9 of "those who seek the Lord through prayer and supplication" before urging his hearers "to humble yourselves and hold onto God until the blessing comes." After an extended silence, several of the pastors present confessed their sins, some sobbing. It was then that Beecher, at the edge of the crowd stepped dramatically forward and got as close as he would get to asking forgiveness for the sordid sex scandal in which he had been the central player. "We confess our unworthiness," reporters afterward agreed that he had said. "And we confess that when we look over our souls, over long periods of time, that we are as a troubled sea. We confess how little we have loved one another and how angry we have been with one another. We confess our pride and how we have fallen into judgment over one another. We have pretended to preach Christ, but the spirit within us has been the spirit of the world. Oh, Lord Jesus, how we have slandered thee!"[75]

Beecher's prayer was big news in Brooklyn and on the west side of the East River as well. The *Eagle* reported that the revival, which had done much to arouse curiosity-seekers and little "to lift the positively depraved from their spiritual darkness," may have helped to heal the wounded among the city's many ministers. The *Eagle*, which had castigated Moody as "an illiterate man who says little," was now willing to concede that Moody might leave "a profound impression on the community" by uniting its ministers. The *Times* reported that Moody and Sankey, after 65 public meetings had shaken the city by awakening many of its ministers. It was their responsibility now to "gather the fruit." Storrs, however, was not so certain. Congregational clergymen would still need to meet to consider the Beecher case.[76] As for Beecher, he was "happy to help the wandering evangelists" and would start by strengthening their theology. He rejoiced "in the success God has given Moody" and acknowledged that "no layman was better able to lift his listeners into the presence of God," but after a two-hour meeting with Moody, Beecher came away disappointed. He told reporters that by Moody's own accounting, the number of Brooklyn's converts seemed small compared to his success across the sea. Beecher thought he knew why. Modern Americans, in his view, needed to know what they could do to get to God. Moody, he argued, had little sense of how society or individuals in it could be "regenerated." Moody had told him "the ship is wrecked" and Christ might return "even tomorrow." That made Moody's mission the rescue of those perishing. Beecher thought that this theology left man out of the picture entirely and would greatly complicate Moody's ministry in America.[77]

AN AGE OF INDIFFERENCE

Beecher's faint praise of Moody's work in the "city of churches" was shared by those in the press who believed that Brooklyn had been behaving reasonably well long before these "earnest, if misdirected ministers" arrived. Nonetheless, from October 24 through November 19, when Moody closed his meetings, the crowds kept coming. The curbstones lined with carriages and the sidewalks thronged with those anxious to enter the Rink struck cultural commentators of the period as "quite a sight to see." True believers and the simply curious had come in good weather and driving rain. The revival had easily passed the "dampness test," but a "nipping and eager air" seemed to signal its end.[78] Some suggested that Moody's legacy might have been the "quickened churches" that he left behind, but all churches hadn't cooperated, and the "positively depraved" of the city had "hardly been touched." More than once Moody had urged the familiar faces in his congregations to bring their neighbors in. Some had done so. Those sympathetic to his movement would tell reporters that "only heaven knows" how many had. Those anxious for their souls did go to an inquiry room, where Moody would meet them one by one, taking their hand in his, before leading them in prayer. All classes were represented. "The shop girl in faded attire sat beside the cultured daughter of opulence," one paper reported. "The gray-haired man and the beardless boy" both sought solace from Moody, as did "the man of business and the hard-handed son of toil." The number of converts, most agreed, was "disappointingly small." The "apathy" of Brooklyn's divided churches, the *New York Tribune* argued, had been reflected in the "coldness of its community." Those who nightly jammed the Rink were out for a skate. It was all in the spirit of "seeing a famous singer or speaker," a spectacle for the bored or simply boastful.[79]

The cooperation of disparate churches that had been so crucial to Moody in organizing his lavishly heralded revival campaign across Great Britain failed him in his first foray at evangelizing Gilded Age America. Moody's characteristic eagerness to be doing "God's work" had led him to minimize the difficulties he would face in starting his big-city sweep in Brooklyn. Complicating his job was the late start that the cooperating churches had made in developing a citywide strategy that would bring the unbeliever in. Moody's star power was now enough to bring the crowds in and to keep them coming, but that was not what he was after. Beecher was right when he said Moody sought to save the lost while there was yet time. And that was why he was "a fire burning all the time" to be at his Master's work.

The press would attach symbolic significance to the start of Moody's big-city swing through Brooklyn. This eagerly anticipated campaign was meant to show whether America was ready for Moody and his methods. The crowds that came three times a day to Brooklyn's Rink to hear Moody speak were spectacle enough for news editors seeking a good story. The relative silence from the inquiry room was more discordant to Moody than to those who chronicled his passage in the press. They were set on seeing the crowds as "a great musical instrument, giving back to Moody an answering note to every chord he touched." For the time being, Moody could be forgiven for offering a theology that "hasn't kept up with the nineteenth century." The city, for its part, "got the revival it anticipated," a little like a great show when it opens, has its run, and then closes.[80]

The decision of Brooklyn's ministers to quickly abandon the Rink once Moody was off to Philadelphia simply confirmed to some what Moody faced in his plan to awaken America from spiritual slumber. Moody and Sankey, all agreed, were original workers—simple, square, modest, energetic, and direct. They were "believing men in a doubting age." It was as if in returning to America after a long absence they had forgotten their place of origin. How else could they be so "red hot in an age of indifference?" Americans were not only in the habit of hiding their sins, but a great many wondered whether there was sin in the world. "They are a tremendous sensation," the *Sunday Sun* observed, given "the tentative preaching of our times. They are men who scorn personal gain in a day of self-seeking." Time would tell whether "these men are right and the age wrong."[81]

"*It's Harder Getting into the Depot than Heaven*"

FOUR

MOODY IN PHILADELPHIA, NOVEMBER 1875–JANUARY 1876

I t was half past seven, and the largest choir that anyone had ever seen in the biggest building any Philadelphian had ever been in were just finishing "What a Friend We Have in Jesus" when D. L. Moody began reading the fifth chapter of Mark. It was the story of Jesus meeting the man with an unclean spirit. "No one could bind him anymore," he said hurriedly, as seven stenographers from the city's leading dailies strained to keep up. "Night and day he was always crying out," Moody seemed to be saying, "and crying out with a loud voice." But many of the 13,000 present could hardly hear him. "The solemn stillness was rudely broken," the *Philadelphia Times* would later report, by someone trying to "kick his way into the reporters' box."[1] It was a gentleman of the press who had arrived late and been barred from the biggest spiritual story to hit the centennial city since Franklin had hosted Whitefield a century and a half before.[2]

Philadelphia's Gilded Age press, known for its "cautious conservatism" and "business-like seriousness," found the former shoe salesman "sincere" and "earnest" if "unremarkable."[3] His results in "stirring a sensation" seemed to stem from organizational acuity and canny public relations, his critics claimed, in which the press played no small part.[4] While the overly eager reporter was finally admitted to the press box, others lacking his status and denied admission could not be consoled by any of John Wanamaker's 300 company employees who served as blue-badged ushers.[5] In the crush of those locked out of the Pennsylvania Railroad Freight Depot and unable to see the spiritual spectacle going on inside, an elderly man could be heard shouting, "I've been to a good many religious meetings in my time, but I was never kicked around in this way before." Event organizers had "gone into show business," another man groused. "It's harder to get into the depot than heaven," complained a third, as they made their unlucky way down Thirteenth Street.[6]

More than one million people did get in to see what many would affectionately remember as the Grand Depot Revival. It opened to a packed house on November 21, 1875, and closed nine weeks later when delegates to a Christian Convention heard Moody explain how the momentum of revival might be sustained. Those who passed through the civic spectacle had never seen anything like it. They delighted in keeping scrapbooks of press reports that included verbatim transcripts of Moody's every utterance during 250 mass meetings. Seventeen thousand anxious inquirers met with Moody and his workers after these meetings, and 4,200 prayed to become Christians. For them the meetings had a special significance. On the fortieth anniversary of Moody's Gilded Age meetings in Philadelphia, a capacity crowd at the Garrick Theatre remembered the centennial city's season of spiritual excitement. One hundred stood to say they became Christians through those meetings. Many more had their own stories to tell of prodigal sons who had returned home, dissolute husbands reconciled with their wives, young men and women fresh from the country who were saved from the seductions of the city.[7]

Philadelphia's business community joined hands with Moody in staging a spiritual extravaganza for a city in the throes of "turning itself inside out."[8] The rise of streetcars and commuter railroads had permitted some to escape the crime and congestion of America's second city. Others were left behind to endure the crowding and contagions of expanding warehouses, city street gangs, and substandard housing.[9] Among those remaining were 160,000 families who belonged to 530 religious congregations. Annexation and industrialization had produced a population of 800,000, a quarter of these foreign-born Irish and Germans, and this population was growing at a faster rate than the Protestant majority.[10] Youth gangs fought over turf and pecking order.[11] Artisans were being displaced by mechanization and felt the depressing effects of the Panic of 1873. So did the small businessmen and the city's financial institutions. The usually upbeat *Public Ledger* understatedly admitted: "The signs of the times are not in every respect propitious."[12] The city's political machine operated for cynical civic amusement and was dominated by ward healers of little vision and less energy. The Republicans had saved the Union, spoilsmen argued, leading one voter to boast: "I'd vote for the Devil, if he was running as a Republican." If simple sentiment didn't work, patronage and intimidation did. "King James" McManes, ruler of the Gas Trust, employed 5,500 people and enjoyed a $4,000,000 annual payroll while overseeing a municipal debt of $70 million. The corruption of machine politics was symbolized by a half-finished city hall that had been begun four years earlier. Those who protested too loudly might face thugs who had police protection.[13]

While it would be D. L. Moody's ties to Philadelphia's evangelical elite—John Wanamaker, George Stuart, Anthony Drexel, and Jay Cooke—that made headlines, much of the revival's success rested on self-made men, new to the city and not yet acculturated to its corruptions. These were the clerks and salesmen of rural backgrounds who filled the pews of Philadelphia's evangelical churches and its communal fellowships such as the YMCA. They were appalled by what they saw as the city's indifference to moral blight and led the campaign to do something about it. They were drawn to Moody's earnest appeal that Christians overcome denominational barriers in proclaiming an old familiar faith to a population that resisted instruction.[14] Through it they hoped to strengthen the social order in the centennial city, while saving souls for the next. While their arrangements in revival planning were "ever so perfect," they warned fellow Philadelphians and its establishment newspapers on the eve of Moody's meetings that an "entire people must be awakened" if the city's slothful citizens were to be reached.[15]

PHILADELPHIA'S PRESS ON THE EVE OF THE REVIVAL

"There was quite an excitement in Frogtown," the *Catholic World* told its readers after warily watching Philadelphia's press welcome Mr. Moody to their city. "The Rev. Eliphalet Notext," the *World's* name for Mr. Moody, "was in town." Brother Notext was no theologian, the *World* reported, but he knew "the business of getting up a revival." That meant creating "a sensation," so "he began with the newspapers." Hoping to stimulate circulation, "a few friendly newspapers chronicled his wonderful success." Then their competition got in on the act. Readers were told that "the numbers of converts was miraculously large." The curious came to see for themselves. The crowds swelled. You could hardly get a seat. By then "Mr. Notext's machinery was in full blast."[16] The paper reflected the sense of estrangement that many Philadelphia Catholics felt from the machinery of Mr. Moody's revival. They had grown to 42 churches, geographically dispersed throughout the city, and could look to their cathedral on Logan Square and the Seminary of Saint Charles Borromeo in Overbrook as sure signs of Catholic permanence. Their significance was sealed in

1875 when the Philadelphia-born bishop James Frederick Wood became the city's first archbishop. The diocese had an allergy to periodic Protestant excitements, particularly when led by the self-taught. Their celebrants shared their antipathy.[17]

The *North American and U.S. Gazette*, then in its ninety-first year of service as the oldest daily paper in America, shared this skepticism. "Adroit heralding" by a sympathetic press, the paper editorialized, had made the excitement of Moody's meetings "not a spontaneous manifestation of the spirit's moving" but the direct result of "a carefully planned success."[18] The paper's publisher, 67-year-old Morton McMichael, had had a long association with Philadelphia's "better" classes, and he couldn't see where Moody's revival would do them any good. He argued that Moody would be better served "saving the souls of those poor wretches" of the Western Pennsylvania coal fields. Such men were "a stain upon our civilization." Their "dark souls typified the black mines where they dig, delve and conspire."[19] An intimate of Webster, Clay, Seward, and Chase, McMichael became Philadelphia's mayor in the late 1860s and a spokesman for its commercial community. His sons Walter, who became the paper's general business manager, and Clayton, who served as managing editor, saw the world as he did.[20] Philadelphia's "intelligent citizens" deplored "religious entertainment" because "no action that is sprung purely from excitement can be trusted."[21]

Speaking for "the better people," the McMichaels disdained Moody's ministry, while the *Sunday Dispatch* chided him for championing the cause of those "who profess to be better than their fellow man."[22] The oldest existing Sunday paper in Pennsylvania had from its founding been a bit of an outcast. Its inaugural number in 1848 made only 28 cents. It had been boycotted by the better people. The daily press ignored it. The Protestant community deplored it. It took the city directory three years to list it.[23] It was published on South Third Street below Walnut, where it developed a reputation under the veteran editor and civic historian Thompson Westcott of tweaking the establishment. "We are nothing, if not critical," he proudly boasted. The paper saw itself as a friend of the workingman and a sworn enemy of the interests. It had mounted an unsuccessful campaign to force the city to take possession of municipal railroads and to lease them to the highest bidder. And it had fought the removal of houses from the middle of Market Street, charging it was "a scheme of the market house monopolists" and their friends in city hall to push the small-time peddler out.[24]

Westcott identified Moody with the special interests and the newspapers that supported them. These were the men who "have the chief seats in the city's churches, who are clad in broadcloth and fine linen and fare sumptuously every day." They were building up "a loud-mouthed braggart" whose "matchless affrontery" sold religion as if it were "a cheap, patent medicine."[25] Moody was "an untiring blower of his own trumpet," but he had help. The crowds that came to the tabernacle to hear him had had "their curiosity piqued by newspaper accounts." Westcott considered Moody "an ignorant impostor" whose "eccentric evangelism" was being promoted by the press in hopes of keeping the public in their place. The suggestion that each night Moody preached to capacity crowds was "the biggest lie in the history of Philadelphia journalism," the *Sunday Dispatch* said. It preferred, as did its readers, "the religion of those who mind their own business."[26]

Philadelphia's competing establishment papers, however, were firmly on Moody's side. Led by the city's most popular paper, the *Public Ledger*, they viewed Moody as a "great commander" directing an "efficient army" of workers in "meetings of moral grandeur."[27] The paper's publisher, George W. Childs, disputed Westcott's claim that only the *Dispatch* defended the public interest. Childs, the "boy barterer," had come up the hard way, buying and selling books. When he won control of the *Public Ledger* in 1864 it was $100,000 in debt; within three years he had put it on a paying basis and opened its new offices at Sixth and Chestnut.[28] He consciously courted respectability, removing from the paper any language and advertising that might offend an eight-year-old. He built a reputation for fair-minded philanthropy, negotiating a wage package with his workers that included profit-sharing and a pension, before endowing a burial plot in Woodland Cemetery for the Typographical Society of Philadelphia.[29]

When the Moody revival opened on the evening of November 21, 1875, in the Old Freight Depot building of the Pennsylvania Railroad at Thirteenth and Market Streets in Philadelphia, it was not surprising to see the 46-year-old Childs sitting on stage with 400 other invited guests. The daily press would note how he attended many of the 250 meetings that followed. So did his managing editor, Colonel William V. McKean.[30] Their presence signaled, as forcefully as any editorial could, the acceptance by the establishment press of Moody's work in Philadelphia. McKean, who had helped establish the Philadelphia chapter of the YMCA in 1854, was a private collector of Cotton Mather sermons.[31] He seemed certain that "the grandest century in the history of men" would have a fitting climax in Moody's meetings. That was why all those committed to the "moral progress" of the less fortunate were "heartily in sympathy with this work."[32]

The *Philadelphia Times* was certainly in sympathy with Moody. By publicizing Moody's meetings, it sought to strengthen its hold on the second-widest circulation in the city. Its 47-year-old editor-in-chief, Alexander McClure, was a man in a hurry and on a mission. As a country editor and lawyer he had been a founding father of the Republican Party and a state legislator who had helped elect Lincoln. He had won a state senate seat running as a Liberal Republican and narrowly lost the 1873 race for mayor of Philadelphia while running as an Independent.[33] While his competitors seemed satisfied to encounter Moody at his meetings, McClure sent a reporter to interview the celebrated evangelist at the home of John Wanamaker, where he stayed during the crusade. Moody admitted he was tired. Two and a half years of daily preaching in Britain had been quickly followed by a month's worth of meetings that had drawn 300,000 persons to the Brooklyn Tabernacle. McClure warned readers that Brooklyn's church leaders had been "full of hypocrisy" and that that had "impeded progress." That was why "the whole city will turn out" to "insure success" in Philadelphia.[34]

McClure saw Moody's meetings as symbolically significant. The centennial meant that all eyes would be on the city. That was why the meetings could not be allowed to fail. "The outside world is watching us with profound interest," McClure editorially observed. Reporters and local pastors shared the responsibility, as he saw it, of moving the momentum of Moody's meetings forward. Together they could stake a claim on America's second century.[35] Nowhere was this view more elegantly put than at the *Philadelphia Inquirer*, where L. Clarke Davis had established a reputation as a first-rate writer of fact and fiction prior to becoming managing editor in 1870 at the age of 35.[36] He had graduated from Philadelphia's Episcopal Academy with a dedication to worthy causes; first abolition, and later care for the insane. Faith and experience had convinced him that "the grandest accomplishments of our race in all the world and in all time have been achieved through the power of religion to control man's will and work." So the sentiment of the *Inquirer* would be "to forward the work of these evangelists to the extent of our ability."[37]

The *Inquirer* proclaimed "The Great Awakening" in a nearly unprecedented nine-line front-page boldface lead on the eve of the Moody meetings. Its daily stenographic accounts of Moody's every public utterance, occupying column inch after column inch, indicated its hope that coverage would be good for the city's spirit and the paper's business. The *Evening Bulletin*, locked in a crowded competition for late afternoon and early evening readers, advertised its coverage in the *Inquirer*, promising a "full report" of the day's events. It was a serious-minded promise from a newspaper that was well respected but not widely read.[38] Gibson Peacock had obtained the job of editor after his father bought a share of the floundering paper in 1847. Struggles followed. The paper was sold at public auction to generate revenue, and Peacock cast about for a good story to stimulate a slender circulation.[39] He thought he had found it in Moody's revival. "Two years of hard times," the *Bulletin* observed, identifying itself with the anxious and vulnerable, had made "the fields ripe unto harvest." The people could use a savior. That was why "everybody desires the success of these meetings."[40]

Revival organizers advertised meetings in the *Bulletin* and other co-operating papers. The *Daily Press,* the *Evening Telegraph,* and the *Public Record* each benefited from that advertising revenue. Event organizers benefited most from the popular *Press* and its warm embrace of the meetings. John Wein Forney, the 58-year-old founder of the *Press,* was a Philadelphia editor with a national reputation and influence. He was a Jacksonian Democrat whose support had proved crucial in the 1856 election of James Buchanan to the presidency. Then he broke with his longtime friend over the extension of slavery into Kansas, and he later became a Republican and an intimate of President Lincoln. Contemporaries considered Forney the dominant figure in Pennsylvania journalism.[41] The *Press* never supported or opposed anything "by halves."[42] "Except a man be dead," the paper argued, "it was impossible to resist" the moral meaning of Moody's message.[43] The paper's weekly edition steadfastly predicted that "the largest number of converts in American history" would emerge from the meetings at the Depot tabernacle.[44]

On the eve of the campaign's opening, the *Evening Telegraph* reported "an enthusiasm never seen before in the city." Even the unexpected death of Vice-President Henry Wilson was shunted to the side to make room for news from the crusade. Charles Warburton, the paper's publisher, had no doubt that part of Moody's popularity was a nostalgic appeal "to a more innocent time" before liberal theology began to chip away at public confidence in the familiar faith of their fathers. That, however, did little to deter the crowds "anxious to shake Mr. Moody's hand after every service."[45] William J. Swain, publisher of the *Record,* saw his penny paper "as a welcome guest at the fireside of the poor man" and believed his readers would share the city's enthusiasm in welcoming the well-known evangelist. The long months of highly publicized work by his organizing committee seemed to ensure curious crowds. If Moody could succeed anywhere in America, the *Record* argued, it would be in Philadelphia, where church leaders appeared to be "united with great earnestness and eagerness for the coming of the evangelists."[46]

The anticipation that Moody's union meetings at the Grand Depot would succeed in an unprecedented way had been carefully cultivated through the organizational acumen of two men Moody had known for years: George Stuart and John Wanamaker, who had served with him in the earliest days of the YMCA. Each was eminently well connected to do Moody a great deal of good in Philadelphia, and each understood the importance of publicity and the effective use of mass media in doing that good. They saw to it that Philadelphia's Protestant community and its establishment press were well disposed to Moody and his methods before the first sermon was preached. Their contribution to the story of Moody's success is a case study in the role of advertising and the power of publicity in crafting the modern mass media revival.

STUART AND WANAMAKER

"The very report of what God is doing in one region can raise hope and effort in another," George Stuart predicted in the summer of 1875, when he financed one of the first summaries to appear in America of D. L. Moody's revival work in Britain and Ireland.[47] The 59-year-old Philadelphia linen importer, whose company had branches in New York and Manchester, had time and money on his hands. He put both to work in helping to make Moody the best-known evangelist in the English-speaking world before bringing him to Philadelphia. This made the well-connected Stuart a "sycophant" in Moody's service, according to his critics at the *Sunday Dispatch*, "as garrulous as a crazy old woman" when it came to bragging about his protege, Mr. Moody. They claimed that the merchant's personal wealth was more responsible than the Associated Press for first bringing Moody's transatlantic work to the attention of American audiences.[48]

Moody first came to Stuart's attention in 1860, when he was a 22-year-old Sunday School teacher working the slums of Chicago.[49] At the outbreak of the Civil War, Stuart recruited Moody to serve in the U.S. Christian Commission, an organization dedicated to meeting the spiritual and material needs of men in uniform. Stuart chaired a committee of 12 who directed humanitarian relief from the organization's national headquarters at 13 Bank Street in Philadelphia.[50] Stuart, by this time, was recognized as a national leader in Christian work and philanthropy. His parents were Scotch-Irish Presbyterians who impressed on their son from an early age the beauty of a Christian's civic responsibility. Stuart became an early advocate of temperance and served as elder and Sunday School superintendent in Philadelphia's First Reformed Presbyterian Church.[51] In 1851, he met George Williams, a farmer's son who became a clerk in a London dry goods store, before establishing the YMCA in 1844. Stuart was struck with the organization's zealousness in improving the spiritual condition of young men new to the city and its seductions. In 1854, he launched a YMCA in Philadelphia, becoming the chapter's president and chief recruiter.[52]

Stuart's most important recruit was the man he chose in 1858 to serve as chapter secretary. John Wanamaker was a 19-year-old clerk in the Tower Hall clothing store, the largest in Philadelphia, when Stuart offered him $1,000 a year to stimulate interest in the work of the organization and to increase its service to the young men of Philadelphia. By the end of his first year of employment, the local chapter had expanded by 2,000 members. "I went into the byways and hedges and compelled them to come in," Wanamaker observed in the aggressive certainty that would make him a superb salesman.[53] For three years the organization expanded its membership among white-collar clerks and merchants by offering lunch hours that combined speakers with fellowship, prayer, and praise. Workers who were strangers to the city were given a sense of group identity and spiritual support. They eagerly told others what they had found.[54] Wanamaker was a practical Presbyterian, a Sunday School teacher determined to make a difference in the lives of the young boys he would collect on the streets and deliver to the Chambers Church on Broad Street below Chestnut. "The Sunday-school," he was certain, "comes closer than anything else in answering the greater needs of the human race."[55]

Stuart's and Wanamaker's introduction to the importance of organization and communication technology in furthering the purposes of evangelism was the revival of 1857–58. By March of 1858 the 3,000-seat Jaynes Hall on Chestnut Street was barely large enough to contain the white-collar crowds who came for noon hour sessions of prayer and praise. Four months earlier, barely a dozen listeners could be found. That was when event organizers decided that if the crowd wouldn't come to them they'd go to the crowd. In a preview of the Moody meetings, hard-working volunteers posted announcements in public places and handed out tracts to men as they arrived at work, where they banked, and as they rode home on public transportation.[56] A media campaign was initiated too. Friendly newspapermen were enlisted to publicize the meetings. Reduced telegraph rates transmitted the good news to cities along the Atlantic seaboard. Eventually, the newly formed Associated Press, always in search of a good story it could sell to subscribers, gave the meetings national play.[57]

Between 1858 and 1875, Moody would come into Stuart's and Wanamaker's orbit, and eventually they into his. The day after Fort Sumter was fired on, Wanamaker launched a clothing store at the southeast corner of Sixth and Market Streets, spending $24 of the first $24.67 he made on advertising his latest line of "ready made clothing."[58] In November 1861 he accompanied Stuart to New York, where they established the U.S. Christian Commission through the cooperation of YMCA chapters in the North.[59] Immediately, Moody impressed Stuart as "one of our most efficient workers." His work in the field, where he led daily services; in camp hospitals, where he offered support to the suffering; and with reporters, where he publicized the commission's work and needs helped assure that "there was no organization which had a stronger hold on the hearts of the people than ours."[60] Stuart

John Wanamaker, the department store magnate, had known Moody since their early days in the YMCA. Each appreciated the power of publicity in getting their messages out.

helped Moody's transition to evangelist after the war by securing for him Philadelphia's Central Presbyterian Church for a series of revival meetings in 1866. Wanamaker, by this time a highly prosperous merchant, was dubious. Moody's fourth-grade education meant "he murders the King's English."[61] The crowds came anyway, and by the time Wanamaker heard Moody address the YMCA convention in Albany two years later, he became a convert to Moody's cause. A friendship followed. When Moody came to Philadelphia in 1871, he was Wanamaker's house guest. When the Great Chicago Fire burned down Moody's home church in that city, Wanamaker and Stuart led a national fund-raising campaign to put the evangelist back on his feet again.[62] When Moody began to make money through the sale of a popular hymnal, the funds were administered by a board of trustees headed by Stuart.[63]

Stuart and Wanamaker fully expected that Philadelphia would be honored as the first American city to host a crusade by the famous evangelist following his highly successful revival work in Britain and Ireland between 1873 and 1875. The Academy of Music was available, but Stuart wanted to make a bigger splash. When Moody made plans to open his North American revival work in Brooklyn, Stuart and Wanamaker decided to stage Moody's Philadelphia campaign in the old Pennsylvania Railroad freight warehouse at Thirteenth and Market Streets. Wanamaker had secretly secured the site months before as the future home of his burgeoning retail business. Now he made it available to Moody and event organizers rent free. The six-week run up to Moody's grand opening on November 15, 1875, was a sure-fire headline stealer. Addison Hutton, perhaps the area's best-known architect, redesigned the shed and waived his fee. Two hundred workmen were dispatched. The construction started an avalanche of free publicity.[64] Railroad tracks were ripped up, and a properly pitched board floor was installed. One thousand gas jets were placed overhead. A tiered platform, large enough for several hundred singers, was next. Stuart got a Connecticut firm to contribute 10,000 chairs at 28 cents a seat. It was the largest such order ever. Wanamaker saw that it was publicized and added eight seats to the invoice to make an exact number of 10,008, an even bigger impression in the press than a round 10,000, which might have seemed hyperbole.[65] As was the case with everything else in the Grand Depot campaign, little would be left to chance.

ORGANIZING AND PUBLICIZING A REVIVAL

Weeks before D. L. Moody set foot in Philadelphia, the elaborate plans to bring him to town were having the desired effect. Daily headlines reported the creation of coordinating committees charged with organizing the event. A committee of 15 ministers beseeched God and participating churches to do their part. A committee of 13 laymen, led by Stuart, made sure men would do theirs. Six hundred singers were sought.[66] Three hundred ushers were found. Many of the singers were from Wanamaker's Bethany Presbyterian Church Bible study, the largest in the nation. The blue-badged ushers were clerks in Wanamaker's store, which by 1875 was the busiest in the nation.[67] Acoustics experts created a wooden shell that would allow Moody to be heard in the auditorium's back row. Wanamaker added a series of speaking tubes to connect his chief usher to all corners of the hall. One hundred eighty police officers were put on special detail to handle the anticipated crowds. A telegraph connected them to city police headquarters.[68]

The sheer size of the undertaking was unprecedented. It assured that the curious would come when the tabernacle opened its 10 large doors to the public on the evening of November 21, 1875. The event was already making municipal history. The one-story tabernacle was the size of a city block, extending 373 feet from Market to Kelly Street and 250 feet from Thirteenth to Jupiter. It was an organized universe crossed by eight aisles and occupied by 8,904 seats and a speaker's platform of 1,304 more. When filled, it created the impression that "the whole city had turned out."[69] The importance of keeping the crowds coming was very much on the minds of executive committee members. "Our entire people must be awakened," the committee secretary, Thomas Cree, claimed, "if we are to avoid the unutterable sadness of failure." Philadelphia's centennial celebration gave a unique opportunity "to exert an influence that will be felt all over the world."[70]

Cree, a longtime YMCA leader in Philadelphia, was given a publicity budget of $30,000 on the eve of the meetings. He knew what to do with it. Much of the money went to advertising in the daily press, the production of large sheet posters and the distribution of small circulars. On one Saturday alone a fleet of volunteers circulated 162,000 notices of Moody's meetings at the tabernacle, while a team of workers visited congregations within 50 miles of Philadelphia.[71] Cree and his coordinators received their marching orders from Moody himself. Those who deplored his merchandising the gospel needed to understand the reality of modern living. America's sacred institutions and religious work, he argued, now competed against theaters and places of amusement for people's time and attention. He believed newspapers were one of the principal places where the battle lines were drawn and the competition fiercely waged.[72] Wanamaker strongly defended Moody's decision. "I owe my success to newspapers," he would often say, and proved it by rarely going a single day without placing an ad of his own.[73]

So that there was no uncertainty about Moody's meaning or message, he met with his coordinating committee and local supporters on the eve of the meetings. Jay Cooke and Anthony J. Drexel, leading bankers of the city, who could be seen passing the collection plate at the meetings, were present, along with the publisher of the *Public Ledger,* George Childs. Cooke, who had helped finance the Civil War, was recovering from his speculation on the Northern Pacific Railroad that had led to his personal bankruptcy and a nationwide panic only two years before. Drexel, who had helped finance Childs's purchase of the *Ledger,* was conservative in finance and cautious in his public involvements.[74] Moody told them that if they expected to lead others to Christ, they must be ready themselves to meet their Maker. Addressing each man by name, he asked, "Are you ready?" The tension was considerable until Moody got to Wanamaker. "John Wanamaker," he said, "are you ready?" "Yes," the merchant replied, "ready-made," repeating his often advertised assertion that suits need not be made to order.[75]

The two friends almost certainly spoke of Wanamaker's mild eruption that night on the way home, as the Moodys settled in with the Wanamakers for the nine-week meeting schedule. Moody would address the large meetings at the tabernacle and Wanamaker the nightly overflow meeting for young men in a Methodist church nearby at Broad and Arch streets. A lifelong friendship would be solidified in the weeks that followed, and years afterward Wanamaker would proudly show to those entering his office one of his most prized possessions. It was a bit of cardboard, faded and very much worn—his usher's card at the Moody meetings that were to make Philadelphia history.[76]

COVERING MOODY'S MEETINGS

Reporters had been warned to come early if they wanted good seats at Moody's inaugural meetings, but they could not have imagined that it might mean hours in advance. The doors were supposed to open at seven for the 7:30 services, but the crowds that came to the tabernacle by midafternoon spilled over the sidewalk and swelled into the street, blocking traffic. The tabernacle's doors were ordered opened before six, and within minutes all 12,000 seats in the auditorium and on stage were occupied. Choir members and ministers among the 10,000 on the outside looking in attempted to take the clamor as a sign of God's abundant blessing. Reporters, locked out of the day's big story, did not share their enthusiasm. A reporter from the *Philadelphia North American & U.S. Gazette* who did break through found "there was not an available seat anywhere in the building." That included the press box, which was overridden "by persons who had no business being there."[77] A *Philadelphia Inquirer* reporter got in after Moody had begun and complained he "couldn't see the speaker."[78]

More than once, the *Evening Bulletin* editorialized, people posing as members of the press had swindled their seats. Some admittedly were reporters from small-town papers miles away. Others, however, were "young gents who know as much about reporting as a duck does about Latin."[79]

The press appealed to Moody's coordinating committee for a remedy. The *Daily Press* publicly called on the Committee of Arrangements to straighten things out so that "the humble chroniclers" of the press could "ply their profession."[80] Their appeal showed how aware they were of the news media's contribution to the success of modern revivalism. The curious come because they read of Moody in the papers, the *Press* said. Then they are "brought under the influence and power" of Moody and the spectacle of his services. "The evangelists regard half their work done," the paper observed, "when the people become interested."[81] The press was no less "devoted to the service of Almighty God" then the men who preached the Good News, claimed the *Bulletin*. That was why "smart young men who beat their way into circuses, variety theaters and other small shows" should not be allowed to succeed at the tabernacle.[82]

The meeting's executive committee responded to the "credentials crisis" by creating a "Reporters' Department" under Cree. It announced it would now reserve specific seats for reporters. Violators would be subject to prosecution.[83] It was becoming apparent to meeting organizers that the press needed a good story as much as event organizers needed the free flow of positive publicity. Instead of incurring the expense of advertising the meetings, Cree's committee decided to simply send a circular to interested editors giving them a schedule of future meetings. Reporting the schedule became front-page news.[84] Moody's text was news too, reported fully and faithfully each day of the campaign by stenographers scurrying to record column inch after column inch. But the spectacle of revival was its own text. "We had never before seen anything like it," Cree could remember, years after the campaign closed. "Thousands desperately seeking admission were turned away" while "everywhere you looked, stretching in long rows from side to side and a way to the back, it was a scene never to be forgotten."[85]

John Forney had seen revivalists come and go in nearly three decades as the city's chief chronicler, but as the tabernacle meetings unfolded he observed: "there has never been a similar meeting in the city's history." It was not only the size of the meetings but the method of their execution that impressed Forney. From the very start, Moody and his coordinating committee "have been as systematic as an astronomer," Forney wrote, offering a new form of evangelism that was not "content alone to trust some higher power." Instead, Moody's first week of messages targeted believers, not unbelievers, with what they must do to revive themselves if they expected to revive others.[86] The *Public Ledger* saw symbolic significance in this approach. The growing anonymity of large-scale urban living in America's second century produced isolated people in search of community. In Moody's meetings "of moral grandeur" they knew they had found it. That was the "electric touch of human sympathy" that was bringing "a mutual thrill to the hearts of thousands."[87]

Reports of Moody's meetings brought President Grant, his cabinet, and the justices of the United States Supreme Court to the Grand Depot on the evening of December 19, an attendance arranged by George Childs, with whom the president was to be staying while touring the city's centennial preparations.[88] Rarely had so many men of power and influence been gathered under the same roof to hear the gospel preached, a significance not lost on Philadelphia's chroniclers of the sacred and secular. Stuart's account of the evening included the "arrest" of the justices at the corner of Thirteenth and Chestnut and their police escort into the tabernacle, where they sought to avoid "mingling with the throng."[89] The nation's most acclaimed historian, George Bancroft, then immersed in revisions of the centenary edition of his *History of the United States*, was also a witness to history that night. So were the former Speaker of the House, James G. Blaine, Grant's heir apparent; James A. Garfield, a future president; and leaders of Congress. Moody did not disappoint. His text from the fourteenth chapter of Luke, "I pray thee, hear my excuse," detailed the reasons people gave for not becoming Christians and the moral urgency to do so while there was yet time. His advocates in the press had never seen Moody more "powerful." Grant, a Methodist, sat on the stage, behind Moody and to his left. After the meeting he told reporters that Moody's message was just what the nation needed. Blaine, always available for a quote, considered Moody one of the country's most "useful" of men.[90]

When word of the president's attendance at the tabernacle reached readers outside Philadelphia, the excursion trains with discount fares began bringing them to town in unprecedented numbers. Tickets issued in advance were designed to make sure the passengers had a seat when they got there, but even that failed to keep the crowds down. Newspapers kept daily score in a kind of competition generally reserved for reporting baseball. Lancaster brought 1,000 attendees; Harrisburg 850; Wilmington 700; Trenton 600; West Chester 300; and Merchantville 150—most of the Christians in that New Jersey town. Each day brought a new team to town. Townspeople from along the West Jersey Road and villagers on the North Pennsylvania Road as far as Doylestown were finding "it's quite the thing to come."[91] Allentown excursionists were combining shopping with matters of the spirit. Even reporters were

Moody strikes a characteristic pose for the "pulpit portraits" that were widely circulated in Sunday supplements and news magazines across the United States during his Philadelphia campaign, exposing Moody's ministry to a nationwide audience.

getting in on the evening entertainment. By special permission they could bring their lady friends to the press box; for them it became date night at the tabernacle.[92]

While the spectacle was something to see, it was the man Moody, the centennial's celebrity evangelist, who attracted the most attention. The close of the meetings only intensified the public's appetite to have one last look of him. The *Sunday Dispatch* had an allergy to the civic celebration. It groused that a poor likeness of Moody, selling for two dollars in the marketplace, was sold out. As an incorrigible self-promoter, Moody knew no equal, the paper lamented. His "pyrotechnic display of mendacities" appeared to bewilder his fans into believing his "feet were not of clay, nor his head wood."[93] The sight of his statuette hawked outside the tabernacle struck the *Philadelphia North American and U.S. Gazette* as a crass commercialization of religious sentiment.[94] Even the redoubtable Dr. R. V. Pierce was getting in on the act: the patent medicine manufacturer advertised in many Philadelphia newspapers during the weeks of the tabernacle crusade under the title "American Genius—Moody and Sankey," in which he likened his elixir to clean out the blood and liver with the purifying work of "the great revivalists."[95]

REMEMBERING MOODY'S MEETINGS

Moody came to Philadelphia on the eve of America's centennial to make converts. When it came to the city's press, however, he was essentially preaching to the converted. The papers in the city that had hailed his coming helped build his following and then praised the mighty works he had done. The opposition press that was hostile to his coming was generally glad to see him go. The *Sunday Dispatch* seemed certain that Moody's "sacrilegious absurdities," despite their constant repetition in a sympathetic press, would have no permanent effect on the city or its sinners. "Salvation of the slop-shop character" made "a travesty of Christianity," the paper argued, deploring Moody's link to the professionally religious within the business community. The paper particularly scolded Moody for his claim near the close of the revival that the Jewish rejection of Christ was tied to their rejection by men. "In a city of 800,000 only women and drunks" warmed to Moody's "bitter prejudice," the paper remarked.[96] The remark flowed in part from Moody's work among women and for temperance, his meetings for each yielding the largest crowds of women participants ever seen in the city.[97] Blacks, however, participated far more marginally in Moody's meetings. When a "colored woman" stood up during a women's meeting in the center of the hall and shouted "glory," thousands of women suddenly stood, many fearing fire. Moody awkwardly asked everyone to rise and sing, and that's just what they did as the woman was led out. Moody's critics had charged him with "sensationalism," but a better description of his meetings was their businesslike efficiency. The Methodist and Episcopalian black churches of Philadelphia had a long and proud tradition of noisy revivals. Black Baptist churches seemed boisterously to be in continuous revival. The mood of Moody's meetings and the color line that separated church attendance tended to exclude Philadelphia's 22,000 African Americans from substantial participation in the tabernacle campaign.[98] The *Nation* noted the underclass was little represented at Moody's meetings. Moody was preaching to the choir, it argued, because his hearers were already familiar with his message or curious about it.[99]

The *Catholic World*, which had caricatured Moody as "the Reverend Dr. Notext," successful only in the power of his publicity, predicted that "every trace of the great tidal wave of revival" would "disappear" when he did.[100] The *American & Gazette*, however, which had criticized the heavily advertised meetings at their outset, certain they would have little "lasting" effect, observed as the meetings closed that "immense gatherings" yielded "crowded inquiry rooms filled with penitents." There was every reason to believe, the paper admitted, that "much good was done" in meetings that the paper hoped could be continued in the evangelist's absence.[101]

At the close of Moody's meetings he thanked the press for their faithful summaries of the tabernacle services.[102] In turn, the *Daily Press* editorially thanked him. His three months in Philadelphia had been "the most remarkable in the history of the city."[103] The word "revival" was taking on municipal meaning. Even advertisers were getting in on it. Jabez Jenkins, a South Tenth Street salesman, promised that his tea "revived" the family as Moody had the spirit.[104] Philadelphia was reported "loathe to part with him," and Moody's followers cashed in on the enthusiasm.[105] In a bid that raised $220,000 for the local YMCA on the evening of its twenty-first anniversary, everything associated with the revival was auctioned off, down to Moody's Bible stand and private towel. It lifted the organization out of debt and placed it on sound financial footing.[106]

Thirty-five hundred persons attended a converts class as the revival closed. The more than 17,000 who inquired about becoming Christians during the campaign were sent Christian literature embossed with Mr. Moody's facsimile signature.[107] Many of these converts found their way into Christian churches. The Presbyterians reported a doubling of new members after Moody's meetings and considered the revival the greatest in the city's history. Methodists reported about the same.[108] Evangelical churches in Delaware and New Jersey reported gains as well. Years after the event, private citizens would show off chairs and planks and gas lamps that had had their temporary homes in Philadelphia's Grand Depot. Still others would carefully preserve newspaper accounts of the event in family scrapbooks.

Moody's loyal lieutenants seemed satisfied with the campaign's conclusion. Years later, Stuart wrote that Moody's success in Philadelphia solidified his "wide reputation" and provided impetus to his evangelism of Gilded Age America.[109] Cree came to the same conclusion. The revival's effects were felt far beyond Philadelphia, he observed, focusing on Moody's influence on evangelical ministers across eastern Pennsylvania and within the mid-Atlantic region. This included a revival at Princeton College and through it a student movement to evangelize college campuses across the country.[110] Moody's mission included drawing Wanamaker into full-time Christian work. Two years after they had teamed up so successfully in evangelizing Philadelphia, the nation's most acclaimed revivalist preached repentance to the country's foremost merchandiser. "I cannot get you out of my mind," Moody wrote him. He was determined "to make one more effort to get you out of your business." Moody urged him to "close out before the end of the year" as Moody had years before when giving himself completely to Christian service. "If I only had you with me," he implored, reminding Wanamaker of their "blessed" work at the Grand Depot. "We have no time to lose. What a blessing you would be to this work."[111] Wanamaker, however, had other plans. His new store at the site of the Old Depot opened on May 6, 1876, to a city that was now widely familiar with the Thirteenth and Market Street location.[112] The cynical might charge Wanamaker with using Moody's tabernacle to publicize his department store, but that belies Wanamaker's lifelong commitment to evangelism. Instead the opening symbolizes the intimacy of business practice and the machinery of Gilded Age revival. The connection was not lost on Wanamaker. To his mind, principles of "business efficiency" needed to be brought into "Christian service." The church was a pay-as-you-go operation every bit as much as the department store. Both required a "permanent system of collections" to keep their doors open. Those that incurred debt risked consequences.[113]

On the first day of the last year of the nineteenth century, Wanamaker, then 61, stood in the pulpit of Bethany Presbyterian Church, at Twenty-third and Bainbridge streets, and offered a tearful tribute to Moody's memory after the evangelist died on December 22, 1899. "No man had accomplished more," he said, in remembering Philadelphia's revival 24 years earlier, "in helping his fellowmen."[114] Had he lived, Moody planned to revive Philadelphia at the dawn of the new century, hoping, he told Wanamaker, to light a fire in the East that would sweep across the nation.[115] At Association Hall, one week later, speakers praised the building Moody had helped build. "He made no inventions," the YMCA reported that day, "and made no new discovery" but "made such an impression on the city and the world that the dying century had seldom seen."[116] Moody was as "irreplaceable" as Lincoln, Wanamaker told a memorial assembly, and like Lincoln was one of the century's great men.[117]

The great revival in the Grand Depot had its critics, those who viewed the religious sensation at Thirteenth and Market as a temporary intrusion into the predictable pattern of the institutional church and its inhabitants. Others complained that any crusade that did not lead to an amelioration of social deprivations brought on by industrialization and recession was not much of a crusade at all.[118] Such criticism failed to capture the essence of this new moment in mass-mediated evangelism and how it excited celebrants anxious to create the new Jerusalem. "Sure it's sensational," the *Evening Bulletin* observed at the height of the excitement. "The American people like sensation!"[119] There were those who had hooted at Moody and his methods as he strolled through Philadelphia's centennial streets, but there were a great many more who stood for hours in long lines before the tabernacle and couldn't get in.[120]

America's second century would be "the grandest in the history of man," Philadelphia's press seemed certain, because it would see "the supremacy of intelligence, justice, and good will" in the affairs of men.[121] But the gentlemen of Philadelphia's Gilded Age press believed that communal life required one thing more. The "onward sweep of progress" could "re-civilize the world only through Christianity," they predicted.[122] And the new times required new methods. That had been the charm of Moody's meetings to the faithful and their conservative chroniclers in the press. From the outset they had realized that "curiosity" was important to Moody's ministry and the daily press was an important instrument in mobilizing the curious.[123] Reading their columns on Moody's mission became an exercise in unabashed public relations. "Journalists are fact-finders," the *American & Gazette* maintained, in reiterating its social responsibility to readers, but when it came to reporting Moody and his time at the tabernacle, many publishers and editors shared the hope of his eager audience that Christ's kingdom of gentle mercy was at hand.[124]

John Forney believed he'd witnessed Napoleon when he watched Moody and his mighty minions marshaling their forces in Philadelphia's centennial year to wage war against slothfulness and sin. His efforts were "singularly blessed by heaven and man," and that was the point.[125] Revival movements in the future would be mass media spectacles in which newspapers would let readers in on everything. They would be staged to reaffirm the founding faith of the community, and they would be communicated through a press equally anxious to remoralize their communities while turning a tidy profit. In exactly that way Moody's mission to Philadelphia on the eve of its centennial celebration got the party off to a good start. And revelers would remember well into America's second century their time at the tabernacle and the press that carefully captured the excitement in its pages.

"The Greatest Show on Earth"

FIVE

MOODY IN NEW YORK CITY, FEBRUARY—APRIL 1876

Halfway through D. L. Moody's 10-week campaign in New York City, *Harper's* portrayed the lay exhorter in the pulpit of P. T. Barnum's Hippodrome, his left hand raised high over his head, summoning his audience heavenward. Barnum himself had been illustrated almost identically by the same publication, when, as a latter-day Noah, he besought his circus animals into his ark at Twenty-sixth Street and Fourth Avenue to give "the greatest show on earth."[1] The world's best-known showman had now taken his act on the road, leaving the world's largest indoor arena to the world's leading evangelist. Both men were Yankee farm boys who had grown up in the Connecticut River valley, without their fathers. It had thrown both of them back on their own resources, which proved considerable. Each became an eager supersalesman—Moody in ministry, Barnum in the big top—but before their names became known, Moody sold shoes and Barnum Bibles.[2] Each had chosen an enterprise that suited his "natural inclination and temperament." For each, a "pledged word" was "sacred." Whatever either did, it was done "with all one's might" through the use of all available means.[3]

Those means often meant for each man the effective application of the persuasive art of advertising. Aggressive advertising had been the customary protocol that Moody's executive committee had used in preparing the soil for the Hippodrome campaign. Barnum said he "fully

Dwight Moody

God's Man for the Gilded Age at the height of his powers and influence, as he appeared in *Harper's Weekly*, on March 11, 1876, when he competed with P. T. Barnum in staging "the greatest show on earth."

appreciated the powers of the press more than any man," adding he took every opportunity "to invoke the aid of printer's ink." Barnum issued handbills and circulars by the tens of thousands and used placards to tell customers that his menagerie with its assorted curiosities was in town. Each man believed that it was necessary "to advertise your business." To do otherwise would be to "hide your light under a bushel." The reference might by biblical, but the admonition was all Barnum. If one's "calling" needed public support, he reasoned, one must advertise "to arrest public attention." Moody's meetings with regional ministers at Christian conventions, where they learned to put on a revival, could not have put it more prettily. Barnum boasted that "whatever success I have had in my life may fairly be attributed more to the public press than all other causes combined."[5] Moody's faith in godly grace would have precluded such a claim. Barnum's sense of self-satisfaction wasn't shared by Moody. The man who advertised himself as "a fearless advocate of truth and liberal principles" happily humbugged paying customers with exhibitions of George Washington's 161-year-old nurse and a "Feejee mermaid" in the form of the head of a monkey sewn to the tail of a fish.[6] But the revivalist puffed by the press as God's man for the Gilded Age said he considered himself "the most over-estimated man in America." Before his Hippodrome campaign he reportedly remarked: "I don't know what will become of me if the newspapers continue to print all of my sermons." The papers had given Moody celebrity status. Their stenographic accounts of his every utterance had magnified his reputation and outreach. Now, wherever he went, the curious came. But he was only "a lay preacher" with "a little learning." His stock would be "exhausted by and by," he felt certain, when readers came to realize that he was repeating "the old ideas" he had taught in city after city. The physical proximity of Manhattan to Brooklyn and Philadelphia would test his uncertainties and expose his limitations.[7]

The nationwide depression, now entering its third year, had been good for Moody's business but not Barnum's. The 65-year-old impresario had survived fires and suits and floods but nothing as devastating as the Panic of 1873, which had spread westward from Wall Street when Moody's ally, Jay Cooke, went into bankruptcy and took leading speculators with him. Financial misery made men suddenly serious about their souls but in no mood for amusements. Barnum had bought the old Harlem Railroad site and spent $200,000 to open his Hippodrome in April 1874 to satisfy "the public thirst for excitement."[8] He had never staged such a circus. Three rings were simultaneously overrun by 1,500 animals, birds, beasts, reptiles, and "marine monsters." Three hundred artists and performers walked on high wires, soared on trapezes, flew balloons, and were shot from cannons. There had never been anything like it.[9]

Moody wasn't the only performer who could attract a president. Grant and his cabinet were among 10,000 spectators who saw Barnum's staging of the great Congress of Nations. It was an unprecedented world's fair, a procession three miles long that wound its way along an oval track nearly 425 feet long and 200 feet wide. Ancient and modern monarchs and their royal retinues shared the proceedings. Queen Victoria and Confucius could be seen waving above their golden chariots. The sultan of Turkey seemed preoccupied by his harem. Napoleon, the pope, the pasha, the czar of Russia and the emperor of China all received salutations, but none like the Goddess of Liberty, who got into the spirit of the centennial by lighting fireworks. Revolutionary War soldiers took a bow, Indians hunted buffalo, cowboys lassoed cattle, ladies in silks rode thoroughbreds, and Romans raced chariots—all for only two bits.[10] But by the end of 1875, a deepening depression left sales slumping. Barnum, an eternal optimist, was compelled to cut costs. Elephants were sold for $4,500 a piece. Tigers, lions, and leopards fetched $600. A monkey could be had for $8. Tapirs, hyenas, and kangaroos attracted no bids whatever.[11]

While what was left of Barnum's circus went on tour, the old man stayed home, serving as the mayor of Bridgeport, where he preached before the Common Council on temperance, against prostitution, and for strict enforcement of the sabbath laws. A convert to Universalism, the former Presbyterian was denied membership in Bridgeport's YMCA. He took his defeat philosophically.[12] When Moody's organizing committee of YMCA laymen came calling, Barnum offered to rent them the Hippodrome for $1,500 per week. The deal was struck. Another $20,000 was found to sweep the old sawdust out and make the arena ready for Moody's meetings. J. Pierpont Morgan and Cornelius Vanderbilt, both Episcopalians, helped underwrite the cost. Morris K. Jesup, a banker and philanthropist who was a past president of the YMCA, opened his Madison Avenue home to Moody.[13] Certainly they hoped for a spiritual revival in their city, and almost as decidedly did they pray that the excitement might overwhelm the public's growing disaffection with national scandal and depression.

PANIC IN A SUPREMELY SECULAR CITY

Eleven months short of his death, the 81-year-old Cornelius Vanderbilt, sea captain, railroad magnate, and commodore, supported both Moody and seances in trying to divine the future. His fortune, buffeted by three years of deepening panic, had dwindled to a mere $100 million. He presided from his red brick house at 10 Washington Place, where the famed feminist Victoria Woodhull put him in touch with the departed spirits of family and friends. Woodhull had first published reports on Henry Ward Beecher's affairs in the interest of promoting free love. And Vanderbilt had helped her open a stock brokerage in the interest of promoting spiritualism's powers of prediction.[14] "Mrs. Satan," as Thomas Nast and other humorists liked to call her, was certain that hard times were "an elixir of life" for those investors who got their financial houses in order. If elected president, she promised to throw the rascals out and to give clairvoyants a chance in managing the nation's postwar speculation.[15]

The Old Commodore and his railroads had played their part in the acute suffering of the 1870s. His public battles with Daniel Drew and Jay Gould for control of the Erie Railroad plundered its stock. Joined by Jim Fisk, a Vermont peddler turned circus con man, Drew and Gould helped create a money panic in their attempt to corner the gold market. Jubilee Jim was shot and killed for his trouble; Tammany called out a 200-piece brass band to make his passing an obstreperous moment of municipal mourning.[16] A billion and a half dollars had to be borrowed from abroad to finance America's overbuilt rail system by the summer of 1873. Jay Cooke's Northern Pacific needed $300 million to meet its payroll and other obligations. Five thousand commercial houses fell into bankruptcy after he closed his doors. Twenty-eight New York life insurance companies quickly failed or merged, with $159 million in losses to investors. Many leading stocks lost half their value.[17] There had been nearly 3,000 business failures in 1871 and more than 4,000 in 1872. The panic's first full year led to another nearly 6,000; its second nearly 8,000 more. The year Moody ministered in New York would be the worst yet. More than 9,000 area businesses closed their doors in America's largest city in the nation's centennial year.[18]

The suffering was particularly painful in New York City, where a metropolis of 1.1 million people, built on the mad pursuit of money and huddled together on an island sixteen miles long and three miles wide, saw the beginning of bread lines and the growth of soup kitchens. From its earliest history, Manna-hatta, a gateway to the New World, had been all business. Locals liked to tell of the city's first scam, when 60 guilders separated what would become the world's most valuable real estate from a native population that knew no better. Like the ancient city of Gotham, New York would be endlessly self-creating and tirelessly self-promoting, a supremely secular city, flowing with milk and honey for those embracing the nation's democratic privilege of freely pursuing one's love of gain.[19] Peter Stuyvesant, a minister's son, may have imposed fines for missing church and carnal contact with the Indian, but his Dutch overlords were more interested in his ability to put their "island for the distressed" on a paying basis.[20] For 54 years, the Dutch encouraged "people of tender conscience" to come to a commercial Eden where capitalism would work itself out with little impediment. Early patroons got land grants on either side of the Hudson if they brought 50 persons to New Netherland, and the city had been on the hustle ever since.[21]

GOTHAM AND THE GOSPEL

From the beginning, New Yorkers drove a hard bargain. The Weckquaesgeek wished they had never turned to their white neighbors for help when fleeing a raiding party of Mohawks. Neither women nor children were spared the slaughter, and the Canarsie fared little better. The Dutch would have their day until a four-ship English squadron arrived to raise the English flag above Fort James, but settlement was slow. Seventy years of British rule found barely 10,000 making their way in lower Manhattan, and yellow fever threatened that.[22] A fifth of them were in attendance on the afternoon of November 15, 1739, when George Whitefield preached on the necessity of a "New Birth" in an open-air meeting on the city common. The city's newly emerging press reported that some scoffed but many wept. When he returned the following year, preaching repentance and the dignity of the individual before Christ, 7,000 gathered, many of them slaves and the city's underclass.[23] His words of warning fell on deaf ears. When several businesses were mysteriously burned in the spring of 1741, suspicion turned toward the city's slaves. Fourteen were burned at the stake, eighteen hanged, two gibbeted, and seventy-one expelled. Four of their white "defenders" were executed, including a Catholic priest charged with popery.[24]

Wartime privateering and providing provisions for His Majesty's forces to fight the French made New York merchants their first fortunes. Shipping provided their second. The city's first families—the Beekmans and Waltons, the Livingstons, Roosevelts, De Lanceys, and Bayards—built Georgian mansions, imported Chippendale and Wedgwood, and self-consciously wore silk. Their critics claimed that "the art of getting money" was "the highest improvement they could pretend to." Trinity Church reflected the Anglican self-confidence of many of New York's money men. Specialty shops in Hanover Square reflected a widening circle of wealth.[25] The enthusiasm, however, was short-lived. Britain's taxing policy enraged the city's merchants and the lawyers who trailed behind them. Revolution was followed by British occupation and ashes. Half the city burned in 1776, and half its population bolted. When Alexander Hamilton returned to 57 Wall Street after the war, the city was in ruins. But within two years, the Continental Congress became his next-door neighbor and New York emerged the new nation's first federal city. Its commercial culture was financed by the Bank of New

York and guided by a chamber of commerce that was top-heavy with former Tories. They joined in the applause when Washington took the oath of office from Federal Hall. In New York, business prevailed over sentiment.[26]

Critics seized on the city's secularism and spirit of speculation in advocating the removal of the nation's capital to the banks of the Potomac. The metropolis of a million and more that greeted Moody had been anticipated in the great grid of 1807, which laid out the city's 12 avenues, 155 streets, and 2,000 blocks. That was before the construction of the Erie Canal linked the Hudson to the rapidly expanding West. In the decades that followed, the city surpassed a population of 300 to the acre, none of whom could grasp the settlement as a whole. Twenty daily newspapers along Printing-House Row chronicled the city's spasms of violence, building, and bankruptcy. The city's Five Points slum erupted in brickbats at the suggestion that the Irish would have their own regiment in the National Guard. A year later, 700 buildings worth $20 million burned, bankrupting the city's insurance industry. A fire in 1845 destroyed 345 more. Twenty people were killed in 1849 in an argument over American and English actors. A financial crash in 1857 destroyed 985 businesses, leaving $120 million in liabilities. Rival police departments fought for control of the streets as many died of starvation. *Harper's* wrote that "nothing has gone as it should." The *Times* thought New York "the worst-governed city in America."[27]

What municipal government didn't do, its churches did. The interdenominational New York Sunday School Union sent 1,000 two-person teams into the city's most destitute wards. The Fulton Street neighborhood was organized under the missionary Jeremiah Lanphier of the Old Dutch Church. His noon prayer meetings, begun on October 7, 1856, began to attract jobless clerks from the financial district. By late January of the next year, overflow crowds were gathering at the John Street Methodist Church just around the corner. Lanphier helped persuade the *Herald* it was a good story. Headlines followed. By late February Horace Greeley's *Tribune* got into the spirit of the civic celebration. Within six weeks, 20 prayer meetings had broken out all over the city in what a special edition of the *Tribune* was calling the "Fulton Street Revival."[28] Laymen led nightly meetings at the Music Hall and Burton's Theatre that attracted thousands. It seemed to some that the Lord had used perilous times to dissolve barriers separating sects. The press prophesied that New York might find "a unity of purpose" in this "unusual season of grace."[29]

Perilous times produced rioting instead. New York City's merchants, bankers, and brokers had long profited from the slave economy of the South. More than 2,000 merchants met at Cooper Union in October 1859 to assure the South that New York City stood with them. Many in the city's working class feared that free blacks would compete for their jobs. Lincoln won only one-third of the city's votes. When southern states began seceding, the mayor, Fernando Wood, told the Common Council that the city should do the same. Several of the city's leading banks said they wouldn't finance the fighting.[30] By 1863 the Garibaldi Guard and Irish Brigade were decimated, the Sisters of Charity ministered to broken bodies in a field hospital in Central Park, and the recruiting tent in City Hall Park was taken down for lack of business. Labor shortages and high inflation led to strikes for better wages. Free blacks were brought in to break them. Lincoln's Emancipation Proclamation outraged Tammany Democrats, who bitterly protested the prosecution of "this Black Republican war."[31]

On the morning of July 13, 1863, hundreds of workers from the city's shipyards, machine shops, and construction sites beat copper kettles in front of the provost marshal's office on Third Avenue, protesting the government's draft. The army guarding the city had been called to Gettysburg, and there was no one to stop the volunteer firemen in Black Joke Engine Company 33 from setting the office ablaze. Jeering crowds cut down telephone poles, stopped rail cars, and stoned commuter trains. Fifth Avenue homes were looted and burned. Thirteen were killed when a Second Avenue armory was sacked and burned. Blacks and Republicans were particularly targeted in the riot's second and third days. The Colored Orphan Asylum at Fifth Avenue and Forty-third Street was torched. Publisher Henry Raymond had to protect his *New York Times* office with a Gatling gun. Horace Greeley's *Tribune* building was burned. Black homes and businesses along Bleecker and Carmine streets were attacked. Before federal troops using howitzers suppressed the violence, 119 had perished, 18 of them blacks. Three thousand were left homeless. William Tweed, the grand sachem of Tammany Hall, the Democratic political organization that ran the city, stepped in to negotiate a cease-fire, with vague promises of "bringing those responsible to justice." It signaled where the city's power center would lie in the immediate postwar period.[32]

A MORAL CORRUPTION

Newspaper editors saw Moody's mission to New York as an effort to remoralize the city and nation after a period of unparalleled corruption. The case against William Marcy "Boss" Tweed was a case in point. A suit against this chairmaker turned firefighter sought to recover $40 million he had looted from the city as head of Tammany Hall. Tweed had worked his way up from his father's brushmaking business to chairman of the New York City Board of Supervisors, which spent $8 million over three years while failing to complete a county courthouse that should have cost half a million.[33] Tammany particularly preyed on the two-thirds of New York City's population who were foreign born, greeting them at the docks when they first arrived and offering coal and clothes, flour, and a little money when times got tough. In turn, Tammany was returned to office every municipal election, sometimes by margins greater than the number of voters registered.[34] Contracts for construction, paving, parks, public printing, and sewers all went through the Ring (Tweed's gang of grafters at the Board of Supervisors and its appendages), and contractors paid for the privilege of doing business. Tweed's take was a million dollars a month. State Republicans, led by the long-time Albany editor Thurlow Weed, worked out a deal for postwar power-sharing: Tweed could have his way in Manhattan if Weed had his in Albany.[35]

On the eve of Moody's mission to Manhattan, the *New York Times* congratulated itself on uncovering the civic plundering that had put Tweed behind bars. But years into his administration they editorially praised him as a reformer with results. The *World* under Manton Marble considered him a civic savior. The *Sun* sought a statue in his honor.[36] Indeed, 89 newspapers received patronage from the Boss and his cohorts between 1867 and 1871; 27 expired when the spigot was turned off. Auditors later found that with three exceptions, all of these newspapers had needed advertising from Tammany to show a profit. The *Transcript* was the big winner at three-quarters of a million dollars. The *Daily News* netted half a million from the Ring. Joseph Howard, owner of the *Star*, personally pocketed a quarter million. The kept press puffed Tammany in column inch after column inch. Investigators later found petty evening papers received $1,000 a month to see things Tweed's way. The City Council awarded bonuses at year's end to friends in the press who had been particularly cooperative.[37]

Henry J. Raymond, who founded the *New York Times* in 1851, eventually soured on Tweed and Tammany. His Republican Party rectitude made him a champion of good government and an enemy of Irish immigration. As the speaker in the state assembly and later as lieutenant governor he surrounded himself with bright young men who shared his sentiment that moral corruption threatened the new nation. His election to the House of Representatives in 1864, a year after his narrow escape in the draft riots, gave him a wider platform for his policies. Two years later he organized the National Union Convention and gave the Philadelphia Address, demanding an end to venality in public affairs.[38] After Raymond's death in 1869, the editor George Jones, the editorial writer Louis J. Jennings, and the chief political correspondent John Foord continued the crusade. Jennings was a no-nonsense Englishman and Foord a recently arrived Scot. Both were equally contemptuous of Tweed's tactics. In September 1870 the *Times* triumvirate went on the attack. All New Yorkers, they claimed, who had not "sacrificed honor for private gain" regarded the Ring's swindling "with indignation and abhorrence." A series of investigative reports followed, detailing the bribes and kickbacks that depicted Tweed and his allies as little more than "a gang of burglars." The *Times* editorially excoriated "the Irish Catholic despotism that rules the City of New York, the Metropolis of Free America."[39]

The *Times* was greatly aided in its attacks on the Tweed Ring by Thomas Nast and *Harper's*. The Bavarian-born illustrator had an allergy to injustice and predatory politics and found both in the Tweed Ring. Nast began his work in caricature at *Frank Leslie's Illustrated Magazine*. Nast had trained under Barnum, who groomed his young protege in the old master's art of ridiculing the powerful for fun and profit. His portrait of the Tweed Ring as a bunch of vultures picking over the bones of city taxpayers was entitled "Let Us Prey." Another drawing depicted a corpulent, pear-shaped Tweed and members of his overweight ring making off with the city treasury. The cut line warned: "Stop Thief!" Another posed a flattened Manhattan under the giant thumb of the Boss. The Tammany Tiger was shown in another issue at a Roman forum devouring Christians. Emperor Tweed watched approvingly and dared: "What are you going to do about it?"[40] Nast was proving more of a threat to Tweed than the *Times*. His constituents couldn't read, he groused, "but can't help seeing them pictures." The Boss offered five million dollars to Nast and the *Times* if they'd stop their series. The attempted bribe became part of the evidence that eventually sent Tweed to the Ludlow Street jail.[41]

The day Moody arrived in Gotham to check the acoustic properties of Barnum's Hippodrome, New Yorkers could hear the scurrying of the city's police force. Tweed, sentenced to 12 years imprisonment, had bribed his way out of jail, and rumors were rampant that he had fled the city he had fleeced. For many New Yorkers it was a dispiriting scene in a season of moral corruption and public scandal. The sex scandal involving Henry Ward Beecher, an icon in the Protestant Church, had been a headline writer's delight. The impeachment of the secretary of war, William Belknap, for accepting bribes had brought "public confidence in the integrity of public men to an unprecedented low." It had followed revelations that President Grant's private secretary and old army buddy Orville Babcock had headed a "whiskey ring" that had conspired to defraud the government of whiskey revenues. When Grant's solicitor general and treasury secretary, Benjamin Bristow, exposed the ring, the president sided with Babcock, and Bristow was forced to resign. Bristow's predecessor, William Richardson, had himself resigned before facing congressional censure in awarding contracts. The Congress itself had been ridiculed for voting its members retroactive pay increases in the notorious "Salary Grab Act."[42]

New York and the nation needed a spiritual revival, the *Times* told its readers, to overcome "the corruption and rottenness of public life." Postwar profits in speculation had now been displaced by paralyzing economic uncertainty. It produced "a distinct class of public men" whose "sense of honor was weaker" than "the temptations to indulgence" they faced. The modern world seemed suddenly sympathetic to "the novel machinery of fraud, peculation, dishonesty, jobbery and greed." As the *Sun* saw it, New York, like the nation, listened to its clergy respectfully but inattentively. Moody, it predicted, would find a city sunk in "pervasive and palpable irreligion" that had become "rich in living wickedness and practical infidelity." From the slum to the fashionable quarters of the city, "in business and the workshop, in politics and the press, in society and the household," Moody would find "every form of falsehood, duplicity, dishonesty, swindling, pollution, profligacy, backbiting and slander" known to man. And all the sermons of the city's highly paid clergymen had done little to change the way people lived. The "hard-hearted and hypocrite, the fighter and the foul-mouthed" attested to "the widespread prevalence of practical unrighteousness" in everyday life. "What we need," the *Sun* said, "is a strong dose of practical religion" to "purify the atmosphere."[43]

"NO MONEY FOR TOMORROW'S NEEDS"

The venality of political corruption was joined to economic panic on the eve of Moody's arrival in New York. This was shown in January 1874, when a mass protest in Tompkins Square was brutally broken up by city police.[44] The state general assembly investigated but did nothing. A generation earlier, when Barnum had brought Jenny Lind to the city, she had remarked, "Have you no poor people in your country?" By the mid-1870s, poverty was everywhere apparent. Local charities reported that they were out of money and food "because of the unprecedented demands made upon us." Twenty-five thousand women and children were "utterly destitute" and were "suffering acutely." In 22 of the city's wards, 365,000 people were housed in 17,110 buildings in rents that varied from three to seven dollars a month. For many families even that was too much.[45]

The city's cramped, airless settlements were a breeding ground for disease and helped make New York the most stricken city in America. Typhus, cholera, smallpox, and yellow fever had afflicted the urban poor since colonial days. The Metropolitan Board of Health waged war against deadly fevers and intestinal infections with depressing results.

New York's underclass had twice the death rate of the national average. Seventy-seven out of every thousand persons died from diseases that simple sanitation could have prevented.[46] Social organizations were reporting conditions "pitiful in the extreme." The Commissioners of Charities was reduced to giving nothing but coal for the winter season. The Society for Improving the Condition of the Poor ceased operations. The Master of St. John's Guild urgently appealed to the public for aid in helping "the deserving poor." There was "no money in its treasury for tomorrow's needs" and "no supply of food in store." It would soon be compelled "to bar the door against the prayers and tears of thousands of women and children who are in utter destitution and terrible suffering."[47] Thieves and "young drunks" were becoming "an army of tramps" who "menaced the peace of the community." Critics claimed that only a few were seeking to end their homeless ways. The rest were vagrants on whom "the bread of charity would be wasted." One suggested abating the growing "tramp nuisance" by requiring roadwork in exchange for overnight accommodations.[48]

The failure of the Bank of the State of New York in mid-March 1876 only added to the municipal gloom. The savings of thousands of depositors melted away overnight, while newspaper investigations revealed that bank directors had pocketed hundreds of thousands of dollars in unsecured loans. Ann Polhamus, a West Side widow, decided to take matters into her own hands. She hustled her lifetime savings out of a Central Park bank, only to find her bedroom ransacked and $10,000 in life savings stolen from a dresser drawer. Israel Atwood, a physician who practiced in the 1200 block of Broadway, couldn't stand it and chloroformed himself. One landlord was demanding the right to sell the body of a debtor for a $25 dissection fee. Adam Hilt had had enough and began beating his wife. When the Ninth Precinct Patrolman Jewell entered the apartment, Hilt began hitting him too. The press reported that domestic battery by drunk and disillusioned husbands was becoming a "municipal epidemic."[49] A citywide survey found its building trades were in "a paralyzed state," with union membership earning one-third of what it had been at the start of the panic. Carpenters, plumbers, gasfitters, and painters were particularly hard hit. What had been a daily wage of $3.50 was now $1.50, for the few who could get it. Twenty-nine leading businesses were reported at a "standstill" with little hope for the future. Price cutting had little effect. On the eve of Moody's meetings, conditions were as bad as they had been in municipal memory. What the city needed was a savior.[50]

ALL EYES ARE ON THE DOOR

One hundred fifty policemen were in place, 500 ushers trained, and 1,200 choir members prepared. More than 10,000 tickets had been issued, but throngs of the curious many times that size came anyway, massing on Madison Avenue and crowding out the carriages along Twenty-sixth and Twenty-seventh streets just for a look at the man. Moody's publicity had preceded him. Reporters anxiously awaited the opening of Barnum's big doors on Madison Avenue. This time no hippopotamus would go through, or pretty ladies riding bareback. At 7:30 in the evening on February 7 in America's centennial year, the entrance was opened and the largest audience ever seen in the city began taking their seats. Fifteen thousand dollars had been spent to fill two adjoining halls with 11,000 chairs and two stages of several thousand more. Within minutes everyone was in place. Reporters recognized leading lawyers who had come to analyze Moody's powers of persuasion. Scientists were there to see if his arguments were within reason. Clergymen came to find how he moved masses. Physicians attended to witness his care of the sick. It was an altogether respectable crowd of "orderly, intelligent, respectable people without a tramp or vagabond to be found," though many could still smell Barnum's sawdust.[51]

Onlookers saw the state's governor, Samuel Tilden, take his seat on the stage. He would become the Democratic Party presidential nominee later that year and would win the popular vote while losing the election by a single disputed electoral vote. He exchanged greetings with Thurlow Weed, the veteran publisher and Republican Party organizer, who knew the meaning of political defeat. This longtime Albany editor and glad-hander who had helped elect Zachary Taylor and advised Lincoln, was now nearing 80, and saw himself pushed to the periphery of power as a harmless relic of New York's political past.[52] He would become a curiosity in his nightly attendance at Moody's meetings, occupying his customary seat in the reporter's box when not ambling on stage to lend his authority to Moody's brand of spiritual surgery. Weed's deteriorating health had forced him into semiretirement and led him to a self-conscious reassessment of his spiritual uncertainties. Other celebrities might come to the revival because it was a socially sanctioned ceremony, hoping they might see and be seen, but Weed went in the hope he might be revived. When Moody and his messengers went into the inquiry room to meet with those uncertain about their souls, Weed often followed. At prayer meetings, he was always present and could be found a little to one side, solicitous and silent. The old editor was a major financial contributor to Moody's mission and a personal project of the evangelist. Moody told the former printer's devil that he would accept Weed's gift when Weed accepted God's gift of grace.[53]

"A living, restless mass of more than a block" remained outside, shivering in the cold and listening to the singing inside. Every 10 to 15 paces they were besieged by vendors hawking hymnals and *Lives of Moody and Sankey*. Not a few had their pockets picked by thieves who must have found "the largest crowd ever seen in the city" a new Eden. Those who couldn't get in, despite special pleadings, overflowed the sidewalks, blocked Madison Avenue, and were backed up all the way to Broadway. Street boys and peddlers met them there with counterfeit pictures of Moody and his singer Sankey that sold swiftly at five and ten cents apiece to worshippers who had never seen the faces of their stars. Some, through desperation or ingenuity, followed reporters, ministers, and singers to a side entrance. There police separated wheat from chaff. Those with credentials went in; the unelected were kept out. The chief usher, seated by the stage, had "telegraphic communication" with the all-important "man in charge of the door," and it was ordered closed. This enraged many in the crowd who "clamorously demanded admittance" and "became abusive when it was denied them." The "uncommon curiosity" of those who couldn't get in would have to be satisfied another day. Moody's publicity "machinery," the local press observed, had worked well in whetting such a substantial appetite. Barnum would have loved it.[54]

Like Henry Hudson, D. L. Moody had led a band of evangelical explorers who surveyed both sides of the river, from Williamsburgh to Newburgh and from Newark to Poughkeepsie, where they found fertile territory for their mighty mission. Moody had commanded the operation as "an experienced generalissimo." Hudson came for commerce, and men of commerce had "kindled revival fires" across the city and its suburbs in advance of Moody's meetings. Their prayer and praise meetings were reported along Third and Sixth avenues, Eleventh and Fortieth streets, on Greene, Laight, Bedford, Water, and Vandam streets, and within Washington Square. Presbyterians, Baptists, Methodists, and Episcopalians were joining hands, the press reported, along with "many ministers who heretofore have stood aloof from such movements." They were encouraged to mute doctrinal differences in the cause of Christ. The message was sinking in and getting out. The "sagacity, skill and comprehensiveness" of Moody's armada was without precedent in the city. Cooperating dailies wondered at its "perseverance and pertinacity."[55]

Just before eight, everyone seemed in place. The *Tribune* reported that the "momentary appearance of the evangelists" created a "nervous expectation" in the crowd. "All eyes turned toward the little door behind the stage" through which Moody would walk. A presidential appearance, it suspected, could have been no more anticipated. At exactly eight, ministers and ushers hovering at the door parted, a little like the

Red Sea, one wag noted, while Moody and Sankey, holding their Bibles, came out on stage. Each appeared oblivious to his central part in this spectacle. Sankey sat silently at his melodeon as Moody bowed his head in prayer at a railing near the center of the stage. An awkward murmur arose from the lips of hundreds who hoped they weren't being heard. "Let us all bow our heads in silent prayer," Moody admonished them, before burying his massive bearded face in his hands. For two minutes a deep silence stilled the sanctuary, where even a whisper would have disturbed the quiet. Moody's mastery, reporters noted, was already apparent.[56]

In the "breathless quiet" that followed, reporters peered across a vast concourse crowded to capacity in every direction from the main floor to two distant galleries that reached distant alcoves. They could see that Moody was kneeling now, and the whole congregation appeared to be a single organism, sharing his sentiment, for he was its head. Few reporters remained utterly unmoved by the spectacle. Even those who felt uninspired could not help but be impressed by the "great depth of earnestness" of the proceedings. Not merely in numbers "but in intelligence and respectability, the city had never seen such an audience," reporters noted.[57] The Hippodrome's great and smaller hall could accommodate 11,000, and the struggle to be among these favored few had few parallels in municipal history.[58]

Moody began by admitting that he "always dreaded going to a new place" because "it took so long to dispel illusions." His sudden celebrity status, created by a press he had openly courted, attracted great crowds, who invariably focused on the man and not his message. "I am the most over-estimated man in the country," Moody told his admirers. The drumbeat of publicity needed to encourage curiosity led "many people to look upon me as a great man." Instead, he was a lay preacher "with only a little learning" and a most reluctant celebrity. Sixty-five salesmen from Philadelphia were hawking photographs of Moody and Sankey in the streets outside the Hippodrome. Moody urged his followers "not to buy them." The pictures "ain't anymore like us than they are like you." Moody hadn't had his picture taken in eight years and didn't plan on doing so anytime soon. "The papers in Philadelphia puffed us up," he told his New York audience, "and big crowds came. But there was no revival until the people realized the work was God's."[59]

Moody faced a paradox in his use of the press and their use of him in creating precampaign excitement. His organization assiduously courted positive publicity in the days leading up to the opening of his New York crusade, but the attention turned all eyes on what Moody and his men were doing and not what God and His Spirit "is doing in our midst." The tendency of the press to make Moody and not his mission the focus of their stories did "the cause of Christ great injury," he told his New York audience. They commented on the crowds, the choir, their surroundings, the ushers, or the many ministers and civic officials they saw seated on stage, or those who weren't there. "We have got to get our eyes off these things," he admonished his listeners, "and we must give God the glory, if any solid work is to be done here." Moody was a good enough manager to know that organization was necessary in any business, including the business of revival, but press and public preoccupation with man's means in staging revivals was "a great obstacle" in bringing genuine revival. "If God is with us we are going to succeed," he told his listeners. "If we take God out of our plans we are going to fail, and we ought to fail." Three days before he began his New York campaign, 146 items from the Philadelphia Depot, down to Moody's personal towel and his walnut coat rack, had been sold at auction. Buyers were thrilled to bid on the nightstand with the Italian marble top where Moody had washed his whiskers and the gilt-framed looking-glass where he had beheld his countenance. His set of stone china toiletware and the crimson plush on his personal pulpit fetched a good price too in spirited bidding. The iron spoons and salt shakers he had used, the stone jug that poured his favorite tea, and the deep yellow bowl he took his meals in would all find a happy home. So would the feather duster, the dustpan, and the wastebasket he'd once held in his hand. The money would go to Christian work but reflected in Moody's mind a very un-Christian attitude. "We have to sink the self," he implored his audience. "We have to get our eyes off these things and toward the Cross." God would stir New York if New Yorkers "looked to God, not men."[60]

GOING THROUGH THE ROOF

Four of Gotham's leading dailies, the *Tribune*, the *Sun*, the *Herald*, and the *Times*, usually agreed on very little, but each was prepared to give Moody, his message and mission, every encouragement. When one man who was determined to enter the crowded and guarded hall couldn't get in, he could be heard on the Hippodrome roof, seeking another way in. Editorial writers were reminded of the palsied man let down through ceiling tiles to the room where Jesus was. The *Tribune* thought Moody had a similar sincerity and power that moved masses. It began preparing *Glad Tidings*, a bound volume of Moody's sermons at the Hippodrome, as reported in the pages of the *Tribune*. The paper promised its forthcoming book would be "the only complete and adequate publication of Mr. Moody's sermons either in this country or in

New York's Hippodrome had long been home to "the greatest show on earth." In America's centennial year, it was Moody, and not Barnum, who was behind the civic spectacle.

England."[61] Moody was deeply ambivalent about the *Tribune* initiative. An estimated one and a half million men and women would attend two months of meetings in New York, but several million more might read about them in the press. Those who never read of revivals in religious tracts were exposed to the good news in the pages of the secular press. But he didn't "know what will become of me if the newspapers continue to print all my sermons." His revival schedule prevented him from preparing new sermons, and he feared editors and readers would tire of hearing the old ones. He jammed newspaper clippings into sermon envelopes, hoping the latest news would freshen old material. And he realized that every week one could read in newspapers "a score of better sermons than I can preach."[62]

The *Tribune's* senior staff was made up of men eager to benefit from Moody's popularity. Chief among them was 38-year-old Whitelaw Reid, who had developed a national reputation as a Civil War reporter for the *Cincinnati Gazette* before joining the editorial staff of the *Tribune* in 1868 and becoming its managing editor a year later. When the paper's publisher, Horace Greeley, ran against Ulysses Grant in the 1872 presidential election, he elevated Reid to editor-in-chief. Reid proved himself a man of careful habits, adept at building coalitions that furthered his own interests over Greeley's. He ousted Greeley as the paper's publisher, which made him, Reid, a favorite of "regular Republicans," who seemed unmoved by the scandals of the Grant administration. Reid developed an antipathy toward Greeley's pious Universalism, which saw its expression in idiosyncratic support for liberal causes such as collectivism.[63] Reid saw the paper as a voice for "the respectable classes" who were the critical backbone of the city's commerce. Backed by the financier Jay Gould, Reid advocated the election of "honest men the country can trust" and lower taxes. Even before it began, Reid was promising readers "a great religious revival" to lift the city's spirits.[64] He promised readers "the truth, the whole truth and nothing but the truth" in revival reporting that "no intelligent person" could do without. To these readers he emphasized that "only the best class of people," New York's "most respectable and intelligent classes," and not "the poor and the lowly, tramps and vagabonds," were flocking to the Hippodrome. Readers needed to know that the city had never seen such crowds.[65]

The 56-year-old Charles A. Dana, then in his eighth year of editing and publishing the *New York Sun*, had worked on the *Harbinger* for Brook Farm, the experimental transcendentalist community, before a 15-year tour as city editor on the *Tribune* under Greeley deepened his interest in liberal causes. On the first days of Moody's meetings the *Sun* had a daily circulation of 130,000, more than three times what it had been when Dana took it over. Dana promised his readers "a daily pho-

Moody ministered to capacity crowds while in New York. He may have imagined he was "the most over-estimated man" in America, but understood "puffing in the press" helped produce the citywide extravaganzas that made his work such good copy.

The paradox of Moody's success was that he and not Christ was made the star of a spiritual showcase. Press accounts made him a celebrity evangelist and his citywide crusades an entertainment for the masses.

tograph of the whole world's doings in the most luminous and lively manner."[66] Dana editorialized on behalf of "practical religion" that would attack the social problems stimulated by urbanization and industrialization. Moody's meetings would be a success if they "purified the atmosphere" by beating back "the widespread prevalence of practical unrighteousness." Dana wrote that Moody needed to know that New Yorkers were "religious" already and it had done precious little "to turn them from their evil ways." He urged him to combat "the drunkenness, dishonesty, wrongdoing, crime and evil" that had descended on the city. Noting that the veteran editor Thurlow Weed had taken to the meetings and been publicly prayed for, the combative Dana observed that "more than one editor similarly stands in the need of prayer."[67] Dana had every reason to hope that journalism could serve the interests of Christianity by assaulting "the prejudices and enmities well established in our community." The *Sun* offered a "scientific" service to its readers in reporting Moody's revival. In doing so, it celebrated "the sacrament of reason" that raised the sights of all men by appealing to their better natures, urging them "to live in harmony with one another" while behaving as members of "a civilized society ought to behave."[68]

Dana might have meant James Gordon Bennett, Jr., the 34-year-old operator of the New York *Herald*, when he observed that competing publishers might well benefit from Moody's message. The dissolute son of the man who helped invent the penny press was much more at home racing his yachts than getting out a paper, but the death of his father in June 1872 elevated him from managing editor to the paper's head. Humility was not one of Bennett's keener attributes. He told the *Herald's* 100,000 worldwide readers that "the advance of our metropolis" owed much to "the willingness of the *Herald* to instruct society in the elements of Christian civilization for a very small amount of money, paid annually in advance." Bennett would self-indulgently spend an estimated $30 million of that money in unrivaled pursuit of pure pleasure, his public intoxications derided by competitors who jealously sought his circulation. The spectacle of Moody's meetings in Gotham would be quickly followed by a spectacle of a different sort. Bennett would be flogged by his fiancée's brother after urinating in a fireplace at an uptown social event. The engagement was judiciously broken off, and Bennett fled to Europe.[69] The item failed to appear in the pages of "the people's paper." Instead the *Herald* scorned "the immorality of ministers" who went to the theater and "those who mistook churches for dormitories." It hoped the ecumenism of Moody's meetings would end an era of "aristocratic religious worship" by reducing "the class divisions so common in metropolitan worship."[70]

John C. Reid, the newly arrived managing editor of the *New York Times*, would not yield to Bennett or any other paper the contest for "that favorite place in New York City households." The paper's circulation was beginning to slide in a crowded and competitive morning field, so Reid scurried with editor Louis J. Jennings in search of something to balance the scandal stories that were beginning to bore readers. They hoped they had found it in boosting Moody's meetings. "In an age when the teachers of infidelity are so numerous and so active," the paper observed, "Moody's work deserves the warmest sympathy and encouragement." By its complete coverage of Moody's stay in New York City, the *Times* hoped "the truths of Christianity" would "reach many thousands who are beyond the sound of his voice." Jennings and Reid argued that promoting the revival was a means of serving its readers "with news that can be safely admitted into every domestic circle." The paper preached that "there is a truth behind Moody greater than he is" and that only a message that transformed the human heart would succeed in "stemming the tide of greed and peculation."[71]

ALMOST PERSUADED AND THEN PERSUADED

For the *Sun* and the *Times*, the story of D. L. Moody's meetings at the Hippodrome was the tale of a veteran editor who was "almost persuaded" and then finally persuaded by Moody's message. The tall, gaunt figure of Thurlow Weed would have been recognizable to any New York editor even if he had hoped to remain inconspicuous. He was born to the eighteenth Century, and few men had had his political influence on the nineteenth. First at the *Rochester Telegraph* and later at the *Albany Evening Journal* he helped put John Quincy Adams, William Henry Harrison, Zachary Taylor, and Abraham Lincoln in the White House and DeWitt Clinton and his own close friend William Seward in the State House. The political partisanship of the press, however, was beginning to look about as old and faded as Weed himself appeared in America's centennial year. Barely one-third of the state's newspapers were politically affiliated in the year of Moody's meetings, compared to more than half at the close of the Civil War, and the majority of these claimed loyalty to party principles, if not its policies and candidates.[72] Weed retired from journalism in 1863 before attempting an unsuccessful comeback four years later as the short-lived editor of the *New York Commercial Advertiser*. Then deteriorating health forced him into a second retirement. Weed was 78 when Moody came to New York City in the winter of America's centennial year and when he became a widely reported fixture at each evening service and often at the noontime prayer meetings as well.

Weed told a reporter from the *Sun* that "the Hippodrome revival is the most remarkable religious movement of the century." He indicated that he had "an unbounded admiration for Moody and Sankey" and that he was "fascinated at their ability to move the masses." Weed, however, appeared to be one of their holdouts. He admitted that he "had never been a religious man" and that while hundreds had made profession of their new-found faith through the meetings, he was not among them.[73] It was reported that Moody had developed "a special interest" in Weed's welfare and that "he would doubtless be unusually happy" to find that Weed had committed his life to Christ. Weed was a heavy financial contributor to defray the costs of the Hippodrome campaign. The generosity put Moody in an awkward position. "I am at a loss to know what to do," the famed evangelist wrote the famous editor. "I wish you knew how anxious I am for you and how I long to see you out and out on the Lord's side." Moody told "my dear friend" that he could not "bear to leave the city and leave you out of the Ark that God has provided for you and all the rest of us." Moody held out the hope that Weed would soon convert and become "my brother in Christ."[74]

The success of Moody's revival meetings in New York was well established by the end of February. Additional services had to be added, often bringing the daily attendance to 30,000. The press reported that Fourth Avenue passenger cars dropped "load after load of chilled wor-shippers" at the Hippodrome. The *Sun* said that "the hope of seeing or hearing Moody and Sankey" had become so strong that "some risked being crushed into a state of semi-unconsciousness in trying to get into the hall." Ushers asked police to help them control the crowds. Even that was not always the answer. One night, finding each of five entrances blocked, crowds surged down Madison Avenue, "creating quite a com-motion" in the back of the building. One police officer had to be hos-pitalized when he was "seriously hurt" trying to keep a crowd from breaking down a Hippodrome door. Officer Wolf was trapped between the throng and the hinges of the door as "the fastenings gave way and the people rushed in, trampling Wolf until he fell senseless." Moody's personal physician reported that Wolf suffered from shock and internal injuries but the trauma "was not life threatening." People impersonating reporters temporarily got through an entrance on Twenty-sixth Street that had been set aside for preachers and the press. Reporters couldn't get in "because the elect wouldn't come out." O. N. Crane, billing himself the "Weedsport revivalist," added to the fun. He told reporters that he'd traveled more 300 miles "to be of service to Mr. Moody in New York." He was dressed in the same farm overalls he'd worn in Weedsport, New York, and carried a "finger-worn hymn-book" under one arm and "the good book" under the other. It was as if the metropolis had gone "mad for Moody," with a desire to be at his meetings "enchaining everyone," leaving "the Devil himself to wonder who really ruled in Gotham."[75]

Friday, March 11, 1876, dawned sunny and unseasonably mild. Thurlow Weed knew what that meant. Since Moody would not be speaking on Saturday, which had become his well-publicized custom, an inordinately large crowd would hear him that night. Two days earlier Weed had sat among friends at a reporters' table, when Moody preached on the blood of Christ. "My friend," Moody said, as he finished his sermon, "what you want is to have the blood applied to you and your sins. You want to be cleansed by it. That was what the blood of Christ was shed for, to cover sin and to bless us and wash us and prepare us for God's kingdom." Moody hoped one day he might "sweep through the gates washed in the blood of the lamb." He told Weed and his other listeners: "Your time will come, and then it will be grand to die with these words upon your lips—'I am sweeping through the gates washed in the blood of the lamb.' "

When the message was over, Weed joined a long line of equally anxious attendees who would speak to Moody and other Christian counselors in an adjacent inquiry room. There, Moody moved about mightily. "Are you a Christian?" Moody wanted to know, pressing the hand of a well-dressed young man, who whispered something to Moody. Weed watched as the two men knelt in prayer. Perhaps a hundred inquirers had come to the room, "and about a hundred working Christians were exhorting them to come to Jesus," a *Sun* reporter said. Weed saw the spectacle similarly. He recognized the sergeant of the Prince Street police station, dressed in civilian clothes and praying with Moody. Weed heard their low whispers joining the chorus of those who were making a decision that he found so difficult to make.[76]

Not surprisingly, Friday evening's meeting was full. The *Tribune* reported that "many had to find seats on the steps leading up to the choir," with the less fortunate "finding no seats at all." They were urged to satisfy themselves by reading "unparalleled revival reporting" in the pages of the *Tribune*, which "during the Moody and Sankey meetings, because of popular demand," would "assure same day coverage by fast train from Albany to Philadelphia and all intermediate points along the way." Weed needed no such assurance. If he had planned to write his own story on Moody's meetings, he had given up on the idea. The event was no longer simply a civic spectacle to excite readers and stimulate circulation. Its puzzling meaning was becoming personal. He looked into "a sea of upturned faces" that crowded every corner of the auditorium, the congregation rising into the galleries that reached around the building and extended far back beneath the roof until the last lines of onlookers was lost in the diminishing light. A quiet prevailed that "would have been worthy of sitting statues," the next morning's paper would say. Weed could see Moody come out on an elevated stage and take his customary seat beside the pulpit perhaps 30 feet from the outermost limit of the audience. He surveyed the man. Short in stature, stoutly built, inclining to obesity, with shoulders slightly stooped forward, Moody seemed utterly unremarkable despite the remarkable thing he was doing. His neck was short and his face round and compact, its expression earnest and not altogether unpleasant, with a ruddiness the press attributed to health and not blood pressure. The inevitable long black beard appeared over a Prince Albert coat, buttoned in three places. With an abruptness Weed had grown used to, Moody spoke, citing the name of the first song to be sung. Every eye appeared to be on him until he sat in his chair, and then Weed heard a gentle rustle, as he and thousands of others settled back into their seats. Moody's strange hold on them and him was beginning, again.[77]

Commodore Vanderbilt, who sat beside Weed, almost certainly did not share his enthusiasm. Moody began that night by observing that "Christianity suffered more from those who have accumulated too much than from those who have too little." He likened the wealthy "to balloons that have too much ballast." They have to "lose weight before they can hope to reach the skies." Moody cited Matthew 6:19: "Lay not up for yourselves treasures upon earth, where moth and rust doth corrupt, and where thieves break through and steal, but lay up for yourselves treasures in heaven, where neither moth nor rust doth corrupt and where thieves do not break through and steal." The *Tribune* likened Moody's delivery to "a great radiating center" from whom "sermons seemed thrown off by a centrifugal force of their own rather than by mental effort." Their power was not so much the thought "as the feeling behind the thought." It was this "moral force" that gave the assertion its own authority.[78]

Moody told his audience that he couldn't agree with a man who told him men made their heaven here on earth. To Moody "a world of sickness and sorrow and sin" was no heaven at all. A friend had urged Moody not to preach to New Yorkers about heaven but to give them something "practical" instead. Heaven, however, was where Moody planned to make his home, and as any man might, he wanted to find out all he could about the neighborhood and his neighbors before moving in. To those who argued that that was something no one could know, Moody observed that the Bible talked of heaven quite a lot, and Christ Himself had said He was going to prepare a place there for those who followed Him. "If you do not know today that your name is written in heaven," Moody warned his listeners, "if no spirit bears witness with your spirit that your name is written in heaven, do not sleep tonight until you know it! It is the privilege of every man and woman in this house to know it if he will."[79]

Moody remembered a day train he had been on from London to Liverpool. He and his friends were looking forward to staying the night at the North Western Hotel. They'd been there before. When they arrived they found the hotel was completely booked and had been for days. The party started to go out, but one lady insisted on staying. "Aren't you coming?" they asked her. "No, I have a room," she answered. "But how," they insisted, "every room is taken." She had telegraphed ahead several days before. "That," Moody told Weed and his other listeners, "is just what God wants you to do. Send your name on ahead. Don't neglect your home beyond the grave. Don't neglect your soul's salvation." The way to make a reservation was the way of salvation, Moody assured his audience. Christ had telegraphed ahead for everyone who accepted his invitation. He was willing that none should be excluded. What was now needed was for men and women everywhere to accept what He had done on the cross for them. "His hand is open to every sinner who takes it," Moody said, "You have nothing to do then to bring about a reconciliation. God is already reconciled to us and is ready to save us."[80]

The *Herald* reported that Moody called the congregation to three minutes of silent prayer. The *Times* reported that Moody's energy and earnestness seemed inexhaustible that day after appearances at five separate meetings. The *Tribune* reported, as its competitors had, the long lines of inquirers who clogged the aisles after worshippers sang "Shall We Gather at the River." Only the *Sun*, however, sent its reporter into the inquiry room that night, and there found Moody. "The work is going well," he said, in answer to a characteristic question. He had just "knelt in prayer" with "one of his most promising converts." Thurlow Weed, the aged publisher and politician, the paper told its morning readers, had "risen that night and become a Christian."[81]

"A WEEDY EDEN"

By the third week of April, Moody's 10-week run at the Hippodrome was ending, and Dana of the *Sun*, who had had high hopes a dose of "practical Christianity" would do his town "great good," was distressed by what he saw. One of Moody's minions had elicited an outburst of applause when he predicted that had the revival gone on six months more "the police force of New York might be disbanded." Dana saw little evidence that "virtue, good will, truth, honor, justice and honesty would acquire complete ascendancy over the

Moody inside the Inquiry Room. A *New York Herald* reporter feigned that he was "anxious over the condition of his soul" to catch Moody solicitously speaking to penitents who had come to his crusade. Thurlow Weed, longtime New York editor, was one of them.

life of the community." Instead, despite the vast throngs who listened to Moody's message, "things yet look very much as they used to in the days before the flood." The well-intentioned "Hippodromists," Dana told his now 140,000 readers, had done little to alter the course "of the brokers on Wall Street, the downtown merchants, the Broadway, Bowery, Third and Sixth avenue shopkeepers, the residents of the fashionable quarters, the politicians of the Custom House and Tammany Hall." Their influence among "members of the various churches and the clergymen who preach in them" could only be guessed at. There was little to suggest that "six months more of revivalism would turn this weedy soil into a Garden of Eden."[82]

At the close of his meetings, Moody had characteristically asked "the blessing of God on the reporters, without whose kind cooperation this work would never have obtained its magnitude in New York City." The *Times* had been among those steadfastly supporting Moody's mission, but at its close it shared some of the *Sun's* ambivalence. The *Times* thought it a little too much to ask Moody to alleviate "the thousand-year agonies of humanity" in 70 days of sermons. "Whatever skeptics may say," the paper nonetheless argued, "the work accomplished this winter in this city for private and public morals will live." It saw evidence everywhere that "the drunken have become sober, the vicious virtuous, the worldly and self-seeking unselfish, the ignoble noble, and the impure pure." The staff of the *Times* had hoped only that Moody's "new influence over Protestantism" would not have been directed only at its oldest members. Although Moody had urged Christians to bring nonbelievers to his meetings, the *Times* thought too many of his celebrants "were people of comfortable circumstances." The poor had hardly been touched. If "the densely populated poor" of the city's East River wards had come to the revival, "we might have seen results that would fairly astonish this city and country."[83]

Moody and Sankey thought the more than 30,000 inquirers who had prayed to receive Christ or renew their faith in him made the Hippodrome campaign one of their most successful. The *Herald* heartily concurred. It editorially appealed to "city churches and pastors to carry on the work that Moody and Sankey have begun." The secular press "had been a powerful instrument for sending abroad the Word," thereby "helping the work of revival." Moody was "a man who spoke like the Evangelist John from the depth of his heart," and he had raised "a Christian army encamped around this citadel of Satan." The paper's editors even made a good Democrat out of him, putting paraphrases into his mouth to attack a scandal-plagued president. When Moody preached on the character of Daniel, the *Herald* had him "lamenting the want of such a man at the present day, when offices are bought and sold and the highest positions in the land are given away for money." It obtained another "exclusive," certain to amuse its working-class readers, when it claimed, without naming names, that "a number of well-dressed, uptown, men and women" had "gone mad from religion" when overcome by Moody's message. A psychologist suggested they may have been suffering from "religio-mania," a condition in which "sensitively organized people of delicate fiber, have their fragile constitutions overpowered by Moody's message," it making them appear "drunk and disorderly" to arresting officers. An overnight stay in lunatic asylums, the paper told its readers, calmed its victims "from their religious frenzy," allowing "friends of the unfortunate" to spirit them off into private care, so that no other newspaper, save the *Herald*, would know.[84]

Just as New York's newspapers cast Moody in narratives of their own making, the *Tribune*, the paper that covered his meetings most thoroughly, saw in revival work what it wanted to see. The city's "better classes" as much as its underclass needed reviving, and the crowds that came nightly to the Hippodrome proved the point. The paper predicted that "a remarkable work will begin" and promised to report "the growing interest as it progresses." The "lawyers, physicians, scientists, and even editors" who came to the meetings listened to "an illiterate man whose grammar was a gross violation of rules learned by schoolboys." What they found was "a man of moral earnestness and inflamed zeal" who challenged skeptics by saying: "It seems like we can have enthusiasm in everything these days, except religion."[85] Moody "saw God in everything," and his powers of description helped hearers see it too. He "clothes Biblical narratives with reality and life" so that "you can picture Old Testament prophets, priests and kings walking the streets of New York." It left one with the impression that "Moody is a man of more ideas than he can ever hope to express," a mind so agile and searching that "he seems wholly unable to find relief in only words."[86] The *Tribune*'s strongest impression of the citywide work that it had helped to create was that "the real work was done by men who had nothing to gain from their immense effort, neither position, nor money, nor reputation." Instead, Moody's genius for organization had created a civic spectacle that no one could have predicted—"a community of believers who unite in disinterested cooperation to achieve great purposes." They were led by a man "who propels his Christianity with a heat and power that carries all before it." It was "a fire and passion that only those insensitive to religious impressions remain wholly unaffected by." Every night "the anxious assailed each of six crowded entrances, wedging their way in" with a determination so acute that "the whole city police force would scarcely have been able to keep them out." What the crowds found was a man "absorbed by one idea. He acts as if there is not another man in the world to act."[87]

An old railroad depot on Fourth Avenue in the middle of Manhattan had long been the scene of strange civic spectacles and enchantments. It became the Hippodrome with Barnum's sensational circus and menagerie. With a cataract on one end and a beer tunnel on the other, it would next serve a municipal thirst for satisfactions as Gilmore's Musical Coloseum. In the hands of the enterprising Sheridan Shook it promised to be "a place of unparalleled amusement." In the decades that followed, however, tens of thousands would remember it as "Moody's Meeting Place," where "the sound of many feet on the boards of that building was like the roar of the mighty sea." The secular press freely admitted that "New York society has been suddenly seized by an unwonted fervor of devotional sentiment." The greatest "social excitement of this or any season" had given New York "the odor of unaccustomed sanctity." As Moody prepared to leave the city, the aroma appears to have reached the uptown offices of the old established *Evening Post* and its editor, the 81-year-old William Cullen Bryant, who was then writing a popular history of the country's first 100 years. The conscientious chronicler of late Puritanism and poet of "Thanatopsis" did not concede the accuracy of Moody's promises of immortality and admitted to no deity higher than nature. Nevertheless, he saw in Moody's meetings a certain civic wonder and moral grandeur. Moody's magnificent "executive ability" and "glorious self-assurance" had allowed the skeptical heart "to shape itself into a temple," Bryant wrote, in which "every aspiration ends in God."[88]

"From the Curbstone to the Ashpit, the Fix Is In"

SIX

MOODY IN CHICAGO, OCTOBER 1876–JANUARY 1877

D. L. Moody was determined to shake Chicago to its sinful center, but first he took on an overly excited celebrant who wouldn't let him finish. The *Chicago Tribune* reported many at the Christian convention were "shocked" when the 32-year-old Moody came down from his pulpit and "unceremoniously" hustled the poor man out. The episode was warily reported in 1869 by Chicago's leading paper, the *Tribune*, as an admonition to a favorite son. The paper warned that Moody was too "impulsive and excitable" to be taken fully seriously. As a young colt he would have to be "brought to harness" if he expected to amount to much in the Lord's work.[1] The "fatherly advice" was from 46-year-old Joseph Medill, the editor and publisher of a paper that boasted "no superior in power and influence among Republican newspapers." By 1869, the overly eager evangelist and the unctuous Presbyterian who had studied law and helped elect Lincoln had had a long and sometimes strained relationship. "Crazy Moody" had alienated Medill and other members of Chicago's frontier press by barging into newspaper offices and demanding coverage of evangelistic efforts "to lift Chicago out of its darkness."[2]

On the eve of Moody's mission to Chicago in America's centennial year, the prophet found he was to be honored in his own country. Moody's sudden star status meant that he would be eagerly embraced by the same circulation-starved papers that had all but ignored him years earlier. Some in the city's press now thought "the fix was in." There would be no escaping Moody and his message now. "From curbstone to ashpit" the great metropolis of the Northwest was being made ready for "the greatest day that our city has ever seen."[3] Moody's trusted confidant and longtime benefactor John V. Farwell saw the situation similarly. In a letter to Moody he put it bluntly: the press that had once scorned him was now "converted."[4] Over three and a half months, an estimated one million people, more than twice the city's population, would see and hear the man whose "pluck, push and enterprise" reflected Chicago's optimism and "capacious energy."[5] Through the daily verbatim stenographic accounts that appeared in Chicago dailies many millions more could follow the campaign. Those accounts "heat to redness the iron of public sentiment," Moody's detractors in the press protested, and led to "a conviction that breeds conviction."[6] It was why, they argued, Moody "thanked God for the press" and why their circulation managers thanked God for him in an ethos of reciprocity that served each well. One even sold a bound edition of Moody's many messages, later boasting that it was "the largest and most complete" record of Moody's mighty work "that has yet been offered to the public."[7] It supplemented the scrapbooks of the many faithful who clipped and saved these newspaper accounts of their local hero as a personal record of God's presence in their midst.

MOODY, MEDILL, AND FARWELL

Joseph Maharry Medill knew a self-seeker when he saw one because he was one. Chicago, the fastest-growing city in the country, was a magnet to many of them, as it had been to him. Medill was one of six children raised by Scotch-Irish parents on a family farm near Massillon, Ohio. He had solicited subscriptions for Horace Greeley's *New York Tribune* and drifted into journalism through his father-in-law's country weekly in New Philadelphia, Ohio. He ran newspapers in Coshocton and Newark, Ohio, but quickly tired of being paid in chickens and trousers.[8] With borrowed money he made Cleveland's *Daily Forest City* and *Morning Leader* a success and himself a reputation. In April 1855 he brought his wife, two daughters, and three brothers to Chicago to take over the *Tribune*, then in its eighth year. The city was the West's third largest, behind Cincinnati and St. Louis, and its cholera capital. The city smelled from raw sewage and slaughterhouse waste and had a lakefront dominated by mosquito marshes. But Chicago was also America's rail and lumber center. Seven dailies waged rhetorical warfare Chicago style, to the amusement of the city's 110,000 spectators; the *Tribune's* emphasis on church news, moral values, and all things Republican was winning 100 weekly converts to its cause.[9]

Civil war at the *Tribune*, now ensconced in a four-story marble palace in the center of the city, began just as the nation's ended. Medill was ousted by major stockholder Horace White as managing editor in 1865 and plotted his return.[10] Moody, in the meantime, returned to the city after seven stints at the front, where he'd preached to the troops and cared for their wounded as a member of the United States Christian Commission. The commission was an undertaking of the nation's YMCAs aimed to spiritually support men in uniform. The experience had put Moody in the publishing business too. Through the Chicago Association he raised money and helped distribute one and a half million Bibles to Union soldiers, and many of the 1.3 million hymnals and 40 million pages of tracts received by the soldiers.[11] His determination to get the gospel out extended in peacetime to Chicago's YMCA movement. As chief librarian and president of the local chapter, he oversaw the distribution of five tons of religious literature annually, much of it in "gospel wagons" that ranged across large and small settlements in the great Northwest. The association's publications committee annually issued five million pages of tracts and papers, including the association's *Heavenly Tidings*. Two hundred thousand copies of *Everybody's Paper* was circulated annually throughout the city, with the *Watchman* commanding such wide acceptance that it was adopted by the national YMCA as its official organ.[12]

John Farwell was a wealthy Chicago merchant who preceded Moody in YMCA work and shared his certainty that it took all means of persuasion to save a few sinners from themselves. The moving of the Spirit, when whetted to "the power of printer's ink," would save Chicago in spite of itself, both men agreed.[13] Like Moody and Medill, Farwell had seen Chicago grow from a "one-horse mud town" to a western sentinel. Farwell's own fortune had grown apace. The clothier had earned $96 his first year in business and donated $50 of it to help build the city's first Methodist church, which was where where he had first met Moody. The latter often arrived late and sometimes slept, to Farwell's great irritation. Only later did he learn that Moody had been up at an early hour bringing street urchins to Sunday School. Moody's "bodyguard" were "river rats" drawn from the "Sands," a no-man's-land of cholera and crime stuck among the packing plants along the Chicago River. The overly cautious Farwell admired Moody's "instant action to meet the needs of the hour." Together the two teamed to make the North Market Hall Mission the largest Sunday School in the city. In June 1860 Farwell became its superintendent and chief publicist. A photograph of the two men posing with their charges made the mission front-page news. The politically connected Farwell arranged for president-elect Lincoln to see Moody's work for himself. In Farwell's mind, the mission school's 1,500 pupils showed that Moody was Chicago's "most useful man."[14]

If Moody was the city's most useful man, Farwell was its most generous. In October 1867, Chicago's YMCA building, the first in the nation, opened its doors in the heart of the city on land donated by Farwell. Farwell wanted to call it Moody Hall, but Moody, speaking first, suggested another name—Farwell Hall. "If you want to know what's going on in America," the *Tribune* reported, "come to Chicago and see the way our 'Y' is working." The building's nightly speakers and socials were intended as outreaches to the growing community of young men who had come to Chicago hoping to cash in on the city's rapid growth. Moody was among the men who greeted them as they were stepping off the train, inviting them for an evening of clean entertainment and a cleaner room at the local Y. "Let's go to the lost and not wait for them to come to us," Moody charged his comrades on the dedication of Farwell Hall. The wares and allures of the world were "widely circulated in our daily press," Farwell warned, but now it was time to tell the story of what "Christian union" could accomplish.[15]

The *Tribune* took note. Moody and Farwell had "infused new blood into the YMCA's shriveled and shrunken skin," the paper alliteratively put it, while putting down their brand of "experimental religion," which "takes the gospel into dance halls, dog pits, and saloons."[16] Moody and Farwell developed reputations for "ministering to young men in a city of young men," particularly those in the center of the city who had been abandoned by churches that had fled to "nicer neighborhoods."[17] The opening of the YMCA's library to the public in April 1869 was the cause of a widely publicized civic celebration. For the first time in municipal history all the city's daily and weekly newspapers could be found in one place, plus 35 of the leading newspapers across the nation. Letters to the editor asked if Moody could make another miracle by providing water fountains to the city's strangers. "In seventy-five years," the *Tribune* boasted, "Chicago and not New York will be the metropolis of this country."[18]

Farwell took a paternal interest in his young protege. When he heard that Moody had given up his job as shoe salesman to devote himself entirely to religious work, Farwell offered to meet Moody's financial needs, but Moody refused. When he heard that Moody was dining on cheese and crackers and sleeping on prayer-room pews, he offered Moody lodging, which he reluctantly accepted.[19] By 1870, Moody's interests were no longer merely municipal. He wouldn't stand for another term as president of the city's YMCA. The local news noted

Moody and longtime benefactor John Farwell pose with Moody's "bodyguard," street urchins drawn from the "Sands," a wasteland along the Chicago River.

Moody's ministry to children brought him to the attention of President-elect Abraham Lincoln and solidified the evangelist's growing reputation in the Chicago press as the city's "most useful man."

he was often away on evangelistic campaigns. While in Indianapolis, he preached alongside Ira Sankey. When in Chicago, capacity crowds came to see him preach at a church on Illinois Street that the press came to call "Moody's Church." It was there on the evening of October 8, 1871, that he preached from Philippians 3 on Paul's text "This one thing I do." Reporters noted his words of warning: to "forget those things which are behind and reach forward to the things which are ahead." But they never filed their stories. A fire that began in a cow barn south and west of the city's center devastated 15 city blocks, killing 250, destroying 450 buildings, valued at $200 million, and leaving 100,000 people homeless. Farwell Hall, Moody's home, Moody's church, and the Chicago Tribune building did not escape the inferno.[20]

"Cheer up, Chicago!" Joseph Medill told his readers when the *Tribune* resumed publication October 11 in a makeshift edition on a rented press. "Chicago shall rise again!" And the city chose Medill to lead it. The next month he was elected mayor, becoming Chicago's chief cheerleader and publicist as the Phoenix City rose from the ashes. A new beginning for Medill and the city was an end for Moody. For years he had felt a call to preach the gospel, and now the fire finished the work he had spent 15 years building. Farwell begged him to stay, but Moody was determined to preach in Britain. In June 1873 Farwell gave Moody and Sankey and their young families money for the passage over[21] on the trip that would establish Moody's reputation as the best-known evangelist in the Western world. Medill, unexpectedly, would soon join him there. His determination to use police muscle to enforce Sunday bar closings alienated the city's German and Irish communities. Medill saw himself waging war against the saloon and liquor interests that preyed on the city's work force, but many workers saw the war differently. In July 1873, as Moody was beginning his union meetings in Europe, Medill announced he wouldn't be a candidate for reelection and promptly set sail for Europe.[22]

CHICAGO'S PRESS ON THE EVE OF THE REVIVAL

Joseph Medill's arch-enemy, "the severely Democratic" Wilbur Storey, editor and publisher of the *Chicago Times*, was delighted to see "Nancy" go. There had long been little love shown between "that little liar" who ran the *Tribune* and "the delusional incompetent" who controlled the *Times*.[23] Storey purchased the paper in 1861, rescuing it, he immodestly claimed, from "the unfortunate ownership" of the reaper baron Cyrus McCormick. The paper had been the voice of Illinois senator Stephen O. Douglas and relied on party subsidies. Under Storey it made headlines as a peace paper and Lincoln antagonist. Its suspension during the Civil War magnified its Copperhead status. After the war its circulation of 30,000 rivaled the *Tribune's*, although Storey claimed it was three times that and "exceeded all the city's papers combined." Storey liked being the story. Few liked him, but the working class read his paper, and he considered himself their protector and advocate. The aim of the second-place *Times* was to be first. Many were realizing, Storey boasted, that the *Times* "is the leading public journal in the country."[24]

Storey's five-story sanctuary at Fifth Avenue and Washington housed a staff of 50 and an operating budget that Storey "spent without stint." Storey claimed he only sought "to instruct." Critics claimed he "reveled in indecencies."[25] Rumors of President Grant's marital infidelities were front-page news along with tawdry tales of "illicit love" and a simple case of blackmail. The *Times* was sued and Storey was publicly whipped for his transgressions. It only intensified his attack on the established moral order.[26] On the eve of Moody's meetings in Chicago, the *Times* printed letters warning "a spiritual debauch" might flow from the evangelist's "dark-ages twaddle." The *Times* was editorially in sympathy with the warning, remarking that "enthusiasm is a good thing if it is about the truth." The truth that Storey had in mind was spiritualism. He preferred the "science" of a well-conducted seance to the way Moody's "salvation shop grinds out the gospel."[27] This peculiar passion had been prompted by the death in January 1873 of Storey's second wife, Harriet Dodge, and his determination to "make contact" with her departed spirit. Competing papers argued that Storey's spiritual condition made him a perfect candidate for Moody's ministry. Joseph Medill, back from Europe and in control of the *Tribune*, had a reporter interview Storey, on spiritualism, and a Dr. Isaac Redfield, who was certain that Storey suffered from an "insane delusion."[28]

Moody's success in Europe had dispelled misgivings Medill had had about Moody's maturity. Medill was impressed by success and admired the organizational aptitude Moody had shown in uniting England's evangelical churches behind him. When Moody returned to the United States after a two-and-a-half-year absence and a bidding war broke out for his services among America's largest cities, Medill urged Chicago's churches to get to the head of the line. "A religious revival would prove just the tonic needed," Medill argued in an open letter, to lift the city's spirits and, not incidentally, his personal finances. The nationwide panic of 1873 had been devastating to the newspaper industry, which relied on advertising for nearly half its income. Chicago's economy, still reeling from the Great Fire of 1871, was particularly hard hit. Medill "slowly awakened to the painfully realizing sense that I had gone too deeply into debt" and that "no human effort" could generate the advertising income the *Tribune* had enjoyed before the crash until there was "a revival of trade." Medill allowed himself a $100 weekly salary plus an 8 percent dividend on his Chicago Tribune stock. The slump meant he earned half as much money in 1875 as 1874, and prospects for 1876 without some sudden surge of optimism seemed little better. He was now offering advertisers page one displays, but it did little good. Even classifieds were being pulled to the front page—a sure sign of desperation—before the experiment was abandoned altogether.[29]

The front page became a battleground where Medill and his brother Samuel, the paper's managing editor, waged war against those who sought to weaken "the moral system" that undergirded communal relations. In the days before Moody's meetings, the decision to discontinue Bible reading in the city's public schools and the trial of a popular Presbyterian cleric for heresy struck Medill as an intolerable erosion of the consensual values that had once united Chicago's diverse communities. The paper predicted the "breakdown" of moral authority unless the Bible was returned to the city's schools and the Presbyterians let Professor David Swing, the 45-year-old pastor of Fourth Presbyterian Church, alone. The *Interior*, a Presbyterian journal that had attacked Swing, saw Medill's attacks as "wholesale and retail slander." Cyrus McCormick, the paper's publisher, took Medill's assault personally, and it was meant personally. Swing was exonerated and decided to launch a nondenominational church, which met at McVicker's Theatre. Medill was one of his major financial backers. Doctrinal differences "sap the community of its strength," Medill wrote. What the city now needed was the "real religion" that Moody offered, to restore "the old Christian faith of this community," leavened with a bit of "Western grit."[30]

Hard times required "provocative journalism," in Medill's view, and that meant playing the Henry Ward Beecher adultery trial and its aftermath to the hilt. The most celebrated story of 1875 included an exclusive interview with the wronged husband who had brought the charges and, eventually, with his unfaithful wife, along with the publication of love letters Reverend Beecher had written to her. "Our circulation is not of the back alley sort," he asserted, while ignoring this coverage, "nor are we dependent on sensation or scandal." The *Tribune's* readers had an "intense" interest in religion and religious personalities, and Medill was determined to find copy that fed that interest. The paper's business readers were reassured this was still their paper. "Readers in the slums who occasionally invest a nickel in a newspaper are not the class whom we desire to reach." The paper's circulation climbed to over 40,000 in the face of these crusades, only to fall back to 31,000 by the end of the centennial summer.[31]

When it came to promoting moral probity and Mr. Moody, no one outdid the *Chicago Inter-Ocean*. "The Farmer's Bible" had reached a weekly circulation of 300,000 by the eve of Moody's meetings in Chicago by becoming the prairie farmer's preferred paper.[32] Richard Scammon had promised "a Christian paper" when launching the *Inter-Ocean* in 1872. To his mind that meant being "independent in nothing and Republican in everything." When William Penn Nixon, a newspaperman from Cincinnati, bought the *Inter-Ocean* the following year, he was determined "to keep it clean enough that people won't be afraid to wrap their food in it."[33] His credentials for keeping the promise were impeccable. His Quaker forebears had been intimates of William Penn and had long been active in the Underground Railroad. Nixon was an early and eager supporter of Lincoln and a war correspondent for an Ohio daily. The *Tribune* under Horace White had veered from Republican orthodoxy on the tariff and in supporting Horace Greeley's challenge to Grant's second term. Nixon's nationally syndicated paper was paid for playing the party line, a point not lost on his opponents.[34] Medill publicly chided the *Inter-Ocean* on its lack of independence but privately feared its effect on his circulation. Nixon's refusal in April 1876 to quit the paper and work for the *Tribune* further infuriated Medill. The *Inter-Ocean* shared Medill's purpose of "civilizing the city by preaching a gospel of good citizenship." Private meetings between Nixon, his managing editor, William Harrison Busbey, and members of Moody's team assured the evangelist, if he harbored any doubts, that the *Inter-Ocean* was already "converted" to his cause.[35] Moody's name was "better known than any human name," the paper reported, and that was because the Bible was "better than any newspaper." Newspapers told "what has taken place." The Bible told "what is to come."[36]

Melville Elijah Stone had been a city editor and a managing editor on the *Inter-Ocean* who chafed at the paper's political partisanship. The son of a Methodist minister, he became obsessed with creating a truly independent newspaper that would interest every reader who preferred news to views. An experimental edition of the one-penny *Daily News* first appeared on December 23, 1875, wryly endorsing Joseph Medill, "a great and idle man," for president. A week later it made its official debut.[37] Stone was convinced there was a place in Chicago for a newspaper that "gives the greatest amount of news in the smallest possible space" with both "dignity and decency." The *Daily News* was "more than a mere business enterprise." It claimed to offer a "true perspective of the world's developing history" that "a woman could read aloud in mixed company."[38] Stone's parents had met at Knox College in Galesburg, Illinois, and shared the school's evangelical animosity toward slavery. Stone's family, like Nixon's, had been active in the Underground Railroad, reflecting an Arminian determination emphasizing human agency in redressing moral grievance. In 1860, Stone's father became pastor of the Des Plaines Street Methodist Church, just west of Chicago's business district. Their neighbor was a cousin of D. L. Moody. As a Wesleyan, Stone was well aware of the power of revivals in transforming human hearts. Revivals were part of the fabric of living in the West—part entertainment, part diversion, part food for the desolate soul.[39]

Stone called on a former schoolmate, Victor Lawson, publisher of Chicago's *Skandinaven*, for financial support in sustaining the *Daily News* when the struggling paper couldn't afford its $50 wire service bill. Stone, as editor, was given a $25 weekly salary and one-third of the profits, should there be any. Lawson's business dexterity combined with Stone's pithy writing style helped the afternoon paper reach a circulation of 14,000 in its first year, the highest among the afternoon dailies.[40] Lawson's father had made a fortune in Chicago real estate speculation but was all but wiped out in the Great Fire. His death in 1872 left his son well connected but in need of a job. Lawson's Norwegian daily had rented eight square feet of space to the *Daily News* in a four-story walkup on Fifth Avenue, just west of downtown and "somewhere behind a tree," according to critics. The paper that he inherited had more than its share of drunks working for it. A disapproving Lawson was forced to fire a man who danced atop a newsroom desk. He had been christened in a Norwegian Evangelical Lutheran Church and had attended Moody's afternoon Sunday School class as a boy, leading to a lifelong conviction that "religious instruction is of the greatest possible benefit in character building." He felt the Sabbath School kept a great many out of reformatories and thought the YMCA, which he aggressively supported, had the same salutary effect on young men.[41]

Lawson sang in the choir of the New England Congregational Church and there met his wife. They were strict Sabbatarians who banned liquor from their home. The *Daily News* refused liquor ads and closed its doors at 9 p.m. Saturday before reopening at six on Sunday evening. Lawson devised a plan to employ schoolboys by making them *Daily News* carriers. A *Daily News* boys' band made all the parades.[42] Lawson had firm ideas about news and advertising. He shared Stone's enthusiasm for accuracy and impartiality and established a fixed ad rate. He insisted that advertising be listed as advertising and not news. To do otherwise "risked one's reputation with the public." Advertisers who didn't accept that could find another newspaper. One bit of collusion, however, he did permit. Stores were encouraged to hold 99 cents sales so that customers would have a penny to spend on the *Daily News*.[43]

For a penny Chicagoans got a newspaper that preached moderation but practiced a bit of seduction in its struggle to gain circulation, if not self-respect. If the *Tribune* had Beecher, the *Daily News* had its own page one church scandal. A "leading lady" in a West End church, readers were advised, had been expelled from that membership for prostitution. Her church attendance had been her way of hiding her crime, a situation "unparalleled in the history of the West." The incident was just another example of the city's "grievous moral condition."[44] That was why the *Daily News* said it was sympathetic to Moody's mission in Chicago. "The good prophet of Chicago" would hold a great revival only if supported by the churches and the press, the paper argued. Moody's revival machinery was a "monument" to "energy, efficiency and enterprise" and would succeed in Chicago just as it had elsewhere, if only given the chance.[45]

Solidifying Moody's status with the *Daily News* was his friendship with Cyrus McCormick, a stockholder in the paper and a generous supporter of the YMCA movement in the city. McCormick admired Moody's energy and results in lifting the city's marginalized out of their spiritual poverty. He supported Moody's ministry financially as early as 1868 and maintained an active correspondence with the evangelist on the eve of the Chicago campaign.[46] McCormick believed that Moody's preaching would help heal communal divisions that had been opened by banning Bible reading from the public schools, divisions that he thought had been deepened "by the *Chicago Tribune* and other newspapers of the baser sort." Like Moody, the *Daily News* treated "all denominations alike and with equal respect."[47]

The staff of the venerable *Chicago Evening Journal*, at 36 the oldest daily in the city, viewed the prerevival posturing of the press with some amusement and not a little anxiety. Andrew Shuman, the paper's editor and soon to be the state's lieutenant governor, chided McCormick for his reputation as Moody's benefactor by suggesting that "times were hard" and the harvesting king "should put a little of his surplus money where it would do the most good" and pay Moody's campaign costs out of his own pocket.[48] The *Journal* had its own worries. It was losing the afternoon reader to the hard-charging *Daily News*. As Charles Wilson, the paper's publisher, surveyed the situation from the fifth floor of the *Journal*'s fashionable if fading brick manse at 159 Dearborn, he liked to recall the paper's long reputation as civil servant, whose strength and Whiggish spirit chronicled and paralleled the city's evolution from "small frontier village to a great progressive city." The Fire, the Panic, and the pessimism of retailers threatened to sink some Chicago newspapers but, Wilson insisted, not his. The outmanned *Journal* announced in June 1876 it wouldn't be outdone in revival coverage by using its connections with event planners to arrange a page one interview with Moody. It gave Moody a chance to publicly urge city business and church leaders who pled poverty to join hands by building a tabernacle suitable for the occasion.[49]

For years Moody had toiled in relative anonymity in Chicago. The press in those days saw "Crazy Moody" as an annoying self-seeker, eager to publicize Christian works in the city.

"THE NAPOLEON OF REVIVALISTS HAS COME"

The usually upbeat John Farwell feared that Moody had over-played his hand and that it would be difficult to find financing for a new building. Farwell attempted to follow John Wana-maker's example by donating land in the city's center to build a great tabernacle, but event organizers balked at borrowing money to build it. "I don't think you fully comprehend the difficulty," he hurriedly wrote Moody on July 26, "in raising money here to build a building that will be torn down." He had urged Moody to preach in smaller churches scattered throughout the city, but Moody refused. City min-isters needed to know they must unite behind his efforts before he came to Chicago.[50] "What is the devil doing?" Farwell exclaimed in exasperation, as the date for Moody's revival neared and the Building Committee dawdled. "The money comes very hard," they complained, wondering whether the tabernacle could be finished for its scheduled October 1 opening. The problem was inertia, Farwell told Moody. Men might "see the morning star when you come," but as for now, "it has been dark a long time." So the two men determined to use the power of publicity to light a fire under event organizers. The Christian community and its business leaders, Moody and Farwell reasoned, could not be seen as failing the city's favorite son in staging a citywide revival. It would make Chicago a national laughingstock. Once Moody publicly committed to coming, they would have no choice but to pro-vide him with a suitable building. "The Lord wants him to come," Farwell and the lumberman Turlington W. Harvey privately and pub-licly told the city's movers and shakers. The newspapers and the living Lord would show people "how easy it is" to build a building "when you feel like it."[51]

The *Evening Journal* noted that if anyone three years before had suggested such interest would be shown in bringing Moody back to the city "folks would have called them crazy." Crazy Moody wasn't crazy anymore, the paper observed. Now "hard-pressed churches and the city's press" who had often ignored Moody and his message when he lived in the city begged for his return, seeing in him and his associates "a power such as the world has never seen since the Apostles." The paper noted that not only Chicago but the daily press in city after city had taken to the revival story as a sure-fire way to stimulate circulation.[52] Chicago's spectacle started in the spring of 1876 at the corner of Monroe and Franklin, when front-page headlines searched the skies for signs of Moody's coming and began to report the progress of "Moody's Taber-nacle" before the first spade of earth was turned. The Moody watch, the *Inter-Ocean* acknowledged, was "an understandable part of his celeb-rity." Moody stayed away, telling Farwell: "Whether I'm seen or not,

Copyright 1900
Fleming H. Revell Co.

After his huge success in Britain, Moody was hailed by Chicago's press, which had once scorned him, as the city's "favorite son."

newspapers will have a full account of their interview with me."[53] His eventual appearance on May 31 at Farwell's Presbyterian church in suburban Lake Forest created a sensation. Moody's "first public appearance in the West" since his return from Europe was "the most notable day in the religious history of Lake Forest." As word spread a crowd gathered two hours early, anxious to have a look. Those that got in would never forget the man's newly won "personal magnetism" that drew all celebrants to him.[54]

The only thing "new" about Moody, in the minds of his critics on the eve of his meetings, was the free publicity the man now received from the press. Chief among those critics was J. T. Sunderland of the Fourth Unitarian Church, who argued that "Moody's name has appeared in the newspapers of this country during the past two years more than perhaps any other name." The wonder was "with all that advertising why he doesn't draw larger crowds."[55] Moody made it known that unless the building of a tabernacle large enough to hold the crowds that would come to his meetings was done "cheerfully," he wouldn't come. New Haven and other cities had sent petitions begging him to lead revivals in their cities, and these were given wide play in the Chicago papers.[56] Medill and the *Tribune* began to apply public pressure to rally the city's business community and evangelical churches to action. Moody was always "at white heat," the *Tribune* reported, and now it was time for a committee of "best men" to match his enthusiasm. Moody's "tremendous linguistic persistence" had "picturing power," Medill argued, the kind of vision the city needed in building a tabernacle to house Moody's meetings. Moody's reputation "has outgrown the church architecture of his times," wrote W. H. Daniels, the paper's revival correspondent, who had published a bestselling book on Moody's evangelical efforts. He required an auditorium "ten times the size of our average first-class church."[57]

The public pressure worked. George Armour and Henry Field, two of Chicago's wealthiest men, joined the executive committee chosen to pick a building site and finance its construction. Farwell again offered the vacant lot at Monroe and Franklin, and an executive committee of leading businessmen and churchmen committed to raising the $25,000 necessary to erect a tabernacle there. Moody telegraphed from his home in Northfield, Massachusetts, that he would begin the meetings by October 1.[58] Excavations began the second week of August, as the city's rail lines announced plans to run extra cars directly to the building. The Moody watch in Chicago's press daily intensified. The evangelist was variously reported in Vermont and New Hampshire, working, resting, and getting a new round of messages ready. A nationally syndicated story said that several women had been trampled underfoot while others had flung themselves through the side windows of a church when a Moody meeting was moved to the city hall in Springfield, Massachusetts. The town was reported to be in a panic.[59] Farwell told event organizers that "when the records of our meetings are written up" they needed to have the same excitement.[60]

Moody's advance team, which had served him so well in his Philadelphia campaign, came to Chicago in the summer of 1876 and left little to chance. Thomas K. Cree, Moody's longtime friend from his YMCA days, was in charge of publicity. Long before the meetings opened they were extensively advertised in newspapers all over the West, casting the revival as a regional as much as a citywide experience. Large three-sheet posters were put up on sacred and secular bulletin boards throughout the Great Lakes and across the plains. The region was saturated with as many as 50,000 small handbills, distributed by a dedicated volunteer army in a single day.[61] By mid-September, the Chicago press was reporting daily on the progress of "Moody's Tabernacle." It would be the largest the city had ever seen, a building of brick and iron in the very center of the city, 190 by 160 feet, with openings on three sides. The main floor would seat 4,500 and a 40-foot gallery another 2,900. On stage, there were seats for 300 singers and an equal number of ministers and other honored guests. Under the platform and gallery were inquiry rooms and offices, including a place for the press to file its stories.[62]

The magnitude of the buildup created a small stir before Moody preached his first sermon. Some in the press welcomed, others ridiculed the coming spectacle. The "Napoleon of revivalists," an unfriendly *Chicago Times* reported, was coming with a vast army to conquer the city. What consolation did simple sinners have in the face of such a force? the paper wondered. "Everything is ready and in perfect order," the *Tribune* said, after sizing up the preparations of Moody's machine. Moody had "conquered the religious world," the *Inter-Ocean* announced, by "rousing the two most enlightened nations of the world to a pitch of religious enthusiasm." The city had "given Moody to the world," and now it was its turn to "welcome him home."[63] If Moody and revival were sent by God, one skeptic scoffed, why were Moody's posters needed "all over the city, down to curb-stone and ash-pit." The determination of the daily papers to advertise Moody and his meetings as a "power from on high," one reader argued, had made an idol of an "ignoramus." [64]

Ninety-eight participating churches sent volunteers to every Chicago household in the week before the tabernacle campaign with a personal letter of invitation from Moody himself. Demands for copies of the letter reportedly "outstripped supply." Seven hundred singers were rehearsed and ready. Three hundred ushers were given their marching orders. Participating pastors were reported "at one with Moody's meetings." Thirteen rainy days failed to slow progress on the building. It was finished a day before the campaign began, with the *Daily News* calling it "a monument to enterprise and energy." The planning and preparation "seems to assure the success of the scheme." An "evangelical garrison" was "about to open fire on the enemy."[65] Like a heavyweight before the big fight, Moody told reporters he was "healthy," "hopeful," and "ready to go." There were barely 20,000 believers in a city and suburbs of nearly half a million, one cleric reasoned, but now that Moody was in town, the odds were in the believers' favor. One supporter said he'd settle for 100,000 converts and not one less.[66]

Some within Chicago's evangelical community did not share this prerevival euphoria. They argued that publicity and organization might "capture the attention of a sinful city" but that it risked, "like a fire, leaving only ruins." Rescuing the lost was God's doing, they cautioned, and manmade means, by themselves, would never revive men and women from spiritual slumber. The Congregational *Advance* warned that "working toward revival won't bring it. Personal self-search and repentance" did not make headlines in large city dailies but did lead to "personal consecration and a disposition to welcome the Holy Spirit" in one's life. The Baptist *Standard* shared this sentiment. "Let's not over estimate mere instrumentality" in bringing revival, it editorially maintained. "God must bless human endeavor" for it to have lasting effect, it observed, while backing a citywide day of prayer and fasting on the eve of Moody's meetings.[67]

"God will do His work if we do ours," Moody told his supporters on the eve of the Chicago campaign, while warning headline writers that "Christianity had been on the defensive long enough." Now it was the devil's turn to tremble. "We have come to Chicago to work," he told them. If Christ could raise the dead, then it was a small matter to "lift Chicago out of its darkness."[68] Storey and the *Times* remained skeptical. "The Moody machine is in good working order," it told its readers, but time would tell whether "the devil will catch it." Publicity had succeeded in "heating to redness the iron of public sentiment." While touring the tabernacle for the first time, Moody was occosted by a *Times* reporter searching for an exclusive. Moody was "courteous but not communicative." The *Times* suspected "a lot of self-righteous satisfaction" from the meetings before they had run their course. It wondered whether "30 good years of preaching" in the city could be "reconciled with this curious hortatory evangelist."[69]

SAUCEPAN JOURNALISM
AND THE "POWER OF PUBLICITY"

"It's an outrage," an angry gentleman was quoted by streetside reporters as saying. His was a familiar complaint in a crowd of 15,000 who claimed to have tickets but couldn't get into Moody's inaugural meeting at the tabernacle. "The popular outpouring can't be compared to any event in Chicago history," one paper said. "It was as if the city had emptied itself on the streets," reported another. The horse-car companies showing Moody and Sankey signs made a killing, while "the carry-all lines speedily caught the contagion." Hours before the afternoon and evening meetings "human torrents" clogged the streets approaching the tabernacle, clung to its 12 entrances, and filled its window wells, eager for admittance to the tabernacle or a glimpse of the great man himself. Doors were opened early as a means of crowd control. This left thousands holding tickets unable to get in and more than a little put off. "I should like to know what they mean by it," a "hatchet-faced woman in a green shawl" was heard arguing. "Here's a ticket, and what on earth is it good for?" A gentleman at her side suggested she keep it as a memento of Moody's visit to Chicago.[70]

Supporters and opponents of Moody's meetings agreed at the outset that the curious came to see a spectacle that advertising and organization had helped to create. "You can see," said a "hooked-nose, lynx-eyed man with a fob chain," cited in the press, "what advertising will do. Say once that Moody will speak and an ordinary congregation will gather." But "hammer at it in the newspapers for a week or two, spread it on the curbstones, paste it on the walls, keep it staring at a city full of people for a fortnight," and one had a circus. The *Times* remarked that the publicity campaign had "caused a stir in almost every part of the city," presenting Moody with "a sea of upturned faces."[71] Moody opened his meetings by preaching on John 11:39. He urged his listeners to "roll away" any obstacle that would get in the way of Chicago receiving revival. As far as the *Times* reporter could tell, the tabernacle resembled "a field of wheat under a visitation of locusts." The city had never seen 10,000 gathered under a single roof and an equal number gathered outside unable to get in. A *Times* correspondent had to have an usher help him through a rear window so he could report on the overflow crowd at Farwell Hall. An Associated Press correspondent followed his example. "The crowd in the streets could fill several churches," the *Tribune* reported. Everyone seemed anxious for a dose of "sanctimonious common sense." The meetings had "a power and promise far exceeding any religious movement Chicago has ever seen."[72]

The hyperbole struck Storey and the *Times* as an exercise in "sauce-pan journalism." Just as a sauce contained many ingredients designed to tickle the palate, Medill's musings treated the reader to "infernal slush." While Moody was "clearly no clown," he was little more than a popular "entertainer," filling his audience with "wonder, disappointment," and in the end "a certain abhorrence." The *Times* might admire an "earnest and adroit" style that seemed to produce "semi-religious fervor," but there was "no stimulus to piety equal to the advertised presence of Moody at these meetings."[73] Medill was happy to meet Storey insult for insult on the grounds of Moody's meetings or anywhere else. The *Times* "represents the great unwashed," and Storey spoke their language with "cheap wit and coarse buffoonery." Moody deserved "the greatest honor this city can bestow" because he dared "to tell the truth." Chicago was "a great and wicked city." What it needed now was "everyone to play their part" in coming alongside "a favorite son" in "civilizing the city" and "saving Chicago from her sins."[74]

Moody's time at the tabernacle became a way of settling old scores in the newspaper wars then under way in the city. The *Inter-Ocean* had little use for Storey's cynicism or Medill's mendacity. It was early apparent to Nixon that anything the self-respecting citizens of Chicago were for the *Times*, known for having a saucepan of its own, would necessarily be against. Nixon charged that his competitor was read religiously by "the low-bred, ignorant dolts" who could be found in the grog shops. These were the "unhappy men and women" Moody came to save "from the clutches of crime, drink and illicit passion." Medill may have shared Nixon's sentiment but not his scruples. While the *Inter-Ocean* sent a stenographer to each of Moody's meetings and gave verbatim records of his every utterance, the *Tribune* often reprinted sermons as they appeared in W. H. Daniels's book. That was why its account of Moody's message on the prodigal son differed from the version appearing in the *Tribune* and explained how the *Tribune* could report Moody's text on "Daniel" one week before he gave it in Chicago.[75]

The *Inter-Ocean* used its coverage of Moody's campaign to confirm the paper's claim as the city's savior. The religious papers relied on the *Inter-Ocean* for accurate reports of Moody's messages, the paper editorialized, and so should interested readers. It republished plaudits from the Presbyterian *Interior*, commending the paper for "the most complete reports" on the revival, down to its prayers. Nixon solicited Moody for a similar sentiment but settled for a letter from Ira Sankey, who said Moody had never been better quoted.[76] The paper legitimized its claim of exclusivity by securing a copyright for its printed accounts of Moody's sermons. It congratulated itself on "the most complete accounts of the enterprise in all its stages." Letters were published from readers throughout the Midwest praising the paper for proclaiming the gospel that "causes our hearts to be stirred within us." Those wishing extra copies or the bound volume of the complete series of sermons were encouraged to send in their orders at once.[77]

The *Daily News* and the *Evening Journal* used the Moody meetings to fight for preeminence in the late afternoon field. Victor Lawson's first job had been working for $2 a week in the *Journal's* circulation department, where he acquired a healthy respect for the value of religious news in stimulating circulation. He would often ride on the *Daily News* delivery wagon, making long-legged escapes from angry, barking dogs by bounding over garden walls. He knew what readers wanted in a newspaper and knew that overcoming a $300 weekly deficit, brought on by startup costs, required careful chronicling of tales from the tabernacle that could not be found elsewhere. Moody's campaign was described as "an evangelical garrison opening fire upon an enemy that has no cover." The *News* claimed that it alone "chronicled faithfully and promptly all that is done." Its accounts of morning and noon prayer services were often on the street before those of its competition.[78] Readers were assured that the paper's "weak imitators" were too busy "trying to beat two pairs with a flush" to consider the municipal history being made by Moody's mission. For its favors the *Daily News* received advertisements from the revival's executive committee, even if John Gillespie, the paper's advertising manager, awkwardly placed one next to "The Crook," a new ballet opening at the Adelphi Theatre, and another below Wold and Wulff undertakers.[79]

The *Journal* continued to convey a familiarity with Moody, buoyed by its long association with him and his methods. Shuman reported on Moody's presumed willingness "to see everyone and at all hours" at his apartment in the fashionable Grand Pacific Hotel. Visitors would find Mr. Moody "stouter than before and with a longer beard." Otherwise he seemed just as approachable as the *Journal* had always found him but having greater confidence stemming from his experience, study, observation, and "unbounded success." The paper considered him "a power against evil and an unbroken column of strength for good" and urged its readers throughout the Northwest to follow "the Awakening" in the pages of the *Evening Journal*.[80] The paper promised to carefully capture the breadth of the revival movement through 264 reporting churches across the northwest. Cree was happy to accommodate them, issuing daily press releases filed by members of Moody's evangelical team who had spread the gospel to Racine and Rockford, Kenosha and Kalamazoo, LaSalle-Peru and Peoria, Des Moines and Dubuque, St. Joseph, Missouri, Ft. Wayne, Indiana, Belvidere, Illinois, and beyond.[81]

The rules of saucepan journalism required that whatever the competition had that readers liked had to appear in the pages of your paper. That included Cree's daily chronicling of the revival's progress across the

Northwest. Cree had Chicago papers reporting "the outpouring of God's spirit upon the churches" across 14 states. Team members were encouraged to file their reports directly with individual papers that dueled over exclusivity. Philip Bliss and Major Whittle filed for the *Inter-Ocean* from Kalamazoo. Charles Ingliss and Frank Rockwell reported on the work in Belvidere for the *Tribune*. The *Evening Journal* reported a "great harvest" in Oshkosh. Charles Spurgeon's account of Moody and Sankey's work in converting souls in Great Britain was published in the *Daily News*.[82] Medill published an open letter to ministers promising to publish revival reports from their cities. Within days, Jacksonville, Joliet, Jonesboro, Ottawa, Clinton, and Fulton were heard from.[83] By the revival's fifth week, excursionists from as far away as Toronto, Pittsburgh, Cincinnati, and St. Louis were reported on their way to see what all the excitement was about. Nightly, the tabernacle continued to pack out. The head usher told the *Tribune* he hardly had the heart to turn anyone away. The hardest part of his job was closing the tabernacle's doors to men and women who were anxious to get in. The sight of 1,000 inquirers on a single night led the Chicago lumberman Turlington Harvey to tell the press he had "never seen people converted so easily." Moody told reporters "we are on the eve of the greatest work of grace this country has ever seen" and heartily thanked them "for making the Lord's deeds known among the people."[84]

Medill found Moody and his methods "an antidote to the formalism and materialism that have cursed the ordinary methods of religious work." Forty million Americans supported 50,000 clergymen at an average annual salary of $275, Medill wrote, and for what? In ordinary business life, 90 percent fail, 3 percent succeed, and 2 percent shine, he argued, and ministers were no different. The vast majority of them "failed as preachers, failed as teachers and failed as convincers." They could learn a little from Mr. Moody. His pulpit style was simple, his tales tender and homely. When he spoke, "the glad tidings went down into your soul." A Chicago lawyer who had studied audiences for 25 years had "never seen men and women under such control as under Moody." It was quite a position for any man to be in. Special services at Cook County Hospital had "cripples and invalids climbing three flights of stairs" for a look at Moody and a touch from God. "Revival trains" were bringing 1,500 excursionists a night. Hotels were crowded, restaurants filled. The revival was helping to establish Chicago's national reputation as a city that took spiritual matters seriously. What's more, the revival was proving to be good for business.[85]

Storey and the *Times* grudgingly admitted that Moody's "pluck, push and enterprise" reflected the city's no-nonsense approach to business and revival. "He knows how to talk to customers, whether they are looking for dry goods or religion," the paper observed. Moody was a lifelong salesman who lived by the Eleventh Commandment: "Let there be advertising." The sensation had stirred the sanctified, while intensifying the opposition of scoffers who remained unconvinced. For Medill to argue otherwise, Storey said, showed "no respect for the intelligence of his readers," even the "weaker-minded" of them. Medill's "reasoning faculty" had never been very good. It had made his paper a captive of those making the most extravagant claims regarding Moody's meetings. Only "a delivery service of unmitigated rubbish" could claim that Moody had delivered "this sin-stricken city" when he had only sharpened its divisions.[86] The trouble with Storey, Medill told his readers, was that "when he writes his mind is subject to an unconscious bias which renders it impossible for him to tell the truth except with a fraudulent intent."[87]

"A STRANGE AND LONELY FEELING"

The personal price Moody paid in public celebrity became apparent in Chicago. The meetings began with the death of his younger brother and ended in the death of Moody's colaborer Philip Bliss. In between, Moody's daughter struggled with scarlet fever. "A strange and lonely feeling" came over Moody as he rushed back to Northfield, Massachusetts, for the funeral of his brother Samuel during the second week of the Chicago campaign. Samuel's epilepsy had made him a convalescent for many years. To Moody's mind, Samuel's Unitarian views had made him a spiritual cripple as well. The Chicago press played these facts as dramatic narrative. The fateful telegram "Samuel is dead," sent by Moody's mother, had been so unexpected that it left him "nearly prostrate," the *Inter-Ocean* told its readers. Moody's inner circle had been told that "his aged mother had been left desolate." Samuel had been "the Benjamin of Mr. Moody's family," and Moody was hurrying home "to put his arm around his mother" and "to look at the silent face of his brother."[88] Medill immediately speculated what the impact of Moody's absence would be on a campaign "that had been begun with such unprecedented power." Word that Moody would be leaving for the East "fell like a calamity on the city's ministers," the *Tribune* reported, and left "an immense tabernacle audience in tears."[89]

Moody's movements to and from Northfield were traced by the wire service and printed in Chicago's dailies. His occasional comments urging the Northwest to "keep the faith" in his absence were given front-page attention. The *Tribune* thought that if the revival could continue without the revivalist it should show that the awakening was God's doing and not Moody's. His executive committee labored to sustain precisely that appearance. When the curious no longer came and empty seats appeared, the dailies took note. Participating churches encouraged parishioners to "get in on the blessing," and they did. The *Inter-Ocean* thought the evangelical team commanded by Moody had done well in the captain's absence. "Other hands, eager and willing, have taken up the work," it reported, "with a new fervor and earnestness." Storey and the *Times* saw the same thing but came to a less flattering conclusion. It credited the machinery of revival for securing the momentum of Moody's meetings and not the spirit of God.[90]

Moody's return on October 15 confirmed his celebrity status. His appearance and demeanor were front-page fodder. One paper thought he appeared "more subdued" and "somewhat saddened." Another metaphorically mentioned that "the shadow of his grief fell over his hearers" and created a more intimate bond between them. Moody and Chicago had grown up together, the *Tribune* said. "Brother Moody," as he was now becoming known, "is one of us, our friend, neighbor and citizen." Chicago had given him "his first impulse and first encouragement," imbuing him with "genuine Chicago force, grit, and energy in his work." Now, in his moment of personal loss, the city was coming out to see him. Streetcars had to be added and train schedules altered to accommodate the demand. Their conductors asked Moody to reschedule his meetings so that they could stay at home on the sabbath. Tickets given freely were sometimes sold by speculators trying to make a dishonest dollar. Ladies who couldn't get in "rustled their silks" and left the evening air "smelling of roses." Street urchins picked up the scent of sales and hawked Moody and Sankey hymnals outside the tabernacle's Madison Street entrance for a dollar apiece. Others sold "the Moody hat" for just a dollar more. Doors for an afternoon service had to be locked to keep the overflow crowd out after a throng forced open a door and overpowered ushers. One woman who was apprehended said ushers should show themselves to be Christians and let her stay. Another caught the eye of a *Times* correspondent. It was a woman who looked like a lady but only if you overlooked her vocabulary.[91]

The *Times* admitted that "Moody's return has intensified the religious passion of the city" in the way of a star coming on stage at a theater. "There is no concealing the fact that Moody is the star performer of this grand evangelistic exhibition," the paper observed. There was none of the "overcoat fever" seen at so many other ministers' meetings. Those that got in liked to linger in his presence. Those who couldn't often stayed, hoping for the sight of him. That was why the *Tribune* deplored the decision to push Moody's personal preaching desk back 25 feet from the foot of the stage. Reporters were having a hard time seeing him, and celebrants felt the same way. Even the appearance of Moody's wife seated on stage among 400 city ministers and local dignitaries made news. When her husband missed a meeting in which his appearance had been widely advertised, letters to the editor expressed outrage. Later it was learned Moody had gone to the bedside of his daughter who had been stricken with scarlet fever, the leading cause of death among Chicago-area children in 1875. Congregations prayed for her recovery, and the press oversaw her convalescence down to the development of "the strawberry tongue," often characteristic of scarlet fever sufferers.[92]

By mid-November, the Chicago campaign was finishing its seventh week, with reports of 800 new converts and a great many backslidden Christians energized by the proceedings. Moody was not fully satisfied. Tabernacle attendees had a familiar look. The *Times* joked that reporters appeared to be "the only non-Christians present." The city was districted and visited by a legion of volunteers who placed copies of the *Tabernacle News* in 100,000 Chicago area homes and businesses. The paper was produced by Moody's publicity committee and paid for by ads from local businesses. It invited every Chicagoan to attend Moody's meetings and a Christian convention soon to be held in the city. "Dear, unsaved reader," it said, "you intend to come to Christ 'sometime,' but why not now?" No one was promised tomorrow, and the need for action was now. " 'Now' is the only word ticking from the clock of time," it entreated readers. " 'Now' only is ours. 'Then' may never be."[93]

The third week of November saw several thousand delegates converge on Chicago for a Christian convention presided over by Moody. Its purpose was to equip them with the techniques needed in evangelizing their communities. "People say they don't have time to read the Bible," Moody told them, "but it's because they're reading other things." That included newspapers. People who would never pick up a tract might read the same message in their favorite daily. That's why members of the press were necessary partners in spreading the gospel.[94] Modern methods in evangelism involved "reaching the people," he told delegates. Many wouldn't come to the church anymore, so the church had to go to them. "Let us leave the churches to the owls and bats," he said, stunning some and provoking applause in others. When asked how a man could preach without a lectern, Moody answered, "If a man isn't enough interested in his own preaching to carry it in his head, instead of writing it out, how can he expect the masses of people to carry it away?"[95]

Among the mass of people visited by Moody's volunteers were women who worked in houses of "ill fame." Before long theirs became a seductive sidebar within the story of the great revival. On December 13, Moody read at the tabernacle a letter he had received a week earlier from a prostitute who charged that "there are many young girls in this city who are leading lives of shame because of the lustful passions of men who have joined your meetings." But as she read the daily papers she found "you have nothing to say to us and our class." Was she "too low" to be saved? Hadn't Christ died for her too? "Remember," she chided him, "Chicago has nearly as many abandoned women as men," and "we need the comfort of Jesus Christ as much as they." Fine churches "killed religion except for fine people." That's why "sinful girls" needed a tabernacle to go to.[96]

Moody encouraged the writer "and members of her class" to come to the tabernacle the next night. The papers played it up as "fallen women night." Cold weather did not keep the tabernacle from packing out, although how many "harlots" and how many "curious" came that night, no one could tell. Earlier in the day, committees of Christian women obtained from the Chicago Police Department the addresses of several West Side "ranches." They knocked on doors up and down Clinton Street and Fourth Avenue between Randolph and Washington, inviting madams and mistresses to a night at Moody's meeting. "The soiled doves" came "in their handsome furs," the *Times* reported, their attire attracting attention and some "silent stares." The *Inter-Ocean* estimated as many as 1,000 "erring women" had heeded the call to come, judging by the number of new faces in the audience. The *Tribune* correspondent saw every seat taken fully half an hour before the meeting began.[97]

A half-hour of prayer and praise was highlighted by Sankey's singing "Ring the Bells of Heaven" and "Rescue the Perishing." Moody preached on Luke 5:32, "I came not to call the righteous, but sinners, to repentance." He told his listeners: "The world seems to think that if a woman falls there is no hope for her, but the fallen woman has no better friend than the Lord Jesus Christ. He came to lift you up and to save you from your sins." He portrayed them as "victims of the sins of men," implored them to "think of the homes you have left" and "the mother and father who mourn for your loss." He read a letter from a woman who had been shunned by respectable society and saw "no way out." Christ was that way, he said, and good Christian people stood ready to receive again what Christ had restored.

At the close of the service, as inquirers left their seats and prepared themselves for Christian counseling in an adjacent room, they "were compelled to run a gauntlet of eyes" that exposed "a morbid curiosity" on the part of the "good Christians" who delayed their departure, Storey said. "The next time Brother Moody invites the 'fallen' to the house of the Lord," he strongly suggested, "it will be well for him to instruct the elect beforehand in the rudiments of decent behavior." An *Inter-Ocean* reporter singled out a woman who "had the bright badge of her calling." She hadn't wanted to speak at first. "We are none of us monsters to be stared at," she finally said. Moody might be well intentioned, but "there wasn't a family in Chicago that'd take one of us in." A "haggard, hard-featured, veteran of the class" added that civil society "sees me as a wild animal." Storey sent several reporters, "regarded by their brethren as temptation-proof," on a highly publicized "apostolic mission" into the very brothels visited by Moody's volunteers. They were largely amused by what they found there. Lizzie Moss told one "virtuous reporter" that she wished she had had an opportunity "for a few minutes private conversation with Brother Moody." She thought she "could have converted him." Another thought the service all right "if only I had had something to drink." Another was "too tired" to make it to the tabernacle. Another had never heard of Moody. Mrs. White, one of the madams, hadn't gone to the tabernacle. She wasn't "that kind of a woman." Josie Andrews had gone and cried. She had "never done a day's work in my life" and saw no escape. Nellie Mitchell, "a plump brunette," said she had become a convert but would be staying in this line of work for another month to "straighten out her affairs."[98]

Even Moody's allies in the press found the evening out with Chicago's "erring women" a bit of an embarrassment and an awkward ending to an 11-week campaign that played to a large attendance and, for the most part, rave reviews. The spectacle, they argued, hadn't targeted the mischievous or the social parasite, and Moody shouldn't be scolded for their indifference or disdain. The 11-week revival had been beautifully scripted, widely advertised, and bountifully attended. Two thousand new converts attended meetings on December 17, and many of these would find a church home. Scores more were quickened in their faith and were already sharing in their excitement.[99] One thousand pockets had been picked at the tabernacle, the *Times* reported, and 160,000 or so individuals who had come four or five times each may have benefited from their 133 meetings with Mr. Moody. The great mass of the poor, however, had not been reached. Moody preached with conviction that bred conviction to those willing to be convicted.[100]

Moody had long prepared to leave Chicago by mid-December for two weeks' rest before beginning meetings in Boston after the first of the year. He was tired, ill, and largely spent. D. W. Whittle and Philip Bliss had been enlisted to come to Chicago and carry on the work. But there were problems with this plan. The Boston tabernacle wasn't ready and wouldn't be for a month. Moody's daughter remained ill and appeared too weak to travel. Bliss and his wife had plans of their own. They were spending Christmas with his mother in the East. Public pressure began to build for Moody to extend his stay in the city. The *Evening Journal* argued that it would be "a great misfortune to abruptly terminate" the tabernacle meetings before their time. The *Tribune* concurred. "The revival wave" continued to build. As long as Moody preached, the crowds would come. The great evangelist reportedly felt a bit of "a prisoner" of the enthusiasm he and his organization had so assiduously cultivated.[101]

"DIVINE PROVIDENCE" AND A BRIDGE IN ASHTABULA

As late as December 17, Philip Bliss hoped Moody might be persuaded to stay in Chicago and to keep preaching until Boston was ready for him. It wasn't because Bliss was reluctant to serve in Chicago, a city he had first called home in 1864; as a 26-year-old Pennsylvania-born farm boy, he came to the big city to work at the Root and Cady Music House as a music teacher and music sheet salesman. It was in Chicago that Bliss developed a widening reputation as a gifted writer of gospel songs. As choral leader and Sunday School superintendent of the city's First Presbyterian Church, Bliss and his wife, Lucy, first came to Moody's attention. In 1874 Moody persuaded the couple to join D. W. Whittle, an old friend from the YMCA, to conduct a series of evangelistic campaigns at medium-sized cities across the Northwest and Border States. While Moody and Sankey were making headlines in Britain, Brooklyn, New York, Philadelphia, and Chicago, the Blisses sang and Whittle preached to large and enthusiastic audiences in Rockford, Minneapolis, Lexington, and Nashville.[102]

The Blisses left Chicago for the last time on the afternoon of December 15, not knowing when they would be back. The night before they had dined with Whittle and Moody at the Brevoort House and heard of the pressure Moody was under to keep preaching. David Swing had endorsed the meetings and often attended them but was among the few urging that it be brought to an end. He observed publicly what some of the campaign's supporters were admitting privately, that the revival had sapped the strength of many of its warmest admirers and disabled some churches that had given their whole energy to the effort. Swing noted that three months of nonstop services had "broken the health" of many and caused "homes to be neglected" and "intellects distorted."[103] Bliss and his wife were no less exhausted. For weeks they had been small branches on the revival tree and had labored with less publicity but no less diligence with Whittle in Jackson and Kalamazoo, Michigan, and Peoria, Illinois. During that time their two small sons had stayed with her parents in Rome, Pennsylvania. For this reason the couple was anxious be off on a long-awaited Christmas reunion with their family before commitments took them to England, where Bliss's hymns "Hold the Fort," "Almost Persuaded," "I Am So Glad That Jesus Loves Me," and "What Shall the Harvest Be?" had given him a substantial following. Bliss and Whittle were well known and widely

Philip Bliss was a talented composer of gospel music and a loyal member of Moody's ever-expanding evangelistic team.

Bliss and his wife, Lucy, perished when a train bringing them to Moody's Chicago campaign crashed when a bridge collapsed over the Ashtabula River.

admired in Chicago. They had lived and worked in the city for years. But no one needed to say what everyone knew. They would not keep the crowds coming as Moody and Sankey had. No one could.[104]

Bliss was not anxious to come to Chicago for another reason. He needed time away from revival work so that he could do some serious writing. More than 50 of his hymns had been included in the enormously successful *Gospel Hymns and Sacred Songs* that had been used since 1875 by Moody and Sankey in their evangelization of big cities in the East. Bliss had declined any share in the copyright, including $5,000 Moody attempted to press on him to build a home for his family. Instead he began work in the summer of 1876 on a second hymnal he hoped to use with Whittle when they went abroad the following year.[105] "I've declined eight invitations," he wrote Whittle from Rome in May. He was "determined to rest and write." One invitation he did accept was to spend a week with Moody in Northfield. It was not exactly a vacation. Moody preached and Bliss sang in 11 services across Vermont, Massachusetts, and the New Hampshire hills. Bliss wrote Whittle that Moody hadn't lost his touch in "making the best use of his visitors that he could." This tour was wedged around Bliss's commitments to a Sunday School parliament and a Chautauqua assembly. In late August he was still trying to get to unfinished work, while nursing his invalid son George.[106]

Bliss was still writing in October as the Chicago meetings opened. For three weeks he helped in the services by day and collaborated with Sankey by night as they hurried to finish the hymnal.[107] At Cree's request, Bliss sent regular summaries of the work in Kalamazoo, while leaving out his ministry to invalids in hospitals and private residences. Three weeks there were followed by 10 days more at union meetings in Jackson and Sundays spent singing to the 800 inmates of the Michigan State Prison.[108] Bliss did the same at the state prison in Joliet, Illinois, after speaking at Moody's Christian Convention on the use of song in worship. R. C. Morgan, the editor and publisher of the *Christian*, Britain's leading evangelical weekly, caught up to Bliss and Whittle in Peoria, where the two men had opened union meetings at Rouse's Hall on November 25.[109] Morgan renewed his invitation to Bliss to come to England. Several large cities in the Northeast had extended invitations as well. In addition, there was the request of participating pastors in Chicago that Bliss and Whittle fill the pulpit after Moody left it. Whittle's diary shows that from the outset Bliss had "an almost unaccountable aversion" to the idea of returning to Chicago. He would "rather go anywhere else" than have the unhappy fate of following the great evangelist there. Moody promised to preach through the end of the year, allowing the Blisses to spend Christmas with their family in the East. Before leaving for home, Bliss stopped by Cree's Chicago office and, although he was loathe to do it, gave him several autographs that admirers had been asking for. It was part of his continuing introduction to the necessities of celebrity. By December 17, Bliss, en route to Rome, seemed resigned to his return but wrote Whittle: "my feeling is the same."[110] The 10 days that followed were among the happiest Bliss had known. The reunited family celebrated Christmas, with Bliss impersonating Santa, down to a trunk of toys he and his wife had bought and made for the children. That evening he sang at a local church and wrote Whittle that since "I hear nothing definite from Chicago," he assumed he would be staying with his family in Rome. What he didn't know was that his singing in Chicago had already been advertised. It was in all the papers. He was supposed to start in four days. Whittle had been reluctant to telegraph him, but now there was no avoiding it.[111]

The next morning, December 28, the Blisses said goodbye to their boys, who would be left in the care of her parents. As much as they would "love to stay," it was "God's will" that they go. He cabled Whittle from Waverly in the afternoon that they expected to be in Buffalo by midnight and connect with a train that would arrive in Chicago on the evening of December 29. Their luggage had already been checked through. But 10 miles from Waverly the engine of the train broke down. They were delayed three hours and missed their connection. They spent the night in Hornellsville, New York, a lonely outpost on the Erie Railroad. The following day they made Buffalo and transferred to the Lake Shore Railroad, taking a train that was scheduled to arrive in Chicago on Saturday morning, December 30. The Pacific Express was two hours late getting in to Ashtabula, Ohio, as the mists of Lake Chautauqua gave way to a heavy snowstorm that had blown in over Lake Erie. Months earlier, Bliss and his wife had sung "Meet Me at the Fountain" before 3,000 people at Chautauqua's summer school convention; now the blizzard prevented a view of the lake as the two passed the time in the parlor car. A newsboy and a lady passenger saw them there about 5:15. Bliss had his Bible open and appeared to be writing on a sheet of paper he had opened over it.[112]

It was at that hour that Moody, preaching to a packed house at the tabernacle, predicted that Chicago's revival would be well served by Whittle and Bliss. They had planned a watch night service in which Bliss would sing some of his best-known hymns. Moody closed with the congregation singing "There Is a Fountain Filled with Blood." Friends thought Moody seemed unusually somber afterward for a man so incessantly upbeat and assumed it was fatigue or his health. Moody remarked that he couldn't shake a certain sense of foreboding.[113] Bliss and his wife were among those passengers who thought they would be spending the night in Ashtabula. The train was now two and a half hours behind schedule, and the whiteout had forced it to run at 10 miles an hour. After some uncertainty, the twin locomotives, Socrates and Columbia, were given the go-ahead and began pulling the 11-car train out of the Ashtabula station around 7:30. The train was crowded with holiday excursionists. Railroad officials later put the total at 147. Surviving passengers insisted it was closer to 250.[114]

One mile west of town the Ashtabula River is 20 feet wide and runs three to four feet deep. The Lake Shore line crosses it on a 155-foot iron truss bridge, built in 1864, that was 59 feet above the water. Engineers for years had griped to company officials that it was too light. A. J. Manning, an engineer at a waterworks next to the bridge, looked out and saw the outline of a slow train approaching. The lead engine had barely crossed the bridge when Manning heard a cracking sound. J. E. Burchell, a friend of the Bliss family, was in the sleeping car behind them and heard it too. And then he heard a crack in front of the car and a crack behind it and became aware of a sudden sinking feeling. Daniel McGrein, the engineer of the first locomotive, felt the shock and immediately threw open the throttle. Socrates pulled back and lurched forward, breaking the coupling rod with Columbia. The smashing sound of the shattering bridge was heard all the way to Ashtabula and beyond. Manning saw the train fall. The parlor car plunged first into the ice and was instantly crushed by a second car. Other cars toppled in at all angles. Heaters and stoves within the cars ignited. The oil fires burned brightly above the drifting snow, ice, and ashes. Cars that landed intact had survivors. They crawled through twisted metal and out windows. Groans of the injured and shouts for help among the trapped could be heard above the inferno.[115]

The Chicago office of the Lake Shore Line first heard of the disaster just before nine. An hour later the magnitude of the calamity was coming into view. It would be the worst rail wreck in the nation's history. The first Moody and Whittle heard of it was when they opened their Saturday morning papers. Whittle's "heart sank." He "feared the worst." He cabled Rome to see whether Bliss and his wife had left. Before he got an answer, he received a cable from Burchell reporting that Bliss, his wife, and children were among the dead.[116] Whittle and Farwell immediately left by train for the scene of the disaster, amid press reports that Bliss had initially escaped the burning car only to perish with his family when he rushed back into the flames to save them. Special editions of Chicago papers were filled with details of the disaster and the story of Bliss's life and death. Whittle was reportedly "crushed" by the news. Moody, who would have to preach for him, was "inconsolable with grief." Peoria was in "shock." Racine, where he had also ministered, was "in tears." Kalamazoo "couldn't believe" the news. Many Chicagoans shared in the incomprehension. "Divine providence cut it pretty rough for poor Bliss," one man said in a characteristic response.

"Blame it on the bridge," said another. Bliss refused "to save himself," a woman reasoned. He gave his life to rescue others, said another. "No act could have been more characteristic of the great heart of the man."[117]

Competing papers played up the news of "the fatal Friday" as a way of claiming exclusives and settling old scores. The *Tribune* boasted that Whittle had telegraphed it first that Bliss's children had not been aboard the train. The *Inter-Ocean* charged that the *Times* had stolen its lead on the story. The *Daily News* maintained it had been first on the street with the story and that the *Journal* later attempted to steal its story. The *Inter-Ocean* exclusively reported that a gold chain burned black belonging to Mrs. Bliss had been recovered. The *Times* reportedly found his hand and her rib, the *Tribune* her hat. The daughter-in-law of an *Inter-Ocean* reporter who survived the accident was certain 140 people had been killed in the crash, despite an official death toll of half that. The *Times* sent a reporter to South Bend to intercept surviving passengers who were making their way by rail to Chicago. He asked each if they had any news of Bliss.[118]

The interior of the tabernacle was swathed in 1,000 yards of mourning crepe, provided by the department store magnate Marshall Field, who had been in sympathy with the Moody meetings. The tabernacle appeared to be "overshadowed by a pall of suffering and anguish," making its New Year's Eve services "the saddest in the city's history." A grief "lay on every heart," and so many "tear-stained faces, marked with deep lines of suffering" had never been seen in Chicago. Moody appeared "almost broken down by the sad truth." When he could speak at all "it was only in broken sobs and in a low voice that was tremulous with grief." Above Moody's lectern four crowns appeared surmounted by crosses and a garland of white flowers and leaves. "We often don't know who our best friends are," Moody told the crowd, "until they are taken from us." The closing hours of the year, he told his listeners, had always saddened him, "but the world had never looked so cold and deserted" as it did that night. He felt he "would like to lock myself in a room and weep." At such times Christ was his only refuge. That was why he was warning everyone within the sound of his voice: "Therefore, be ye ready."[119]

As midnight neared, Moody read a dispatch from Farwell saying they had found no sign of Bliss. Not a watch, a sleeve-button, a chain, a key, or a ring that had once been connected to Bliss or his wife had come to light. Farwell was returning to Chicago. Bliss, he felt certain, was in ashes. Sankey then sang the famous Bliss song "What Shall the Harvest Be?" "Bliss," Moody said with some difficulty, "was in heaven, reaping what he had sown." Others could know with certainty where they would spend eternity, Moody said, asking all who wanted to receive Christ to accompany him into the inquiry room. He wanted to spend the last few minutes of the old year on his knees in prayer with inquirers. The unconverted were assured "there is one here present in the spirit, who was to have been here in the flesh." He was "bending in love and prayer" over everyone preparing to receive his Savior. As the chorus sang "There Is a Fountain Filled with Blood," Moody made his way to the inquiry room, everyone stood, and many followed him.[120]

MANAGING THE PUBLIC MIND

One third of the one million people who saw Moody at his meetings in Chicago did so in the revival's final month. Fatigue, family illness, the death of Bliss, and delays in Boston had extended him beyond his Chicago schedule and, nearly, his energies. As the date neared for his departure, the appetite to see and hear him took on the quality of "a grand sensational drama," the Baptist *Standard* declared disapprovingly. "The sacred and solemn transaction between the soul and God" became reduced in the popular press to a public spectacle characterized by manmade means. America's second century was being marked by a "peculiar dispensationalism," the dispensation of evangelism, in which personal instrumentality in advertising and organization displaced the divine in calling sinners to repentance. Those in sympathy with human agency in attacking the strongholds of the enemy saw matters differently. "No one who has not been on the ground can understand the many-sidedness of the work going on in Chicago," the Congregational *Advance* argued. The modern mass media had made it possible to declare the message of God's salvation beyond his tabernacle and over the Mississippi Valley, beyond even the walls of the Alleghenies and Rockies. Moody's "practical sagacity" assured that "a national revival of religion" was now possible for perhaps the first time. If Whitefield had had Moody's means of getting the gospel out, it observed, he would have had no need to cross the Atlantic 13 times.[121]

Moody believed the press was both an ally and an enemy in communicating Christ to urban populations that were largely indifferent to instruction. The excitement over Bliss and the Ashtabula rail disaster had shown the public's passion for sensational stories. "The daily papers and the dime novels," he told believers at Farwell Hall, gave the public the "new food" of cheap thrills and risk-free escape more readily than the news of "what's doing in Heaven" or how to get there. That was why he hoped that "the day would come when Sunday papers would be swept away." People filled their heads with startling stories and had no room for the sermon. So he structured sermons and services that told a good story and developed through the powers of publicity, organization, and prayer a revival campaign that became a sensational story of its own.

His defenders in the press appreciated a modern, manufactured revival when they saw one. Moody's work arose from "no passing wind," the *Inter-Ocean* observed, and did not "drift into the proportions and intensity" of a big-city riot without human help. Instead, the meetings were "engineered from general conception to minutest detail with all the power that money and zeal could command." It made Moody "the most consummate manager of the public mind" that the city had ever seen. Never before had men "who put such strong faith in the power of God put more faith in the use of agencies to affect powerfully the minds of men."[122]

The city was having a hard time giving up its evangelists, Bliss to heaven, Moody to Boston. The largest crowd ever to gather under one roof in Chicago, more than 10,000 persons, packed out the tabernacle the night of January 5 in a memorial service for Bliss, presided over by Moody. Police estimated that a far greater number tried to and could not get in, even when some resorted to the most imaginative of excuses. One man warned that a dire family emergency required he immediately contact his wife who was "somewhere inside the tabernacle." A distraught mother presumably sought a sick son. Another posed as a choir member, someone else as an usher. Reporters observing the melee found well-dressed ladies to be the most persistent, with more than one threatening to block the entrance unless she gained admission. Inside, a large and "poorly executed" portrait of Bliss appeared in front of Moody's lectern. The revivalist read a letter sent to the Blisses in care of Chicago on the date of his death. Their children, Paul and George, four and two, were happily playing with the ark the parents had left them and now eagerly sought their return. A collection produced $10,000 that would be held in trust for the children. Worshippers were told that Bliss's trunk had also been opened and a final hymn found. When sung "to a shining sea of upturned faces," even the most skeptical of reporters could understand the tears they saw. "So on I go not knowing," the final verse begins, "I would not if I might; I'd rather walk in the dark with God than go alone in the light; I'd rather walk by faith with Him than go alone by sight."[123]

Chicago's leading dailies may have been quite overwhelmed with the inscrutable sovereignty of God "in taking Bliss like Elijah from our midst," but a *Times* correspondent who saw the spectacle did not share their theology. "Never were mortals more 'instructive' than these pious Christians," he noted, but what was needed was not blind acceptance but "better girders." The sight of nightly crowds struggling to see their redoubtable Moody one last time was one time too many for some critics. Moody's meetings and message had been widely advertised in the Anglo-American world, argued W. H. Ryder, a leading Universalist, in an open letter to the city's press, but not everywhere. That left only

1.3 billion of the earth's 1.5 billion outside Moody's household of "cheap grace." Ryder was reassured by the knowledge that when the publicity of these meetings receded and this generation had hurried to their graves, men would know that it wasn't the blood of Christ but the character of men that reconciled them to God.[124]

Moody's meetings in Chicago ended in the greatest snowstorm to hit the city since the days of the Great Fire. It arrived horizontally, perpendicularly, and sometimes from four directions at once, press accounts claim, "filling the streets with drifts deep enough to cool a horse's belly." But it failed to slow those determined to take their evening at the tabernacle before Farwell converted the space into a retail block. "Pedestrians trotted along sidewalk paths like sheep," a *Times* reporter recorded, "each following the tracks of the one before him." Women "lifted their skirts with impunity," and those "vulgar-minded males" sneaking a little look appeared to be the only ones not on their way to the tabernacle. "Great heavens," exclaimed a man from the rear platform of a Madison Street car, "I suppose people would go to the Moody and Sankey meetings if it stormed pitchforks and cord wood." "It must be a good place to go," replied the conductor, "or so many people wouldn't go."[125]

Inside the tabernacle, new converts and quickened backsliders filled the chamber and its standing room in celebrating an extraordinary season of grace and gratefulness in the city of Chicago. Moody characteristically thanked the press for their participation in what was a civic celebration. He had not found "an unkind word in any of our daily papers." It meant that what the Lord had wrought in Chicago had been trumpeted across the Great Northwest. Editorial writers did not consider the claim extravagant. "Never did one man reap such a harvest since the Reformation," Medill exclaimed. In so doing, he had shown the modern church the way. He had not preached "a thorny, flinty road to heaven over which we must travel on bleeding feet" but instead had emphasized the "common ground" that should serve as a platform for the future of the church. The *Journal* reported that the finale was a tribute to what "money, organization, prayer and the unity of believers" could do. As Whittle and the singer George Stebbins prepared to take up the work, which would be removed to a local church, the *Daily News* seemed assured that "the harvest will be a rich one if harvested properly."[126]

Reporters accompanied Moody and Sankey to the train station just as they had welcomed them three and a half months earlier. Moody would be taking two weeks off before beginning in Boston, and that was news. Moody told them $64,430 had been raised or pledged in a final collection to pay off the debt of the local YMCA, and that was news too. Moody's daughter had recovered from her bout with scarlet fever, and there was no truth to rumors that Moody and Sankey had been quarreling. Nothing had "grieved" Moody more, and he was happy to put an end to the rumors.

As reporters filed their final stories, their editors were left to reflect on what they had seen. The Chicago meetings had been an experiment, the *Inter-Ocean* readily admitted, that could not be allowed to fail. Moody's organization and a cooperative press had seen that this was so. Together they had made the meetings "the center of everyone's observation." Prophecies were printed predicting success. It pressured those with "definite misgivings" and "indefinite reluctance" to mute their opposition. A "warm and steady movement" of church members led many to surrender "day and night, in wet weather and dry" to the cause of the great awakening. Then "placards in every alley and by-way and at every street crossing warned the washed and the unwashed of the meetings," while five daily newspapers attended to Moody's every word and every Sankey song as though they were the utterance of a closely contested political campaign. An army of officials saw that the meetings went forward on schedule and that there was nothing to "provoke displeasure." Then came the short prayers, the short sermons, the gospel songs, the Bible readings, "the hard work and common sense of shrewd men" backed by "strong battalions," who succeeded in "spending money like water" while "a religious fire was kindled in the very bones of the people." Soon, "from house to house, in the streetcars, in the warerooms, from church to church," the multitudes talked of salvation with only a liberal here and an extreme orthodox there refusing to join in.[127]

The major newspaper in Chicago that had refused to join in was prepared to admit that "even Moody's great opponent recognizes that Moody's fervent common sense makes bad men a little better and does no injury to the good." With Moody, the *Times* and Storey wrote, "you see the hard wood at once." The paper that claimed to champion Chicago's working class believed that Moody "belongs to the people"; it was just that "the people are generally outside the churches." While the "devotional mind" was strengthened by Moody's message, the rest of the city's civilian population would have to put up with the "pretentious piety of the new converts," variously estimated at 2,500 to 10,000, or "the sanctimony of the old ones." Twenty-five hundred people had newly affiliated with evangelical churches, and sales of Bibles in the city had quadrupled. Only time would tell what impact this would have on public life. Storey feared "the infusion of cant into commerce" because of the well-publicized claim that revivals in religion led to revivals in industry. The truth was that Chicago had "gained in population and criminality" during the revival and "lost in nearly everything else."[128]

David Swing was in a peculiar position to view the great Chicago revival in the winter of America's centennial year. He had had his run-ins with orthodoxy because of his liberalism and had alienated liberals with his orthodoxy. He hadn't been among those welcoming Moody with open arms, but he had followed his success. Although he hadn't sat on Moody's organizing committee, he had often sat on the stage as Moody ministered. It was a tacit show of support by a man who found himself at odds with much of Moody's message and some of his methods. Brooke Herford, the city's leading Unitarian, argued that Moody's success showed that "modern man must have religion. Even if it is false and ignoble." To Swing, that was precisely the point. The regular church reached "only a few and those not deeply," while Moody and his chroniclers in the press offered their audience evenings of communitarian excitement. The Calvinist, the Catholic, the Baptist, the liberal, the skeptic all had their "scales hung in their little shops" in which they "weighed the world as if one could seize the world through a blade of grass." Then came Moody to show a better way. The wrath of God had given way to the love of the Father, so that "the people come together not in fanatical gloom but in smiling joyfulness." The crowds that came assembled not on their Day of Judgment but as though "they were hurrying to their Father's house." Swing wrote that Moody understood that the human heart had grown weary with religion and hungered for something more satisfying than merely making money. They pitched their tabernacle "in the midst of our orthodox desert," and "palm-trees and bubbling springs emerged in the wide arid waste." Their new style of worship came in a new house of worship, one that was "large, airy, and cheap," designed to bring in the very people the elegant churches had shut out. Here finally was a church composed of celebrants not born in its sanctuary. To this new place came a new man, "a son of Thunder," a "man for the multitudes," who preached the words and works of Christ. Moody was not "a theologian but an impulse." His efforts in Chicago had shown the church its future in America's second century.[129]

Stories that "reach the people"

D. L. Moody and the press of Gilded Age Chicago both had the same idea in mind—they wanted "to reach the people" with stories that would capture and hold their interest. Moody might have done what he did for the Almighty and the publishers of the period for the almighty dollar, but both clearly sought to instruct. Moody's moral mission was to return Chicago to its spiritual senses. Medill and Storey hoped to save the city from the other's politics. "The fight is on," the *Times* put it directly. "It is war in the mud with mud to the neck."[130] The revival had been good for business, and the press, for the most part, had been good for the revival. The *Inter-Ocean* was preparing for sale its bound stenographic account of Moody's sermons. Medill took tabernacle coverage just as seriously. When an "unsaved compositor" misquoted a scripture from the Book of Job, he was editorially scourged, with Medill's promise that it would never happen again. Only a "new man" at his post would fail "to instantly and fully recognize a text of Scripture when he finds it in his 'take.' " That explained why Job exclaimed "Father myself," in the *Tribune* and "I abhor myself!" everywhere else.[131] To hear "reporters and editors speak respectfully" of Moody's meetings "as a work of genuine goodness" struck the religious press as a revelation. What greater evidence could there be, the Congregational *Advance* asked, that the "spiritually blind" had been made to see?[132]

It was Luther who remarked that the printing press was "God's highest act of grace" because the spread of his ideas helped to make the Reformation possible.[133] Moody certainly felt a similar solicitude. "I pray Heaven's richest blessing to rest upon the press of Chicago," he told them in a widely quoted benediction that was adapted for every occasion. "I hope they will continue to spread the Gospel of Christ as they have done during these meetings."[134] He could pay them no higher compliment. Farwell and Harvey, meeting privately with editors of the *Inter-Ocean* and *Tribune*, were assured "they'd keep the coverage up" for a month more. Farwell wrote Moody in Boston that that would be "a great sendoff" for Whittle and would "keep the interest up in country towns," which still remained stimulated by the revival winds that had blown through the Windy City.[135]

Moody and Chicago's mass media grew up together, knew each other, and needed one another. Moody needed to reach those at a distance through the pages of the press. Newsmen needed a good story. Together they crafted a civic spectacle of unprecedented proportions. There was something in the sight of 10,000 penitents under a single roof that "thrilled the soul" of a believer, while reminding the skeptic of a wheat field after the cicadas had gotten to it.[136] The newly appointed bishop of Chicago, William Edward McLaren, spoke for many Catholics and Episcopalians when he declared: "Those claiming to be special messengers of God appear in every age. The church survives them all." Long after the flood of free publicity had run its course, he predicted in the *Diocese*, the true church, "her people and clergy would still be standing in the old paths." They, and many like them, neither "sought nor needed some new thing."[137]

Moody's celebrity as God's man for the Gilded Age grew rather than diminished with time. The occasion of his death, on the eve of the twentieth century, showed the degree to which his reputation had become inextricably linked to the city he had made home more than a quarter century earlier. Newspapers nationwide mourned his passing, but none with the particular passion and parochial pride of the Chicago press. "It was Chicago which discovered him," the *Tribune* gloated. "Chicago gave him his opportunity and then in due time gave him to the rest of the world." "We had the closest personal knowledge of the man and his work," Lawson and the *Daily News* reported, "and today there are no more sincere mourners anywhere at the death of the great evangelist than in the city to which he gave his first strength in Christian effort. It was here he expanded, achieved his first and greatest successes, learned the sources of his power and that secret of reaching the people in which he has possibly never had an equal."[138] Nixon and the *Inter-Ocean* helped develop Chicago's motto "I will." In the paper's appreciation of Moody it was duly noted that "he had." Moody was "a Chicago man," the paper said. "It was here that he passed the days of his earliest humiliation" and his "later greatness rivaling Wesley." The *Journal* thought "few men in the world's history had exerted so wide and compelling an influence." And in an irony Moody might have well appreciated, the most complete coverage of his passing was offered by the *Times,* the paper least likely to be a convert to his cause. Now named the *Times-Herald,* with Storey having long passed from the scene, the paper applauded the life of "the greatest evangelist of the century." Chicago at one time "claimed this mighty preacher, but when he died the whole world claimed him." It seemed only yesterday that the street in front of the tabernacle "was filled with a vast concourse of people struggling for admission" to his meetings. The paper now celebrated Moody's life, as did "the plain people of this city."[139]

Some doubted the wisdom of revivalists joining hands with their "wicked partners in the press." They pointed out that God had given no eleventh commandment at Sinai to "let there be advertising." Clearly the "power of publicity" was with Moody, but what of the Spirit of God, they wondered. They did not approve of "hot-house, high-pressure, forcing systems of propagating the gospel and for converting the world." The very people who had given Moody the cold shoulder when he worked in Chicago earlier, these critics pointed out, now sought publicity in supporting his work. "Moody had not changed" since those days, "but the circumstances seem to have changed wonderfully." He and his efforts were front-page news now. New methods in religious work, it appeared, brought "notoriety" but little of lasting spiritual significance.[140]

The Great Western Revival, as it came to be remembered, repeated a pattern that demonstrated how the power of prayer and publicity could craft civic spectacles that stimulated circulation. By its end, however, it made something else apparent to Moody and those who had the eyes to see it. Sensation produced celebrity that was not without its consequences. It made the personal public and tended to fix attention on the messenger and not the message. It made the star evangelist and his campaign organization to some extent a prisoner of the need to meet expectations or exceed them. It made the Moodys stay in Chicago and hurried the reluctant Blisses to it. Newspapers and their editors had a stake in these narratives; they boosted circulation.

And Moody and his minions were learning to play their parts. It was all for the sake of Western readers, who eagerly embraced the plot line. Now the news would be made in New England, as Moody and his mighty men prepared to stir Boston by first exciting the mighty men of the city's press.

"*It Is a Marvel to Many People*"

SEVEN

MOODY IN BOSTON, JANUARY–APRIL 1877

More than a month remained in D. L. Moody's 1877 New England campaign when the *Boston Globe* promised to issue a bound volume of its stenographic accounts of the great evangelist's revival work for those "anxious to secure and treasure" a permanent record of Moody's winter-long meetings. "So many thousands" had demanded a "complete and authentic" record of Moody's ministry that the paper was constrained to immodestly admit "the general excellence and uniform accuracy" of its reports compared to the competition. The paper loudly boasted the great man's imprimatur. "Never," Moody was inevitably quoted as again saying, had he "been so well reported by any newspaper in the world."[1]

By the time Moody and his men arrived in Boston, they had all but perfected the techniques of courting and capturing a positive press. The Reverend Joseph Cook, writing the forward to the *Globe*'s volume, considered it central to the success of Moody's mission. Many of the 6,000–7,000 people who had nightly filled the Boston Tabernacle to see the spectacle, he felt certain, had first seen stories sanctioning Moody's purposes and practice. "The work of sending religious truths abroad through the newspaper press," Cook commented, surpassed Whitefield's witness of 1740 during the Great Awakening and reflected the proper power of publicity in modern ministry.[2] Moody's official biographer, his son William, came to the same conclusion. Those made curious by

MR. MOODY. **MR. SANKEY.**

Full Reports of Mr Moody's Sermons and **Prayer Meeting Talks in the Great** Boston Tabernacle, beginning January 25th, and graphic and truthful descriptions of the services and inquiry meetings will be given in the

BOSTON DAILY GLOBE.

This paper will be sent regularly every day at the rate of **75** cents per month, or **$2** for three months. Address,

GLOBE PUBLISHING COMPANY, 238 Washington Street, Boston.

Competing newspapers saw Moody's meetings as a means of stimulating circulation. In city after city, many promised to offer their readers the "most complete" campaign coverage. Some, like the *Boston Daily Globe*, sent relays of stenographers to Moody's meetings, attempting to keep up with Moody's 225-words-per-minute. Following his crusades, several of these papers published bound editions of Moody's sermons, which sold well in the marketplace.

newspaper accounts might crowd out those seeking conversion at Moody's meetings, his son admitted, but it was the price organizers paid in starting and seeking to sustain an evangelistic effort of such scope and "catholicity."[3] For their part, Boston's newspapers were quick to notice that "the learned and unlearned, the rich and poor, the high and low" were welcomed in Moody's democratic meetings, where the great evangelist spoke movingly to "the real cravings of the common run of human beings."[4] Chicago had been quick to claim Moody as its native son, but Boston would have none of it. Its papers pointed out that New England pride was on the line in making certain that the East Northfield native and his evangelical retinue were not disappointed by the warmth of New England's response to his entreaties. After Boston, Moody's evangelical team would tour small-town America throughout 1877. In Burlington and Montpelier, Vermont, and Concord and Manchester, New Hampshire, in Providence, Rhode Island, and Springfield, Massachusetts, and in Hartford and New Haven, Connecticut, the techniques of publicity and preevent planning perfected in Boston would be on display. In each, Moody tried to keep the message simple—he was not the story, nor were the great crowds who came. Instead he urged listeners to attend to the greater story of God's unqualified love and what all New England should do in response to it.[5]

"A MAN OF EARNEST PURPOSE"

By the time Moody reached Boston in the winter of 1877, his reputation on both sides of the Atlantic as God's man for the Gilded Age had already been assured. Christ had found that prophets were hardly recognized in their own country, but that was not what Moody found. Chicago had shown and Boston would show again that when Moody came into a community it was as if Christ was coming and headlines followed. Boston's dailies were eager to get in on the interest by marketing Moody as an evangelical superstar "whose fame is in all the world." Typical was the *Globe's* tribute to "this plain, warmhearted man of earnest purpose" whose face was splashed across Boston's press in the days leading up to the New England campaign. That coverage contained Moody's charge to Boston's Christians that "faith and courage" characterize their united campaign to win the day for Christ. The paper was not alone in emphasizing the democratic elements of Moody's organization, in which "dignified Episcopalians, enthusiastic Methodists and contented looking men and women" of no denominational affiliation sat with "Spiritualists, Deists, Free-Thinkers, and Unitarians" under Moody's spell. This "great sea of human faces" struck some as confirming "the conviction that God has chosen Moody for the work he has deliberately undertaken."[6]

Moody's use of all available means in bringing revival had been controversial across the Gilded Age landscape but came under particular scrutiny in New England. The press observed that Moody's revival machine would have struck his eighteenth-century counterparts as human meddling in events better left to God's sovereign grace. In 1722, 1734, and 1734, when the churches of Boston had prayed and fasted to ask God for "the more plentiful effusion of the Holy Spirit," it was understood that this was how God brought revival—by the refreshing and renewing of his people.[7] Contemporary accounts of the quickening of God's people in colonial and early Republican America point to God's initiative, and not man's, in the divine decision to again intervene in human history.[8] Jonathan Edwards wrote of revival in Northampton in 1735 as "a surprising work of God in the conversion of many hundreds of souls." His *Discourses on Various Important Subjects,* published three years later, describes revival as "a work of God" that stood as "a remarkable testimony of God's approbation."[9] Other narratives written during the Great Awakening similarly speak of revival as "a genuine work of God" and "a blessing to the people of New England" on the order of the second chapter of Acts.[10]

The 100-year history from Edwards's labors in Northampton to Moody's birth in East Northfield is a chronicle of communal preservation as much as personal transformation during seasons of revival. Spiritual excitement emptied taverns and forced men to take the sabbath seriously. It restored ministers to previous positions of importance and influence. Neighbors patched up differences. In the wake of revival, women regained their proper respect as nurturers in the home and caregivers outside it. The poor were looked after. Crime rates went down. When communities revived, the twin perils of rationalism and agnosticism were overcome.[11] Clearly, the church and its leadership benefited from each wave of spiritual excitement, but before Moody the pattern was to see revival as God's harvest, not man's making. This is not to suggest that George Whitefield, John Wesley, or others before Moody were indifferent to the press their campaigns received or failed to see the impact of positive publicity in pushing God's cause. Whitefield generally got on well with editors, many of whom profited from the sale of his sermons. Whitefield deplored any suggestion that men could make a revival but lived to see the day when his portraits sold briskly in the marketplace.[12] In the early nineteenth century, Methodists, like Wesley, saw nothing wrong in "cooperating with God" to bring renewal, even if it meant planning meetings and publicizing them.[13]

THE EVANGELIST IN BOSTON

Moody approached Boston warily. Twenty years earlier he had
left a little shoe store on Court Street hoping for better things
in Chicago. During that time the Athens of America had
continued in its warm embrace of liberal theology. Certainly a city in-
spired by Ralph Waldo Emerson, Theodore Parker, and William Ellery
Channing and anxious to "cultivate a professional disdain of religious
enthusiasm" seemed to present "peculiar difficulties" to the old familiar
faith that animated Moody's ministry.[14] That was why he insisted on
painstaking preparations and the unity of participating churches before
committing to the campaign. Generating publicity on Moody's meetings
prior to their startup was part of this plan. It began with the announcement on May 8, 1876, that 78 Boston area churches were working
together to bring the evangelist to their city. When he came on June
28, he met with representatives from nearly 300 churches to discuss a
timetable and organizational structure for the undertaking.[15] A fifty-
member executive committee was established on September 13 to oversee construction of a brick tabernacle on Tremont Street between Berke-
ley and Clarendon streets, located west of the Common in the new
Boston then being reclaimed from the Back Bay. The structure had eight
grand entrances with a seating capacity of 6,000 and a platform that
would hold 800, in addition to a choir of 2,000. By November 6,
$30,000 had been spent or pledged to build it.[16]

Moody could count on many in Boston's evangelical minority to
champion his cause. Chief among them was Adoniram Judson Gordon,
the 40-year-old pastor of Boston's Clarendon Street Baptist Church,
whose commitment to evangelism would later lead to the establishment
of a divinity school that would bear his name. Henry Durant, a local
lawyer and founder of Wellesley College, would host Moody and his
family during their winter-long campaign. Phillips Brooks, an influential
Episcopalian and one of Harvard's most popular preachers, actively endorsed Moody's ministry, as did John Greenleaf Whittier, who shared
Brooks's distaste for some of Moody's methods but respected his ability
to move masses. Joseph Cook of Andover, whose Monday lectures in
Boston since 1874 had been a sensation in their attempt to harmonize
science and religion, shared Moody's pulpit.[17] Tremont Temple Baptists,
Park Street Congregationalists, and Mount Vernon Congregationalists
were early and eager supporters of Moody's mission. They had little love
for liberal theology and less for its arrogant dismissal of the old familiar
faith. They would lead the more than 2,000 volunteers whose door-to-
door canvass of each of Boston's 90,000 households in March 1877
greatly stimulated the interest of the press and public in the tabernacle
campaign.[18]

While workmen prepared the tabernacle for its dedication on January 25, 1877, Moody met with reporters and publishers of Boston's secular and religious press in hopes of winning their support for the coming campaign. They were assured that Boston's evangelical community was united in prayer and preparation for the meetings, and editors were urged to play their part in spreading this sentiment to readers who would be anxious to share in the excitement. "Everything human foresight could devise," the press was told, would be done "to secure the success" of the campaign, including direct mail, newspaper and streetcar advertising, billboards, and prayer chains targeting Boston's unchurched community. The purpose of event organizers, according to the *Sunday Times*, which advertised itself as "the spiciest paper in New England," was to create the impression that "the revival is a big thing" and "there had been nothing like it in Boston for a long time."[19]

Every effort was made to meet the needs of reporters covering the campaign. A reporter's box at the front center of the auditorium would be reserved for the press, regardless of the extent of a meeting's overflow. It meant that anyone who was attempting to cover the campaign under deadline could. Uniformed ushers, trained to bar entrance or egress from the auditorium during meetings, would make reporters their sole exception. Each reporter was given a chair, a desk, inkwells, and, when necessary, the paper to write on. Although the sanctuary was brilliantly lit with gas lamps, Moody made certain that long-stemmed candles were placed at each reporting station to help stenographers keep up with the pace of his speaking, which he had now gotten down to 220 words a minute. Moody's rationalization of the revival process saw no detail as unimportant if it would enhance attendance and press coverage. So each day's program, speakers, and sermon title were printed in advance and published in the daily press. If a reporter wanted to know the name of the minister Moody had asked to offer the invocation, a campaign staffer was sure he got his answer before the morning editions. For those correspondents writing for the afternoon edition, there was always Moody's personal newspaper, the *Tabernacle News*, which chronicled the campaign's progress daily.[20]

The tabernacle crusade coincided with a volatile period in Boston newspaper history and a deepening economic crisis that, as elsewhere, worked to Moody's decided advantage. The upstart *Globe*, founded only five years earlier, was just coming under the control of General Charles Henry Taylor, a publisher who would soon win the praise of Joseph Pulitzer and William Randolph Hearst for his uncanny capacity to stimulate circulation by promoting stories that moved middle- and working-class readers.[21] The "godly *Globe*," as critics were beginning to call it, more than tripled its meager 8,000 circulation by offering daily stenographic accounts of Moody's meetings.[22] This encouraged Taylor to experiment with an evening edition of the *Globe*, the running of larger headlines, and more local news in a newspaper priced at two cents daily. During the 13-week campaign Taylor often worked a 16-hour day, overseeing coverage of Moody's afternoon and evening meetings that included editorials of high praise, from the editor Edwin Munroe Bacon, and sidebar summaries of lives that had been transformed through Moody's meetings, written by the general reporter Arthur Adams Fowle.[23] In four years at the *Globe*, Taylor had moved from private secretary to shorthand writer, reporter, manager, general manager, and editor of the paper. He knew how to encourage loyalty and zeal on his staff. Even competitors admitted: "he is a good friend and a good enemy." If he opposed a man "he said it to his face." But "if he promises a thing, it is sure to be done, no matter what the cost or trouble."[24] Taylor believed Boston's newspapers had a responsibility to disseminate Moody's message of moral reform and salvation by faith to the masses. It was good news for Boston and turned out to be even better commerce for the *Globe*.

Boston's *Herald,* which had won a daily circulation of 116,500 by advertising itself as "a people's paper" that "spared no expense" in giving readers "trustworthy intelligence," was not to be outdone by the ambitions of the *Globe*. The paper's managing partners, Royal M. Pulsifer, Edwin B. Haskell, and Charles H. Andrews, had warily worked their way up through the *Herald's* business and editorial offices by keeping a close eye on the competition.[25] In hiring Edwin H. Woods as their circulation manager, one of New England's first, the paper greatly accelerated the sale of its Sunday edition and became a regional newspaper of note. Woods, affectionately known as "the Colonel" because he had been made lame in the Civil War, claimed to know "half the hollows and hillocks of New England." He visited many of them during Moody's Boston campaign, taking the first train out most Sunday mornings to sell the paper's account of the spectacle directly to newsdealers, bypassing wholesalers eager to share in the profits. The *Herald* claimed that this initiative made it the nation's widest-selling Sunday paper at 64,800.[26]

Its coverage of Moody's civic spectacle confirmed the *Herald's* growing reputation as the city's stealth paper. The Director's Room, where weather strips on the door, the joke went, prevented the leak of exclusives, served as inner sanctum for planning coverage. The paper's personal column was dropped to make room for a "Religious Department" that ran throughout Moody's meetings. A staff stenographer was assigned to capture Moody's every public utterance.[27] This did not mean that Moody could count on the *Herald* for unqualified support. The *Herald* had long cultivated both the readership and respect of Boston's "better classes," many of whose members were cool and indifferent, if not openly hostile, to Moody's methods. The paper was prepared "to bow to the popular interest" in the campaign, but that should not be confused with endorsement of Moody's means of stirring up excitement in the city.[28] The paper gave wide play to Unitarian and Universalist opposition to "the God which Mr. Moody presents." These clerics had no objection to "the reformation of a few drunkards, the reclaiming of a few prostitutes or the conversion of a few thieves" but thought it unlikely that "the intelligent men and women of Boston" would find Moody's simple-minded view of God particularly appealing.[29] For its part, the *Herald* claimed "a living newspaper has no theology" other than to "arouse people to a sense of their responsibilities," while making sure "those seeking entertainment, the simply curious and the overzealous do not have their day."[30]

SEEKING A GOOD STORY

When Moody began his meetings in Boston, the *Herald* was preparing to move its 190-member staff into a new six-story headquarters on fashionable Washington Street. The *Herald* architects built in the imperial French Renaissance style, using granite from the Bay of Fundy, a gesture of uncommon confidence in the midst of a long and deepening depression that had been particularly unkind to the nation's newspapers. The *New York Sun*, the nation's circulation leader, had lost one-quarter of its 140,000 readers in the dreary weeks following the controversial presidential election of November 1876, and other papers, including Boston's *Herald,* were privately reporting that and worse. The war between Russia and Turkey no longer attracted readers, and the Franco-Prussian conflict did even less to meet the paper's weekly payroll of $2,000.[31] Boston's press needed a good story, and the crowds that nightly came to the new tabernacle provided such a story.

Boston's *Journal,* Republican in politics and ecumenical in spirit, boasted that it had "an orthodox Congregationalist, a Methodist, and an impenetrable-shelled Universalist working within seven and three-quarters feet of one another" and "no barbed wire separated them." It believed in Moody's meetings as much as in a protective tariff and was convinced "the great revivalist" could bring Boston back to its spiritual senses.[32] Boston's *Daily Advertiser,* then in its sixty-fourth year of service as the city's "most respectable daily," was an early and eager convert to Moody's mission. The paper portrayed him as a home-grown godly servant who had returned to the city "a revivalist of world-wide reputation." It was persuaded that "those who come under his influence would be made better and truer men and women."[33] The *Post* and the *Traveller* each followed Moody's meetings faithfully and easily found readers who couldn't get enough of Mr. Moody. The *Post,* established in a walkup on Water Street 46 years earlier to further Andrew Jackson's "cause of genuine democracy," saw "an unceasing stream" gathered at Moody's inaugural meeting on the evening of January 28, 1877. They began coming in the early afternoon as the horse-cars on Tremont Street "brought elbow to elbow the gray-haired church veteran and the giggling school girl, the youth about town and the mother who had carefully wrapped a Moody and Sankey hymnal in a pocket handkerchief." The *Post* had never seen an "attraction like it."[34] The *Traveller* was "conservative in matters religious" and certain that "next to his Bible, every Yankee reads his daily paper."[35] For six months it had daily tracked the construction of what it called "Moody's Tabernacle" through the paper's sources at the Park Street Church and Boston's YMCA. This allowed the paper to give intimate and exclusive details on crusade planning and publicity, down to the black walnut desk and accompanying recliner that Moody would use in a special room set aside for him at the tabernacle.[36] It was consistent with the paper's republican desire to "make men truer to themselves and better before the sight of their fellow-men and Heaven."[37]

The *Transcript* was the *Traveller's* chief evening competition and tended to resist causes its opposition embraced. It was to be that way with Moody's tabernacle campaign. The *Transcript* had long positioned itself as the custodian of Boston's cultural life, causing one critic to crack that "all disbelievers in the infallibility of the *Transcript* will be handed over to the proper authorities."[38] Like its nearest neighbor, the Old South Church, the newspaper's office stood like a sentinel at the corner of Milk and Washington streets, warning Moody that because of Boston's "intellectual superiority" a revivalist's "appeal to emotion won't do." It observed that "our people here are less excitable than in other cities."[39] The paper's editor, Walter Alfred Hovey, and its night editor, Edward Henry Clement, editorially endorsed Moody's mission "to turn the community to a deeper contemplation of the moral law, which makes men considerate of their fellows, better neighbors, better parents, and more disposed to carry out the golden rule."[40] This would be sure to assuage the *Traveller's* important female readership.[41] It did not prevent the paper from "risking heresy" by editorially chiding Moody for what it saw as errors in exegesis and theology.[42]

Much like those in other cities that had seen the Moody machine in action, Boston's newspapers saw "a great symbolic significance" in Moody's meetings in America's Athens. The city saw itself as "the center of intellectual life" in America. That was why, its papers maintained, all eyes were now on the city. The *Congregationalist* saw the attention as a heaven-sent opportunity for area churches as they sought to expand their influence by making Moody's mission a success. "Boston is the center of a broader circle," the paper noted. "Lines of influence run out from this great opportunity." If Boston could be rescued from rationalism, there would be no hiding place for the heathen.[43] Moody could expect "the hearty cooperation of Boston's evangelical churches," the Methodist *Zion's Herald* promised. "Even the secular papers will read like religious tracts." All that was necessary now was "the solemn conviction of sin." Readers everywhere, the paper seemed assured, would understand the symbolism when Boston was brought to repentance.[44] The sentiment was not lost on the *Sunday Times,* which worried that "Boston is sweltering in a slough of sanctity." Readers everywhere were urged "to draw the line between religious worship and this broad burlesque of it."[45]

The machinery of revival

Moody preached more than 100 sermons and his colaborer Ira Sankey sang over 300 solos to the more than one million people who gathered during the 13-week revival run at the Boston Tabernacle during the winter of 1877.[46] Even the oppositional *Christian Register* admitted that "there was never a better advertised affair" than Moody's meetings, with daily stenographic accounts in most major newspapers and substantial summaries in the rest.[47] These reports chronicled the "machinery of revival" that Moody brought to bear on Boston. It ensured that large crowds of the faithful would be on hand when the tabernacle opened its doors. This provoked a positive press to daily chronicle the civic celebration and encouraged the curious to come. When weather and mounting indifference had reduced crowds by late February, friendly churches throughout New England were urged to come to the tabernacle through half-price railroad tickets. Moody met with reporters every other day at Tremont Temple and offered sidebar stories on slow news days concerning grocers and market men, furniture and fish dealers, fallen women and faithful journalists who now met to pray and study their Bible. A door-to-door canvass by 1,000 volunteers in mid-March reached each of Boston's 90,000 households with Moody's *Tabernacle News* and an urgent appeal to attend these "life-changing" meetings while there was yet time. The effect was to create a second great rush of interest in Moody's meetings, while evoking a bitter controversy in Boston's press and its pulpits over manmade means in bringing about revival.

Boston's Unitarians thought Moody "an illiterate evangelist" of "very limited intellectual resources" who was greatly aided by reporters "who rush to their inkstands to pen glowing accounts of messages" containing "the most commonplace thoughts."[48] Moody's "businesslike

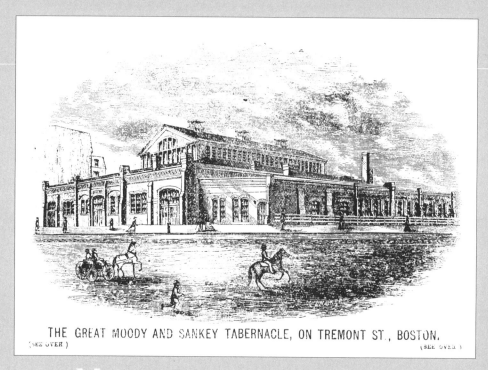

THE GREAT MOODY AND SANKEY TABERNACLE, ON TREMONT ST., BOSTON.
(SEE OVER)　　　　　　　　　　　　　　　　　　　　　　　　　　　　　　(SEE OVER)

Moody's New England campaign at Boston's Tremont Street tabernacle in the winter of 1877 closed a remarkable record of Gilded Age revivals that demonstrated the powers of prayer, publicity, and the modern press in creating civic extravaganzas of unparalleled proportions across urban America.

earnestness and ingenious ignorance" moved masses, the *Christian Register* reluctantly acknowledged, and that was just the problem. Hundreds of "the most thoughtful ruling classes" were turned away by Moody's "heretical views," the paper argued, that falsely relied on the Trinity, man's total depravity, and Christ's substitutionary atonement and warnings of the eternal torments of hell. Man's moral perfectibility, Unitarians were convinced, required "a more rational view of the Divine Nature."[49] To the multitudes, "the depraved and the degraded," Moody offered a salvation that was "easy and cheap." It required little of the very people who were most in need of reform, the *Register* warned. The church should address itself to "sobering men's minds," the *Register* argued, instead of supporting an "artificial" revival. "Our land and time are marked by great excitements," the paper observed, with "conceit and clamor and self-advertisement parading itself in the pulpit."[50] The work of Moody and his advocates in the press was "an organized epidemic of frights and frenzies," detractors claimed, much in the manner of a cheap civic entertainment.[51]

Despite the great crowds that came to Moody's meetings, the *Transcript* concluded that "the religion which the great evangelist dispenses has not secured the confidence of this community."[52] Moody created "machine-made Christians" by "stirring up the city" with appeals to people's selfishness. Who wouldn't want to live forever with friends and relatives who had preceded you to paradise, the paper wondered. As a manager of public penitence, Moody knew few peers, the paper speculated. But even if Boston was now awash in a spectacle of revival, the water wasn't very deep.[53] Moody's "homely audacity" appalled the paper most. His intimacy in seeming to speak for God in matters of man's salvation would make Arnold and Emerson scoff in amusement. The *Transcript* was certain that the skillful staging of citywide services would not overcome the skepticism of intelligent men and women. While Moody's meetings had meant a "moderate advance" of the spiritual interest in the community, those outside the evangelical churches, including Boston's Catholics, had been "unpersuaded."[54] The *Transcript* noted that the excitement of attending the revival had stalled out in early March, leaving crowds from the suburbs and distant settlements to fill in the empty seats. Widely advertised half fares on area railroads had taken scores to the tabernacle. They were encouraged to get in on the history that the revival seemed to be making.[55] Moody's methods of working up a revival had turned off the city's serious-minded Christians, the Catholic *Pilot* opined. The evangelical insistence of "singing, acting, and weeping" had been a performance more fit for stage than pulpit.[56]

The *Herald* shared some of these suspicions. Initially it had "bowed to popular interest" in the revival and sent its reporter to record four

and five columns of tabernacle news nightly, while giving the controversy over presidential succession less than half as much. Even "minor
details were worth knowing," it observed, in justifying its decision to
break coverage rules in reporting news from the inquiry rooms.[57] Five
weeks into the crusade, Moody was receiving 100 fan letters a day, the
Herald noted, a "splendid illustration of what a man of moderate ac-
quirements may do when he means what he says and is really in earnest."[58] From the outset, however, the *Herald* had hoped that Moody's
meetings would revive the local churches, much in the manner of a
mighty general leading a loyal following. The "machinery" of supporting men's souls was already in place. Nearly 200 city churches preached
a gospel designed to arouse Bostonians to a sense of their moral responsibilities. But these Sunday services were lightly attended and little regarded. Church buildings stood otherwise idle, "monuments of the vanity rather than the devotion of the worshippers."[59] By mid-February it
was becoming increasingly apparent to the *Herald* that outlying churches
were disproportionately benefiting from a costly revival that Boston's
churches were underwriting. The majority who came to the Tabernacle
were out-of-towners, the old, the curious, and those "seeking entertainment." By mid-March, 400 regional churches had joined the New
England Prayer Alliance, and each seemed to be sending celebrants anxious to get in on the act.[60]

When it was announced in mid-April that $21,000 was still needed
to pay off the debt of building the tabernacle and that local participating churches lacked the necessary funds, the *Herald* finally broke
with those backing Moody. Conservative pastors of Boston's evangelical
churches had from the first opposed inviting Moody to Boston, the
paper noted, for fear that such a "modern religious enterprise" would
bankrupt their churches and needlessly excite congregates, while ex-
hausting pastoral staffs swept up in the manufactured excitement. Their
warnings were now realized, the paper seemed certain. A national depression had strained the resources of local churches long before Moody
came. Now the debt had grown, and pastors who openly resisted the
extravagance risked being called envious or apathetic. Moody's good
press forced them "to bow to public opinion" and acquiesce. So they
reluctantly submitted themselves to "this illiterate evangelist" and his
noisy assembly. Three months had shown Moody to be "a true child
of religion who marvels most at things he understands least." The *Herald* thought that was the reason unsophisticated suburbanites and out-
of-towners seemed most moved by Moody's message. Their churches
and not Boston's were most likely to benefit from new converts or re-
commitments from old ones. Let them now pay for the "luxury" of
this revival. Boston's faithful were clearly poorer, the paper insisted, for
Moody's having come.[61]

Walt Whitman found a fundamental irony in the *Herald's* criticism of an evangelical campaign it had helped to promote. He had watched the march of Moody and his men from afar from the first day they had landed in his native Brooklyn. Now he had decided to see for himself. Writing in the *Sunday Times,* he recounted a horse-drawn journey to a "heavenly hippodrome" where, "jostled, hurried, squeezed, hat smashed and clothes torn," he took his seat beside "Beacon Street Brahmins, South Cove snoozers, Free Thinkers, Yankees, Germans, and Irish" hoping "to take our peep at Moody and Sankey and be saved." The democratic gathering appealed to Whitman's Jacksonian impulses, but Moody decidedly did not. "Eight thousands I's and irreverent allusions to the Deity" were meted out in endlessly bad grammar. This proved a revelation. "Moody's wonderful murder of syntax," the former editor of Brooklyn's *Eagle* and *Times* observed, had been carefully edited by the *Herald* and other papers eager to sell the story of this revival at two cents a copy. If Moody wasn't "an ignorant charlatan," he was at least a "mistaken enthusiast." The papers that had made him a celebrity and his revival a spectacle were without excuse. They believed neither in Moody's God nor "his method of swaying sinners." It was Whitman's view that the press had made Moody into a commodity much in the manner of a medical advertisement or a police court report. Their reporting on a "religious curiosity" was designed to make readers "Tabernacularly inclined." And they had succeeded beyond their most expansive hopes.[62]

REVIVAL AS MASS SPECTACLE

Moody's defenders in the New England press applauded the very efforts his critics decried. The *Examiner and Chronicle* observed that Moody's success had put the lie to Emerson's assertion of 40 years earlier that "a decaying church" stood behind "decaying unbelief." Moody had shown that modern mass evangelism would be the most powerful force to renovate society and exalt "the sin-ruined man."[63] His determination was to build in the cities of America what Methodists had long constructed in the West—a revival of the spiritually desensitized.[64] To this end he had necessarily enlisted the support of the professing church. And to its prayers and praise he had brought preaching and personal labor "to resurrect the occupants of a burial ground."[65] The principles involved in making a successful revival were no different from those involved in any other human activity. Moody made a business of saving souls and went about it in a businesslike manner. That was why organization and lots of it, with a premium placed on media relations, was a centerpiece in his strategy of saving Boston and other Gilded Age cities from their sins. In religion, as elsewhere, God had arranged that right methods secured appropriate results.[66] Moody's New England campaign was a clinic in applied Christianity, his supporters asserted. The crowds that came affirmed the moral force of Moody's message. No general had ever been more vigilant in his use of weapons. It had Universalism and religious indifference on the run.[67]

Bibles, Bible tracts, and more than 100,000 copies of *Tabernacle News*, Moody's own account of the crusade, were distributed door-to-door by armies of volunteers during Moody's meetings in Boston. It was a major news event that made its own headlines. So were the gatherings, for prayer and praise, of the city's furniture dealers and market men, dry goods dealers and grocers, fish peddlers and shoe salesmen, railroad men and temperance workers, office clerks and flour wholesalers, businessmen and journalists. They had been stirred to action and a new sense of community by Moody's ministry and methods. I.A.M. Cumming, the pseudonym of the *Sunday Times* reporter, was amused that Moody sought to convert "perishing pencil-pushers" into "pious press-men." He noted that that reporter Stephen Stockwell had chaired the afternoon prayer meetings in Amory Hall, at the corner of West and Washington streets, in honor of the *Journal*'s "utmost enthusiasm in reporting a crowded house even on nights when the Tabernacle wasn't two-thirds full."[68] Doubters might scoff at such public displays of penance, but most of Boston's dailies found it no laughing matter. Crowds of more than 100 had forced the triweekly press meetings to be moved to Tremont Temple at the corner of Summer and Kingston streets by the middle of April. Moody and Sankey often led the services to signal their importance. As an "impartial chronicler of passing events," the *Journal* reported that "a deep, pervasive, religious interest" had settled on the meetings and the city with "many finding themselves brought into a perception of spiritual things they hadn't anticipated."[69] The *Traveller* and the *Globe* concurred. The Boston daily press, like their colleagues in Britain, Brooklyn, Philadelphia, New York, and Chicago, reported that their city had never seen anything like it. Before the revival, "a religious article of any length was a phenomenon," observed the *Globe*. "Now all the papers are brimful with religious news" because the city was overflowing with a spirit of revival.[70]

In the final weeks of Moody's great city tour, several newspapers were reporting "a great anxiety to be present" before he closed his act in Boston. Twenty thousand persons packed the assembly hall to capacity to hear Moody's three daily messages. Thousands more were turned away disappointed.[71] Those unable to attend sent messages to Moody's quarters at the Tabernacle, begging for prayer and personal guidance. A secretary couldn't even keep up with autograph seekers.[72] *Zion's Herald* saw the excitement as a modern equivalent of Pentecost. Biographies of Moody suddenly began appearing in Boston's bookstores, depicting him as God's man for the Gilded Age.[73] Men could be heard "talking religion in their cars, by the wayside and in their counting rooms." A Boston editor reported he had reconciled with his son, "with the emotion of a man who had fallen heir to $50,000." Ladies coming from Lynn and approaching Park Street long before the appointed hour found Friday temperance meetings full to capacity. Fanueuil Hall was taken over by prayer and praise meetings of market-men. Grocery-men set up soup kitchens for 125 vagrants. State Street businessmen wondered how their newfound faith could be translated into better customer relations. Hackmen fasted to grow closer to Christ. Shoe-men urgently asked Moody to stay on after his revival meetings closed. Only the spiritually blind, more than one paper observed, failed to read these signs of the times.[74]

Even newspapers that were critical of Moody's brand of mass evangelism admitted that the crusade was of such monumental proportions that it would serve as a historic reference point for those who had lived through it. As a "swift-succeeding excitement," Moody's manner of staging a revival seemed to break with a past in which one waited for God's spirit to move. Now it was man who acted and God, belatedly, who blessed. Whether those blessed had been permanently changed as a result of Moody's mission only time would tell.[75] One thing, however, seemed certain. Modern mass evangelism had changed, and Moody had helped to change it. This did not mean, however, that each of Boston's gentlemen of the press was equally approving. There was as much regret as regard for the phenomenon of revival as mass spectacle that was now coming into view. They found its "thunders and lightnings are fiercely discharged" with "a restless energy" characteristic of business enterprise and moneymaking generally. Something, however, had been lost in "this epidemic of frights and frenzies, of fiery appeals and tearful songs, of noisy demonstrations and pulpit pyrotechnics." Modern salvation seemed more geared toward the circus ring than a silent chamber.[76] In this, spiritual revival was becoming a lot like other aspects of American life. It was filled with fever. What was needed now, some commentators claimed, was less spectacle and more service, less activity designed to excite and entice and more serious-minded ministry to those increasingly alienated from the requirements and anonymity of industrial living.

At the close of Moody's winter's work in New England, an estimated one million men and women had attended his revival at the Boston Tabernacle. An estimated 6,000 new converts and a great many reenergized ones would presumably now take their proper place in the churches of New England and in the spiritual life of the region. Participating pastors were reportedly exhausted from the pace Moody had been keeping.[77] Eighteen hourly messages a week with little more than a sounding board to amplify his voice had pushed the indefatigable Moody to the limit too. In six months of continuous revival work in Chicago and Boston, he had preached nearly 500 messages and prayed personally with thousands of inquirers, while perfecting the organizational apparatus that coordinated and publicized his many meetings. At the very beginning of those meetings in England and now at their close in New England some critics charged he had been in it for the money. Moody wearily observed that he could make more money on the lecture circuit in a night than he had made in Boston in three months.[78] Like Chicago, Boston's faithful were reluctant to give up their prophet. A petition was circulated urging him to extend the revival. To pay off the debt on the tabernacle $21,000 was pledged, and another $10,000 was promised to keep the building open if only Moody and his men would stay. Moody observed that the revival now underway in New England was bigger than any man and would be guided by others to greater heights.[79]

At the close of the Boston campaign, even Moody's critics recognized the historic proportions of what they had seen. Moody was compared not unfavorably with Whitefield, Wesley, Edwards, and Finney in his ability to organize and oversee communal religious excitements. Like them, Moody was in earnest. Each man saw his mission vividly and was able to move other men by this sense of urgency.[80] Intellectuals had scoffed at Whitefield, the *Congregationalist* wrote, and now regretted it. The same would be true, it predicted, when historians analyzed the impact of Moody's mission in New England 100 years hence.[81] Those chroniclers would record that all of New England had been spiritually awakened by Moody's meetings, *Zion's Herald* felt certain, and that "a deep, powerful, persistent force" would continue to energize the region's faithful long after Moody had left for other harvest fields.[82] An analysis of New England's Congregational, Baptist, Episcopal, and Methodist churches showed a gain of 21,000 new converts in 1877 alone and an equal number in the two years that followed. That doubled the conversion rate of Baptists and Congregationalists in the years leading up to the revival and increased by one-third the conversion rate of Methodists and Episcopalians.[83] It is more difficult to measure the spiritual significance of the revival in the lives of those who had already claimed Christ prior to Moody's coming. Anecdotal evidence and press accounts seem to support the view that the winter of 1877 was seen by many as an important moment in the spiritual life of New England's evangelical churches and its secular press.

REMEMBERING MOODY AND THE 1877 REVIVAL

The death of D. L. Moody in December 1899 was front-page news across the nation, with New England's newspapers prominent in their praise of a passing native son. Appreciations particularly recalled Moody's memorable work in the regional revival of 22 years earlier. The *Globe*, which had used Moody's mission at the tabernacle to build its reputation as a daily to be reckoned with, hit the streets with an extra edition. It gave banner headlines to Moody's last words, recorded by loved ones at his bedside in East Northfield, Massachusetts, that "the world is receding and heaven opening," and the paper celebrated "a life devoted to the cause of his Master."[84] The *Transcript*, no friend of Moody's revival work, shared this sentiment. Moody had been the century's "leading evangelist." During this time "no one else had so profoundly influenced the English-speaking world" in winning sinners to Christ.[85] What Moody accomplished, the *Transcript* declared, was "beyond human measurement." One did not have to agree with his interpretation of the Bible to recognize "the prophetic potency of his messages" that gave him "a power of persuasiveness" unparalleled in the country's history. That was why "he will be missed and mourned by the churches as profoundly as by the common people, who regarded him almost as their Moses."[86]

In pulpit after pulpit across the region, pastors paid tribute to Moody in remembering his great crusade. There was little doubt that "Moody has left his mark on this age," observed Reverend Daniel Addison of All Saints Episcopal Church in Brookline. Hardly a church could be found that did not claim at least one celebrant "who date from him their conversion."[87] Two thousand congregates gathered at Tremont Temple to fondly remember the revivalist and his New England campaign. They raised $2,500 to make the final payment on a new chapel that Moody had launched in his hometown of Northfield.[88] Their mood was expressed by Reverend Reuben A. Torrey, who presided over Moody's memorial service in Northfield. "When news of Moody's death reached me," said Torrey, who headed a Bible school in Chicago soon to be named for Moody, "I said to myself: 'The world has lost some of its realness to me, but the world beyond is increased in realness.'"[89] Moody was a unique product of New England, noted Reverend Charles C. Earle, at the Harvard Street Baptist Church. "He was reared in one of those well-disciplined homes of New England, of Puritan type, which have produced so many stalwart men for the nation and the church." Even Universalists, who had little regard for Moody's theology, felt a certain sense of loss. Reverend George L. Perin of Boston's Every-Day Church thought no one in his generation had "better presented the idea of love" to multitudes who felt alienated from the machine age and the life of the church.[90]

A generation had made it clear to editors in towns large and small that Moody's revival had succeeded in renewing religious interest within the region. "All must agree Moody made men better morally," the *Lowell Courier* reported. Not only the region but "the world is vastly better for the work he has done in it," the *Portland Express* observed. "It made him a man among men in the Christian world of his time," the *Keene Sentinel* declared. "He needs no monument of marble or bronze," the *Nashua Telegraph* suggested. The quality of his converts' lives was monument enough.[91] No one could compare to Moody in his "sure seizure of the moment," the *Springfield Daily Republican* reported. It was why "since Whitefield no evangelist can be compared with him."[92] Citizens of Gloucester, Massachusetts, remembered Moody's revival with affection, the town's *Breeze* made known, while those of Norwood prepared to live lives faithful to his teaching, the *Advertiser* announced. Editorial appreciations appeared in Salem and Newburyport, Brockton and Lynn, Fall River and Athol, all in Massachusetts. A pen-and-ink drawing of the evangelist dominated the front page of the *Lewiston Journal*, while the *Bangor Commercial*, the *Concord Monitor*, and the *Rockland Star* were announcing that the ever-zealous Moody had worked himself to death.[93]

The *Foxboro Reporter* suggested that at his death "D. L. Moody was more familiar to the people of the United States than any other man." That this may have been so owed much to the news Moody made in his lifetime and in his death. From beyond the grave he remained his own best witness. The *Quincy Daily Whig* was among those newspapers reprinting Moody's many sayings, including his final sermon, given in Kansas City that fall. "People might sneer at the sensational news of revivals," Moody was quoted as saying, "but I would sooner cut off my hand than speak against revivals. I prefer sensation to stagnation every time. A seaman does not fear a storm as much as a fog."[94] Moody didn't know what the church of the twentieth century would be like. "I stand by the church of the First Century," he liked to say. But the big-city revivals he staged on either side of the Atlantic during the Gilded Age would anticipate the mass media revival of the following century, with its premium on organization and publicity and its deft use of media relations. "There is no excitement in a graveyard," Moody told listeners during his last revival. That was why citywide crusades in the future needed to make their own news if they expected to awaken sinners from sleep.

At the time of D. L. Moody's death, one-third of America's 75 million men and women regularly went to church, and nearly three-fifths of these to evangelical churches. But the press of the period portrayed a church in crisis and threatened with decline. The problem appeared to be churches that had grown fat in their self-satisfaction while inattentive to the problems associated with industrialization and urbanization. All too often penitents were fed "religious services designed to tickle the ear without awakening the conscience or purifying the heart."[95] What was needed in the next millennium, New England's newspapers suggested, in supplements dedicated to Moody's memory, was "less pulpit eloquence and more music to awaken the natural grace inherent in the human heart."[96] Moody had helped to point the way by making the kingdom of Christ and the working of his Spirit more accessible than the seduction of the devil in "a highly publicized career of inordinate usefulness."[97] Moody's passing was the occasion to lament that there were few "honest and earnest men" whose preaching appealed to "learned and unlearned alike."[98] Moody "impressed himself upon the moral and spiritual life of his time with a power that hardly any other individual of his generation could parallel."[99] It made Moody "the colossal figure of the century, if indeed he ever had a prototype."[100]

The revival campaign of Moody and his ministry team throughout the Gilded Age set a standard for the use of organization and the power of publicity in getting the gospel out. "Modern evangelists," the *Globe* predicted, would do well to follow "Moody's ideas in evangelism." If they wanted to be "potent preachers" they had to be great organizers and publicists first.[101] Just as Paul had preached at the crossroads of the Mediterranean world two millennia before, Moody preached through the press as a modern messenger to millions. Cooperating publishers congratulated themselves. Through their pages the press had helped to create civic spectacles that encouraged the curious to come and see for themselves. When they did, bigger headlines followed. The realm of those who could not be reached with the gospel diminished as the modern press reached distant outposts. To his dying day, D. L. Moody was certain it was the Spirit and not the work of human hands that brought sinners to repentance and stood the test of time. But his great Gilded Age campaigns in Britain and across urban America showed what could happen when God and man labored together. The result was a mass media revival that succeeded in reaching the spiritual needs of men and women who were still searching for personal significance and communal cohesion on the eve of the modern era.

The Beginning

EIGHT

Moody in queenstown, june 1873

Shortly before D. L. Moody's death, his longtime associate in evangelistic work, Ira Sankey, wrote in *Success,* for a generation who may not have heard the story, the tale of how the two had gotten their start. "We sailed in June 1873 to England," he recalled. At Queenstown they received word that "the two men who had invited us to England had died." Moody was undeterred. When their ship arrived in Liverpool, Moody told his colleague in widely quoted words of faith that would often be repeated: "If the Lord opens a door to us, we will go in." That night, as Sankey remembered the story, "Mr. Moody found an unopened letter among his papers." It supposedly said: "If we ever came to England we would be welcome at York to speak at the YMCA." It was the sign Moody sought. At once he told his favorite singer, "We will go to York."[1]

For the first day or two, Sankey recalled, "our meetings were not large," but by the end of the week "no building in the city would hold all the people who desired to attend." The story of Moody's sudden success, so often repeated in the press, was part of the widely shared sense at Moody's death that he had surely been God's man for the Gilded Age. And if that success was not sudden, but slow, and the sign not only of divine favor but of human trial and error, who could say? Press accounts of the period seem to tell the story of a largely anonymous revivalist and his coworker arriving on an island that was long indifferent to their labors. Weeks of dedicated work did little to suggest that Moody, Sankey, and their melodeon were anything other than a communal curiosity and summer entertainment. Moody's allies in the evangelical press, however, were telling a different story. They saw Moody's non-sectarian message heralding the old, familiar faith as an antidote to the clerical conformity that was crowding Christ out of the sanctuary. That was why the *Christian* and other evangelical papers rallied to Moody's cause in the north of England, helping to create a certain excitement as Moody and Sankey approached Scotland.

David Beaton was a seminary student in the fall of 1873 when Moody and Sankey came, as their admirers in the press would have it, "to save the spirituality of the Scottish church." Beaton came into personal contact with the revival effort and initially believed that Moody would have little effect on disapproving Scots who "are not influenced easily by revivals or revivalists." This, however, was where Moody's organizational acumen and intensely earnest consecration came in. His preevent protocol now involved meeting with ministers of the evangelical alliance, their allies in the press, and those sympathetic to the movement throughout the Nonconformist community. It was there, Beaton remarked, that many found Moody to be "a man of strong will," even as others found him "hopelessly overbearing." Even these critics, however, could not deny his "unity of purpose" and "popular appeal." One secret of Moody's success, Beaton came to believe, was "his power to attract and interest" celebrants and their leaders as well. "Many great men felt small in Moody's presence," he remembered. The force of Moody's certainty that he was about God's business produced "a wonderful effect." It seemed to propel all before him, leaving pastors and publishers alike to feel "as if they had to submit to his will."[2]

Eighty years later a spiritual son of D. L. Moody, Billy Graham, arrived in Scotland, hoping to build on the foundations that Moody had laid. Everywhere the twentieth century's most sensational revivalist saw the good work fashioned by the most effective evangelist of the nineteenth.[3] By the twenty-first, satellite, broadband, and digital made the wired world a communication community; Graham in a single day could have the hope of reaching ten times the audience Moody had amassed in a quarter century of mass meetings.[4] The crowds who once felt commanded to come out of curiosity to city centers to join those swept up in the sense of civic excitement could now stay at home and sample spirituality against competing entertainments. Others in the new millennium would park their cars at drive-in crystal cathedrals without ever getting out. The press reports it all, if at all, in agate type, having to wait for scandals of celebrity evangelists or pederast priests to have a story that will stimulate circulation the way Moody's missions so often did.

A century after Moody's passing, more than nine in ten Americans still say they believe in God, but only two in three now seem certain. Moody's critics foresaw the trend, even as Moody and his allies strove "to save a few," as Beecher skeptically saw it, "before the boat sank." For a quarter century following those remarks, Moody worked ceaselessly to oppose the modern flight from faith. During that time he perfected his revival instrument, which meshed the machinery of mass media with preevent planning and produced the spectacle of big-city revival that reached its crescendo during his Gilded Age tour of urban America, only to be briefly revived again during the Great Columbian Exhibition of 1893 in his longtime hometown of Chicago. More than 27 million fairgoers would come to celebrate the 400-year anniversary of the great explorer's discovery of America, ignoring the obvious irony that they were a year late and that Native Americans had found it first. Event organizers put on quite a party, stretched along 666 acres of Lake Michigan's shoreline. Out of the swampy sediments rose the classic columns of Daniel Burnham's Great White City, an architect's dream of heaven. Its 150 buildings gleamed like the marble homes believers expected of a celestial city. This paradise, however, was made of staff, a plaster of Paris and jute substitute, that transients would torch soon after the celebration had run its six-month course. Moody's old ally at the *Chicago Tribune*, Joseph Medill, now 70, had ceaselessly promoted the extravaganza, hoping it would be good for business in tough economic times much as Moody's mission to Chicago had been nearly a quarter century earlier. From the top of a 250-foot Ferris wheel, the faithful could look down on the Midway Plaisance, a gladway of invention and consumption, celebrating the arrival of the internal combustion engine, the Heinz pickle pin, Edison's moving-picture kinetoscope, and the waffle cone.[5] In the midst of this melee, some old-timers even found the tabernacle tent of the 56-year-old Moody, grayer and stouter now than in his glory years but preaching still the old familiar faith to reporters and readers who now found him not the show but the sideshow. The great man would have to fight for the front page when he preached the good news now. He had to share the spotlight with the World's Parliament of Religions, whose Congress confidently predicted that it was only a matter of time before modern men and women achieved through education and science a fully satisfactory secular means of salvation.

When Moody died in December 1899 his critics had reason to hope that the "old theology" had also breathed its last. Moody may have been the most beloved man of the late nineteenth century, they admitted, but he was by its end also the most out of date. "Progressive religion" reconciled the ethical and social problems of modern living, they now believed, to the requirements of a "new humanity." Even Moody's allies admitted that "the most powerful religious personality of the century" relied on "an optimism, energy and self-certainty" that seemed an artifact of an older era in America when belief came more easily.[6] Even to the end, as his energy ebbed, the optimism remained strong. "I can see how much better it is to depart and be with Christ," he was widely quoted as telling his family and friends from his deathbed, "but I want to live. I want to see the old century out." He told reporters, "I think there is going to be another revival, and I want a hand in it."[7]

Although he did not live to see the old century out, Moody's methods of evangelism, taught in the evangelical schools he had founded, included plenty of prayer and preevent planning to organize sympathetic churches and stir the faithful to action. This enthusiasm lived on in the revival work of Billy Sunday, Billy Graham, and others. Perhaps most important to those who came after him was Moody's recognition that a great enemy of church life, the secular press, could be harnessed to further the purposes of the church. Those who slept in on the sabbath and opened their morning paper could also be reached, Moody had reasoned, through the devil's advocate. In city after city, Moody's message to ministers was the same. The person who would never pick up a sermon, he told them, might read an account of it in the daily press. He understood that America had entered "an age of advertising" and its many ministers needed to exploit it if they wanted to get their message out.[8] One worked through newspapers to create a sense of civic excitement that encouraged believers "to expect a blessing of unusual magnitude."[9] When the first crowds came, headlines would follow. Readers would be made aware that something was happening—Christ had come to their city—and they would then be eager to get in on the blessing. For their part, Gilded Age editors, or the "saucepan press," as their critics came to call them, were not unaware of Moody's methods.[10] In a time of economic depression, the daily press, weaned from its dependence on political parties for financial support, now needed news suited for every palate. That meant playing religion as civic spectacle and Moody as celebrity evangelist if it succeeded in stimulating circulation. And it did. First in Britain, and then in Brooklyn and Philadelphia, followed by New York, Chicago, and Boston, the saucepan press found stories to satisfy every taste. In times of economic panic and political scandal, D. L. Moody's proclamation of the old familiar faith seemed a perfect antidote to the slump in spirits and, just as important, sales.

An ethos of reciprocity emerged between Moody and his many admirers and occasional critics in the press. They needed and used each other in creating communal festivals of "unparalleled proportions," or so the story went. And whether the excitement was made by Moody or for Moody or through his allies in the press or reflected a sovereign God shedding his grace on a population thirsting for something sacred, it made, in the end, excellent copy. What was widely realized at the time was that modern means of mass communication, seen by some as an enemy of the sacred, could be used to serve its servant. A century later, that old familiar faith, joined to the engine of digital communication, is still surprisingly successful at moving postmodern men and women in ways that would have been easily understood by their Gilded Age ancestors. The search for personal significance in an information age of growing anonymity, alienation, and estrangement seems a need as great at the beginning of a new millennium as it was in the industrial age at the end of the old century. It was perhaps the ultimate irony of Moody's work that he used the machinery of revival to present the love of Christ positively to multitudes who felt alienated from the machine age.

Two terrible wars in the twentieth century and terrorist attacks at the beginning of the twenty-first seemed to spectacularly shatter the kind of American optimism that was embodied in Chicago's White City and was nurtured by those who saw in modernity the hope of a new heaven and a new earth. Postmodern citizens still seek solace and spiritual solidarity in the midst of uncertainty and crisis, much as their ancestors had in Moody's day. They continue to turn to images made in the mass media in their search for certainty and a sense of personal significance, just as many Americans did during the Gilded Age. One of the favorite stories of that generation was the unlikely tale of a New England farm boy, with a fourth-grade education and a gift for selling boots, who became a celebrity evangelist, God's man for the Gilded Age. The citywide spectacles he helped create brought a modern means of mass communication to the service of the faith of their fathers. The unfolding of that alliance has now crossed a century and is a part of a larger narrative that propels their children and their children's children into the next.

Notes

1. THE END

1. Compare competing accounts in *Chicago Tribune*, December 23, 1899, 1, and *New York Times*, December 23, 1899, 4. Moody's summary of his own life appears in the foreword to William R. Moody, *The Life of Dwight L. Moody* (New York: Fleming H. Revell, 1900).

2. *Kansas City Star*, November 18, 1899, 1. *St. Louis Post-Dispatch*, November 18, 1899, 1.

3. Letter from William Jennings Bryan to D. L. Moody, November 23, 1899, D. L. Moody Papers, Yale Divinity School Library, New Haven, Connecticut, box 1, folder 3. All further references to the Moody Papers are to this collection, unless otherwise noted. Letter from Booker T. Washington to Mrs. Dwight L. Moody, December 23, 1899, Moody Papers, box 6, folder 1. Letter from Lenore B. Anthony to D. L. Moody, November 18, 1899, Moody Papers, box 5, folder 28.

4. *Detroit Free Press*, November 19, 1899, 1. *Detroit News*, November 19, 1899, 1. *Chicago Tribune*, November 19, 1899, 8.

5. Letter from Charles A. Blanchard to D. L. Moody, December 1, 1899; letter from Walter C. Douglas to A. P. Fitt, December 23, 1899; letter from Frederick del Booth Tucker to Dwight L. Moody, November 18, 1899; letter from Charles W. Wood of the Yoke Beavers Bible Class to Dwight Moody, November 19, 1899; letter from M. B. Williams to D. L. Moody, December 9, 1899; and letter from Arthur Long to D. L. Moody, November 22, 1899; all in the Moody Papers, box 5, folder 28, Yale Divinity School.

6. Moody's telegrams of reassurance to his wife, Emma, November 17 and November 18, 1899, Moody condolence letters, Moody Papers, box 5, section 28, letter I.

7. *New York Times*, November 19, 1899, 1. *Chicago Tribune*, November 19, 1899, 36.

8. *New York Tribune*, November 20, 1899, 4. *Chicago Tribune*, November 20, 1899, 4. *Boston Globe*, November 20, 1899, 3.

9. Letter from Louis Klopsch, publisher of the *Christian Herald*, to A. P. Fitt, December 15, 1899; the Wanamaker and *North American* telegrams, November 18 and November 19, respectively; Ira Sankey to D. L. Moody, November 22, 1899; all in condolence letters, Moody Papers, box 5.

10. Letter from R. Scott to A. P. Fitt, December 1, 1899, condolence letters, Moody Papers, box 5.

11. Chapman's "tribute to the memory of the greatest apostle of the age" is *The Life and Work of Dwight L. Moody* (Philadelphia: International, 1900), vi and 17–21. Letter from Chapman to Moody's son William, December 18, 1899, condolence letters, Moody Papers, box 5.

12. *Congregationalist*, February 1, 1900, 157–158.

13. Summaries of these stories are in the "Christian periodicals" file, D. L. Moody Papers, Moody Bible Institute, Chicago.

14. *Literary Digest*, December 30, 1899, and *Springfield Republican*, undated, Christian periodicals file Moody Papers, Chicago. See also *Congregationalist*, December 28, 1899, 1010–1011.

15. *Boston Globe*, December 22, 1899, 1. *Montreal Gazette*, December 28, 1899, 1. Henry Drummond, *Dwight L. Moody* (New York: McClure, Phillips, 1900), 123–125.

16. *New York Times*, December 23, 1899, 4. *Boston Globe*, December 23, 1899, 1.

17. The kind comments from editorial writers in *Chicago Tribune*, December 23, 1899, 12, can be compared to a distinctly less charitable tone in *Chicago Tribune*, January 13, 1869, 4, and January 14, 1869, 4.

18. Lawson's private experience at Moody's Midwest revival is chronicled in Finis Farr, *Chicago: A Personal History of America's Most American City* (New Rochelle, N.Y.: Arlington House, 1973), 140–141. His paper's appreciations of Moody appear in *Chicago Daily News*, December 22, 1899, 4, and December 23, 1899, 4.

19. Ira D. Sankey, *My Life and the Story of the Gospel Hymns* (Philadelphia: Sunday School Times, 1906), 21–25 and 78–79.

20. *Boston Journal*, December 27, 1899, 3. *Chicago Chronicle*, January 1, 1900, 4.

21. *New York Sun*, February 4, 1900, 4.

22. *Philadelphia Press*, December 23, 1899, 2. *Sunday School Times*, February 10, 1900, 1. *Philadelphia Public Ledger*, January 8, 1900, 5.

23. *New York Times*, December 24, 1899, 22. *New York Herald*, December 23, 1899, 4.

24. *Brooklyn Eagle*, December 25, 1899, 1.

25. *Daily Telegraph* (London), December 23, 1899, 2. *Evening News* (London), December 23, 1899, 2.

26. *Manchester Guardian*, December 23, 1899, 9.

27. *Westminster Gazette*, December 23, 1899, 9 and 10. *Record* (London), December 29, 1899, 1271.

28. *Belfast News-Letter*, December 23, 1899, 5.

29. *Glasgow Herald*, December 23, 1899, 4.

30. *London Daily News*, December 23, 1899, 3.

31. *Philadelphia Public Ledger*, December 24, 1899, 6. *Philadelphia Evening Bulletin*, December 24, 1875, 4. *Philadelphia North American*, December 24, 1899, 2.

32. *Boston Evening Transcript*, December 22, 1899, 6, and December 23, 1899, 16.

33. The Billy Graham campaign lasted from May 30 to June 17, 1962, at Chicago's sprawling lakeside convention center. Numbers are courtesy of the Billy Graham Evangelistic Association in Minneapolis, Minnesota.

34. Billy Graham, "Crusade Questions," *Moody Monthly* (October 1954), 32–33. In the same issue, see also the remarks of the archbishop of Canterbury under the title "The London Campaign," 80, and J. Erskine Tuck, "The Winning of the Press," 28–29 and 86–90. Billy Graham, *Just as I Am: The Autobiography of Billy Graham* (New York: HarperCollins, 1997), 208–211.

2. "EXPECTING A BLESSING OF UNUSUAL MAGNITUDE"

1. *Liverpool Telegraph and Shipping News*, June 18, 1873, 3. *Liverpool Daily Post*, February 8, 1875, 5.

2. *Birmingham Daily Post*, January 18, 1875, 5. *Sheffield Post*, January 9, 1875, 8. *Glasgow Daily Mail*, March 16, 1874, 4. *London Morning Post*, March 10, 1875, 6. *Dundee Weekly News*, June 13, 1874, 4.

3. *Dublin Daily Express*, October 31, 1874, 3. *Belfast Morning News*, September 14, 1874, 2. *Edinburgh Daily Review*, December 8, 1873, 3, and January 5, 1874, 2. *Newcastle Daily Chronicle*, October 28, 1873, 4.

4. Billy Graham, "Crusade Questions," *Moody Monthly* (October 1954), 32–33. In the same issue, see the remarks of the archbishop of Canterbury, under the title "The London Campaign," 80. *Daily Telegraph*, July 13, 1875, 3, and May 22, 1954, 4. *London Daily Herald*, February 20, 1954, 1. *Daily Mirror*, February 27, 1954, 2.

5. George E. Morgan, *R. C. Morgan, His Life and Times* (London: Pickering and Inglis, 1908), 171–173. Frank Guy Armitage, "The Influence of Dwight L. Moody on the City of York," *Christian Work*, February 6, 1915, 174–178. Paul D. Moody, *My Father: An Intimate Portrait of Dwight Moody* (Boston: Little, Brown, 1938), 116–120.

6. Frederick Francis Cook, *Bygone Days in Chicago: Recollections of the "Garden City" of the Sixties* (Chicago: Clurg, 1910), 305–311.

7. John V. Farwell, *Early Recollections of Dwight L. Moody* (Chicago: Winona, 1907), 8–9.

8. *Chicago Tribune*, January 6, 1866, 4; January 7, 1866, 4; January 8, 1866, 4; January 9, 1866, 3; and January 12, 1866, 4. *Chicago Times*, January 9, 1866, 2, and January 12, 1866, 3.

9. Accounts of Moody's season of preparation in Britain are found in Morgan, *R. C. Morgan*, 169–171. William R. Moody, *The Life of Dwight L. Moody* (New York: Fleming H. Revell, 1900), 131–143. James F. Findlay, Jr., *Dwight L. Moody: American Evangelist, 1837–1899* (Chicago: University of Chicago, 1969), 64–69.

10. *Chicago Tribune*, August 28, 1867, 4; August 29, 1867, 4; and August 30, 1867, 2 and 4.

11. See Moody's fundraising letters to Cyrus H. McCormick, April 15, 1868; November 24, 1871; February 24, 1873; and May 1, 1873; all in *D. L. Moody's Letters*, vol. 1, Moody Bible Institute, Chicago. McCormick financed Moody's plan to put up racks of Christian literature in passenger depots and hotels throughout the city and to train a staff to visit these locations three times weekly. In the first 10 months of the program's operation two million pages of literature were distributed. McCormick's ties as stockholder to the recently established *Chicago Daily News* furthered Moody's positive press from that paper.

For Moody's generally warm relations with the city's dominant paper, the *Chicago Tribune*, see *Chicago Tribune*, January 10, 1867, 2; January 8, 1869, 3; and June 27, 1870, 1. See also *Chicago Evening Journal*, January 11, 1870, 4, and June 8, 1870, 1.

12. Farwell, *Early Recollections*, 110–111. See also the letter from M. K. Jessup to John Farwell, January 17, 1872, Moody Papers, box 8, folder 95.

13. *Chicago Tribune*, March 16, 1873, 12; April 6, 1873, 9; April 13, 1873, 9; May 11, 1873, 9; and May 25, 1873, 9.

14. *Chicago Tribune*, May 25, 1873, 9. Farwell, *Early Recollections*, 111–112. Ira D. Sankey, *My Life and the Story of the Gospel Hymns* (Philadelphia: Sunday School Times, 1906), 18–24 and 40–42. See also "Moody and Sankey" file, Moody Papers, Chicago.

15. *Chicago Tribune*, May 25, 1873, 9. *Christian*, June 26, 1873, 17.

16. Letter from George Bennett to William R. Moody, March 12, 1900, Moody Papers, box 8, folder 95. Also in the same folder see letter from D. L. Moody to John Farwell, June 30, 1873.

17. Letter from Bennett to Moody, March 12, 1900. Emma C. Moody, diary entries of June 20 and June 23, 1873, Moody Papers, box 14, folder 2.

18. *Christian*, July 10, 1873, 28. *Middlesex Mercury and County Advertiser*, June 21, 1873, 1. *Yorkshire Chronicle*, June 28, 1873, 5.

19. *York Herald*, June 28, 1873, 7. *Yorkshire Gazette*, July 12, 1873, 5.

20. *York Herald*, July 5, 1873, 8 and 11. *Yorkshire Chronicle*, June 28, 1873, 4, and July 12, 1873, 5.

21. Emma Moody, diary entries, July 30 and July 31, 1873, Moody Papers, box 14, folder 2. Sankey, *My Life*, 48–49. *Christian*, August 7, 1873, 11.

22. Emma Moody, diary entry, August 25, 1873, Moody Papers, box 14, folder 2. Moody, *Life of Moody*, 164–165. *Sunderland Times*, July 22, 1873, 2.

23. *Sunderland Times*, August 2, 1873, 2. *Sunderland and Durham County Herald*, July 25, 1873, 5, and August 1, 1873, 7. *Christian*, February 19, 1874, 8.

24. Moody, *Life of Moody*, 165–166. Sankey, *My Life*, 57–58. *Christian*, September 18, 1873, 5. Morgan, *R. C. Morgan*, 174–175. *Newcastle Daily Chronicle*, August 25, 1873, 4, and August 29, 1873, 4.

25. *Newcastle Courant*, September 5, 1873, 3. *Newcastle Daily Chronicle*, September 12, 1873, 4.

26. J. Edwin Orr, *The Second Evangelical Awakening in Britain* (London: Marshall, Morgan and Scott, 1959), 31–42. E. R. Cotton, "The Effects of the Awakening in Scotland," *Times of Blessing* (Edinburgh), September 3, 1874, 322–323. "Religious News from England," *Christian Banner* (London) December 1, 1874, 25. Undated

clipping, "The Moody and Sankey Meetings," in "Moody in England," series 3 and 4, vol. 1, D. L. Moody Papers, Dolben Library, Northfield Campus, East Northfield, Massachusetts, box S-2.

27. Edwin Hodder, *The Life and Work of the Seventh Earl of Shaftesbury*, vol. 3 (London: Cassell, 1886), 353–358. *Newcastle Daily Chronicle*, September 24, 1873, 4. *Zion's Herald* (Boston), July 31, 1873, 244. William R. Moody, *D. L. Moody* (New York: Macmillan, 1930), 135–140. "Messrs. Moody and Sankey," *English Independent*, February 18, 1875, 177–178. "Messrs. Moody and Sankey," *Methodist*, April 9, 1875, in History, Moody, "English Revivals," Moody Papers, East Northfield, folder 4, Misc. Memorabilia.

28. Alfred W. W. Dale, *The Life of R. W. Dale of Birmingham* (London: Hodder and Stoughton, 1898), 315–317. George Kitson Clark, *The Making of Victorian England* (Cambridge: Harvard University Press, 1962), 180–186. Owen Chadwick, *The Victorian Church* (New York: Oxford University Press, 1970), 286–298.

29. *Christian*, June 26, 1873, 16. Morgan, *R. C. Morgan*, 175–177. Henry Varley, Jr., *Henry Varley's Life Story* (London: Alfred Holness, 1887), 103–121. *Zion's Herald* (Boston), July 31, 1873, 244. H. W. Clark, *A History of English Nonconformity*, vol. 2 (London: Chapman and Hall, 1913), 17–27.

30. *Christian*, September 18, 1873, 5–8. *Newcastle Daily Chronicle*, September 11, 1873, 3, and September 18, 1873, 4. Moody, *D. L. Moody*, 149–150.

31. *Newcastle Daily Chronicle*, September 18, 1873, 4; September 24, 1873, 4; and October 11, 1873, 3.

32. *Newcastle Daily Chronicle*, October 15, 1873, 3, and October 28, 1873, 3. Emma Moody, diary, September 25, 1873, Moody Papers, box 14, folder 2.

33. *Newcastle Daily Chronicle*, October 28, 1873, 4, and November 13, 1873, 3. *Christian*, October 23, 1873, 8, and October 30, 1873, 4.

34. Moody, *D. L. Moody*, 150–151. *Christian*, November 24, 1873, 4.

35. The British press borrowed heavily from Moody's self-representation. The account in the *London Daily News*, March 10, 1875, 3, is typical of the summaries that preceded Moody's arrival in cities scheduled for his crusade work.

36. *Carlisle Daily Journal*, November 18, 1873, 3. *Christian*, October 23, 1873, 8. Dwight L. Moody, *To All People: Comprising Sermons, Bible Readings, Temperance Addresses, and Prayer-meeting Talks, Delivered in the Boston Tabernacle* (New York: E. B. Treat, 1877), 181.

37. D. L. Moody, *New Sermons, Addresses and Prayers* (St. Louis: N. D. Thompson, 1877), 33–34. Moody, *To All People*, 181. D. L. Moody, *Thou Fool: And Eleven Other Sermons Never Before Published* (New York: Christian Herald, 1911), 78.

38. Stanley Gundry, *Love Them In: The Proclamation Theology of D. L. Moody* (Chicago: Moody Press, 1976), 80–81. Henry Drummond, "Mr. Moody: Some Impressions and Facts," *McClure's* (December 1894), 59–60. George Adam Smith, *The Life of Henry Drummond* (New York: Doubleday and McClure, 1898), 58–61.

39. *Carlisle Daily Journal*, November 18, 1873, 3; November 20, 1873, 2; and November 21, 1873, 4.

40. The *Carlisle Daily Journal*, November 19, 1873, 3, republished accounts of Moody's success at Newcastle. The *Daily Review* of Edinburgh reported news of Moody's work in Carlisle. The pattern was followed in the cities that followed. See also *Carlisle Daily Journal*, November 20, 1873, 2; November 21, 1873, 4; and November 22, 1873, 2.

41. Letter from Emma Moody to her mother, Moody Papers, November 5, 1873, box 8, folder 95. In the same folder see also letter from D. L. Moody to James H. Cole, November 8, 1873.

42. William G. Blaikie, *For the Work of the Ministry* (London: Strahan, 1873), 16–29. *Sunday Magazine* (Edinburgh), February 1, 1874, 5. Emma Moody, diary entry, November 22, 1873, Moody Papers, box 14, folder 2.

43. *Daily Review* (Edinburgh), November 24, 1873, 4. *Narrative of Messrs. Moody and Sankey's Labors in Great Britain and Ireland, with Eleven Addresses and Lectures in Full* (New York: Anson D. F. Randolph, 1875), citing the *British Evangelist* (London), December 8, 1873.

44. *Daily Review* (Edinburgh), December 15, 1873, 2. *Narrative*, 25, citing *British Evangelist* (London), January 13, 1874.

45. Moody, *D. L. Moody*, 168. Moody, *Life of Dwight L. Moody*, 205–206. *Christian*, December 4, 1873, 11. *Daily Review* (Edinburgh), December 10, 1873, 11. See the introduction by W. Robertson Nicoll to *Henry Drummond, The Ideal Life: Addresses Hereto Unpublished* (New York: Dodd and Mead, 1897).

46. *Christian*, December 11, 1873, 6, and January 29, 1874, 5, citing *Daily Review* editorial of earlier in the week.

47. *Christian*, December 18, 1873, 3, and February 12, 1874, 2, citing an editorial in Edinburgh's *Family Treasury* that appeared earlier in the week. *Daily Review* (Edinburgh), December 10, 1873, 7. Similar letters of support can be found in the *Edinburgh Evening News, Edinburgh Scottish Guardian,* and *Edinburgh Courant*.

48. *Narrative*, 31, citing the *British Evangelist* of January 8, 1874.

49. *Daily Review* (Edinburgh), January 3, 1874, 2, and January 7, 1874, 3. *Edinburgh Courant*, January 12, 1874, 4. *Edinburgh Evening News*, January 13, 1874, 2.

50. *Daily Review* (of Edinburgh), December 19, 1873, 2. *Christian*, February 5, 1874, 8. *Edinburgh Evening News*, January 13, 1874, 2. *Edinburgh Courant*, December 18, 1873, 2.

51. *Edinburgh Evening News*, December 22, 1873, 3. *Daily Review* (of Edinburgh), December 23, 1873, 2. *Edinburgh Courant*, January 5, 1874, 4. *Glasgow News*, February 10, 1874, 4. Emma Moody, diary entry, January 1, 1874, Moody Papers, box 14, folder 2. "Recollections of 1874," at page 8 by Mrs. Peter MacKinnon of Campbeltown, Scotland, Archives and Manuscripts, Yale Divinity School Library, group 28, series 1, box 5.

52. *Christian*, March 5, 1874, 3, and April 2, 1874, 6. *Glasgow Herald*, January 2, 1874, 3. *Daily Review* Edinburgh), January 9, 1874, 3. *North Briton Advertiser*, January 13, 1874, 3. *Portobello Advertiser*, January 15, 1874, 3.

53. *Glasgow News*, March 14, 1874, 4. *Christian*, March 19, 1874, 7. *London Daily Mail*, February 21, 1874, 5 and 6. *Glasgow Christian News*, February 28, 1874, 3. *Androssan and Saltcoats Herald*, May 23, 1874, 3. *Dundee Weekly News*, June 6, 1874, 1.

54. *Glasgow Herald*, March 26, 1874, 7; April 4, 1874, 6; and April 14, 1874, 3. Alastair Phillips, *Glasgow Herald, 1783–1983* (Glasgow: Richard Drew, 1983), 7–9 and 78–89. *Glasgow News*, March 3, 1874, 3 and March 10, 1874, 3. *Christian*, March 5, 1874, 5.

55. *Glasgow News*, February 21, 1874, 5 and 6. *Christian*, May 7, 1874, 6. Letter from Moody to Farwell, May 7, 1874, in Moody's Letters, vol. 1, 1854–1879, Moody Papers, Chicago.

56. Emma Moody, diary entries, January 1, 1874; July 12, 1874; and July 13, 1874, Moody Papers, box 14, folder 2. "Recollections of 1874," 1–5. *Daily Review* (Edinburgh), December 8, 1873, 3, and January 2, 1874, 2.

57. "Recollections of 1874," 10–12.

58. The controversy and mutiny within Moody's coordinating committee is described in *British Evangelist*, January 15, 1874, 3, and *Glasgow Christian News*, February 28, 1874, 5.

59. *Porcupine* (Liverpool), June 14, 1873, 4; *York Herald*, July 5, 1873, 8; *Sunderland and Durham County Herald*, August 22, 1873, 5; *Sunderland Times*, August 22, 1873, 5; *Edinburgh Scottish Guardian*, November 28, 1873, 437; and *Glasgow Christian News*, February 28, 1874, 3.

60. Moody, *Life of D. L. Moody*, 423–434.

61. Letter from Moody to John Farwell, November 14, 1874, Moody Letters, vol. 1, Moody Papers, Chicago. Moody, *My Father*, 111–114. *Christian*, July 16, 1874, 8–9, citing the *Huntly Express*.

62. *Evening Citizen* (Glasgow), February 7, 1874, 4. *Glasgow Evening Star*, February 14, 1874, 4. *Liverpool Mail*, February 20, 1875, 6. *Morning Post* (London), March 10, 1875, 6.

63. *Globe* (London), March 19, 1875, 3. *Daily Telegraph* (London), July 13, 1875, 6. Letter from Moody to John Farwell, March 14, 1874, Moody Letters, vol. 1, Moody Papers, Chicago.

64. *Christian*, May 28, 1874, 4–7. *Glasgow Daily Mail*, May 25, 1874, 2. *Glasgow Evening Star*, May 25, 1874, 3. *Evening Citizen* (Glasgow), May 25, 1874, 2. *North British Daily Mail*, May 25, 1874, 3.

65. See Moody's open letter to readers of the *Christian*, June 11, 1874, 6. A similar sentiment on the power and necessity of advertising meetings and their aftermath appears in a second of his letters, July 9, 1874, 6. W. G. Blaikie, writing in the *British and Foreign Evangelical Review*, observed that the religious movement stirred by Moody was "unprecedented in the history of Scotland." See *Christian*, July 23, 1874, 3–5, and September 3, 1874, 7.

66. Robert Peddie, *A Consecutive Narrative of the Remarkable Awakening in Edinburgh* (Edinburgh: Partridge, 1874), was followed by John Hall and George H. Stuart, *The American Evangelists D. L. Moody and Ira D. Sankey in Great Britain and Ireland* (New York: Dodd and Mead, 1875). Rufus Clark, *The Work of God in Great Britain: Under Messrs. Moody and Sankey, 1873 to 1875* (New York: Harper, 1875). E. J. Goodspeed, *A Full History of the Wonderful Career of Moody and Sankey, in Great Britain and America* (New York: Henry S. Goodspeed, 1876). Robert Boyd, *The Lives and Labors of Moody and Sankey* (Toronto: A. H. Hovey, 1876). Elias Nason, *The Lives of the Eminent American Evangelists Dwight Lyman Moody and Ira David Sankey* (Boston: B. B. Russell, 1877). W. H. Daniels, *Moody: His Words, Work, and Workers* (New York: Nelson and Philips, 1877).

67. See letter from Henry Drummond to Mrs. Peter MacKinnon, June 30, 1875, Moody Papers, box 8, folder 96. See also the publisher's preface in M. Laird Simons, *Holding the Fort: Comprising Sermons and Addresses at the Great Revival Meetings Conducted by Moody and Sankey* (Philadelphia: Porter and Coates, 1877), 2.

68. John MacPherson, *Revival and Revival-Work: A Record of the Labours of D. L. Moody and Ira D. Sankey* (London: Morgan and Scott, 1876), 43–44. *Daily Review* (Edinburgh), December 22, 1873, 2. *Christian*, January 1, 1874, 11.

69. "Recollections of 1874," 65–66. Moody, *D. L. Moody*, 207.

70. *Christian*, September 3, 1874, 7. *Belfast Morning News*, September 8, 1874, 2. *Belfast News-Letter*, September 8, 1874, 2.

71. *Christian*, September 17, 1874, 3, and September 24, 1874, 3. *Morning Post* (London), September 22, 1874, 5.

72. *Christian*, September 17, 1874, 17–18. *Belfast Morning News*, September 8, 1874, 2, and September 10, 1874, 2.

73. *Belfast News-Letter*, September 14, 1874, 2. *Northern Whig* (Belfast), September 18, 1874, 3. *Ulster Examiner and Northern Star*, September 19, 1874, 2.

74. *Belfast Weekly Telegraph*, September 24, 1874, 3. *Ulster Weekly News* (Belfast), September 24, 1874, 2. *Witness*, October 8, 1874, 2. *Christian*, September 24, 1874, 6–8.

75. *Belfast News-Letter*, October 9, 1874, 2. *Northern Whig* (Belfast), October 10, 1874, 3. *Dublin Nation*, October 24, 1874, 1.

76. *Witness*, October 8, 1874, 2. *Christian*, October 15, 1874, 12 and 13.

77. "Recollections of 1874," 120. Sankey, *My Life,* 73–74. The "Fair Play" editorial in the *Nation* is cited by Moody, *D. L. Moody*, 189. The *Freeman's Journal* is cited in the *Christian*, October 29, 1874, 8.

78. Letter from Moody to Farwell, November 14, 1874, Moody Letters, vol. 1, Moody Papers, Chicago.

79. *Daily Mail* (Dublin), November 14, 1874, 3. "Recollections of 1874," 91. *Christian*, November 5, 1874, 10–13.

80. Letter from D. L. Moody to W. Crosfield, March 31, 1875, Archives of the Billy Graham Center, Wheaton College, Wheaton, Illinois. Photocopied in Moody Letters, Moody Papers, Chicago. *Manchester Guardian*, November 30, 1874, 2. *Birmingham Daily Mail*, January 18, 1875, 2–3. *Liverpool Daily Post*, January 6, 1875, 5.

81. *Sheffield Post*, January 2, 1875, 4. *Manchester Courier*, December 7, 1874, 7. *Sheffield Daily Telegraph*, January 4, 1875, 4.

82. *Sheffield Post*, January 9, 1875, 4, and January 16, 1875, 7. *Sheffield Christian Messenger*, January 16, 1875, 3. *Sheffield Daily Telegraph*, January 4, 1875, 4, and January 16, 1875, 4. *Sheffield and Rotherham Independent*, January 16, 1875, 4.

83. *Liverpool Daily Post*, January 23, 1875, 5, and February 13, 1875, 5. *Liverpool Mail*, February 13, 1875, 13, and February 27, 1875, 6 and 7. *London Daily News*, March 8, 1875, 2. *Daily Telegraph* (London), June 25, 1875, 5.

84. *Christian*, December 3, 1874, 6. Letter from D. L. Moody to John Farwell, November 14, 1874, Moody Letters, Moody Papers, Chicago. *Record*, March 10, 1875, 1.

85. The publicity work of Moody's coordinating committee for London is outlined in Moody Papers, box 8, folder 96. Aspects of the campaign are also summarized by the London correspondent of the *North British Daily Mail* and the *London Christian World* in the days leading up to the campaign.

86. *Birmingham Daily Mail*, January 18, 1875, 2. *Sheffield Post*, January 23, 1875, 7.

87. *Birmingham Daily Mail*, January 18, 1875, 2, and January 25, 1875, 3. *Birmingham Gazette*, January 25, 1875, 3. *Birmingham Morning News*, January 25, 1875, 4. *Liverpool Daily Post*, February 8, 1875, 5.

88. *Daily Telegraph* (London), March 10, 1875, 5. *Times* (London), March 10, 1875, 3. *London Morning Post*, March 10, 1875, 6.

89. *London Daily News*, March 10, 1875, 3. *Christian*, December 3, 1874, 6. *Daily Telegraph* (London), March 10, 1875, 5. *Times* (London), March 10, 1875, 5.

90. *London Morning Post*, March 10, 1875, 6 *Record* (London), March 17, 1875, 2. *Globe* (London), March 19, 1875, 2. *Spectator* (London), March 19, 1875, 6. *Vanity Fair*, April 3, 1875, 3.

91. Letter from Queen Victoria to the countess of Gainsborough, April 27, 1875, cited in Moody, *D. L. Moody*, 212–213. *London Daily News*, March 16, 1875, 6. *Daily Telegraph* (London), March 12, 1875, 2. *Vanity Fair*, April 10, 1875, 3.

92. The popular impact of Moody and Sankey is chronicled in the Moody Papers, particularly in box 8 and folder 96. The doggerel is first cited in an undated issue of the *British Weekly* that can be found in that folder. Figurines of Moody and Sankey manufactured during the London campaign can be found in the Moody Papers, Chicago. The two men look distinguished but accessible to their working-class fans.

Further recollections of Moody's appeal to London's commoners are in the D. L. Moody Centenary Addresses given in Westminster Chapel on February 5, 1937 by John A. Hutton, editor of the *British Weekly*, and G. Campbell Morgan of Westminster Chapel, which are in the Moody Papers, box 16, folder 19.

93. Typical examples of these early compendiums of Moody's sermons are in Clark, *Work of God in Great Britain*, 375–430. The historic character of the London meetings is described in Hedley Morrish, "The Coming Moody Centenary," *British Weekly*, January 21, 1937, 391, and "The Moody Centenary," *Advance*, February 1, 1937, 65.

94. Dale's comments appear in "London Honours D. L. Moody: The Centenary Celebration, Albert Hall Speeches," Moody Papers, box 16, folder 16.

95. *Christian Standard* (London), June 25, 1875, 3. *London Daily News*, July 12, 1875, 2. *Daily Telegraph* (London), July 23, 1875, 3.

96. *London Daily Chronicle*, July 14, 1875, 4.

97. *Christian*, January 29, 1874, 3.

98. *Signs of Our Times*, March 17, 1875, 162–166. *Times of Blessing*, March 18, 1875, 3. For a discussion of the rise of the democratic marketplace and its impact on journalism, see Michael Schudson, *Discovering the News: A Social History of American Newspapers* (New York: Basic Books, 1978), chap. 1, "The Revolution in American Journalism." For evangelical enterprise in getting the gospel out, see David Paul Nord, "The Evangelical Origins of Mass Media in America," *Journalism Monographs* 88 (May 1984).

99. *Christian*, February 12, 1874, 7.

3. "SIDEWALKS AND ROOFTOPS ARE BLACK FOR BLOCKS AROUND"

1. *New York Herald*, August 15, 1875, 4. *Brooklyn Daily Eagle*, October 27, 1875, 3.

2. *New York Herald*, August 15, 1875, 4.

3. *New York Tribune*, August 14, 1875, 4, and August 16, 1875, 10. *New York Sun*, August 16, 1875, 1. *Brooklyn Daily Union*, August 14, 1875, 1.

4. *Brooklyn Daily Times*, August 14, 1875, 1. *Brooklyn Daily Union*, August 14, 1875, 2. *Brooklyn Sunday Sun*, August 15, 1875, 4.

5. *New York Times*, August 17, 1875, 4. *New York Herald*, September 12, 1875, 8.

6. For Finney's views on the importance of human agency in promoting revivals, see Charles G. Finney, *Lectures on Revivals of Religion* (Oberlin: E. J. Goodrich, 1868), 9–20, and Charles G. Finney, *Memoirs of Charles G. Finney* (New York: A. S. Barnes, 1876), 24–41.

For Jonathan Edwards's understanding of the role of God in initiating and sustaining religious revival, see Jonathan Edwards, *A Narrative of Surprising Conversions* (Lafayette, Ind.: Sovereign Grace, 1972); Iain H. Murray, *Jonathan Edwards: A New Biography* (Edinburgh: Banner of Truth Trust, 1987), 155–176; and Harry S. Stout, "The Puritans and Edwards," in Nathan O. Hatch and Harry S. Stout, eds., *Jonathan Edwards and the American Experience* (New York: Oxford University, 1988), 142–159.

George Whitefield saw preaching and publishing as ways of furthering God's work in reviving his church. See Frank Lambert, *"Pedlar in Divinity": George Whitefield and the Transatlantic Revivals, 1737–1770* (Princeton: Princeton University Press, 1994), 95–133, and Michael J. Crawford, *Seasons of Grace: Colonial New England's Revival Tradition in Its British Context* (New York: Oxford University, 1991), 183–195.

7. Charles G. Finney, *A Sermon Preached in the Presbyterian Church at Troy, March 4, 1827, from Acts 3:3—Can Two Walk Together Except They Be Agreed?* (Philadelphia: Geddes, 1827), 11–19. Finney, *Lectures*, 35–47. Finney, *Memoirs*, 411–417. See also Calvin Colton, *History and Character of American Revivals of Religion* (London: Westley and Davis, 1832), 165–188, and Whitney R. Cross, *The Burned-over District: The Social and Intellectual History of Enthusiastic Religion in Western New York, 1800–1850* (Ithaca, N.Y.: Cornell University Press, 1950), 198–208.

8. Edward S. Griffin, *A Letter to the Rev. Ansel D. Eddy on the Narrative of the Late Revivals of Religion in the Presbytery of Geneva* (Williamstown, Mass.: Ridley Bannister, 1832), 4–14, and Gamaliel S. Olds, *Review of a Narrative by Rev. John Keep* (Syracuse, N.Y.: Smith, 1833), 16–27.

9. *New York Herald*, August 16, 1875, 4. *New York Sun*, August 19, 1875, 2. *New York Evening Post*, October 8, 1875, 2.

10. *New York Herald*, September 19, 1875, 8.

11. *Greenfield* (Massachusetts) *Recorder and Gazette*, September 4, 1875, 1. *New York Herald*, September 5, 1875, 8; September 6, 1875, 3; September 11, 1875, 4; and September 12, 1875, 6.

12. The recollections of D. W. Whittle, Moody Papers, box 8, folder 95.

13. The development of Moody's plans for evangelizing America can be seen in the open letter from D. L. Moody to members of his Chicago church, July 12, 1875, from London, Moody Letters, Moodyanna Collection, Moody Bible Institute, Chicago. See also William R. Moody, *The Life of Dwight L. Moody* (New York: Fleming H. Revell, 1900), 263, and interview with Ira Sankey, *New York Tribune*, August 16, 1875, 10.

14. *New York Tribune*, October 8, 1875, 4. *New York Herald*, October 8, 1875, 3.

15. *New York Tribune*, October 11, 1875, 1.

16. *Brooklyn Daily Times*, October 11, 1875, 2. *Brooklyn Daily Eagle*, October 12, 1875, 2.

17. *Brooklyn Daily Eagle*, October 14, 1875, 2. *New York Graphic*, October 9, 1875, 2.

18. *Brooklyn Daily Times*, October 12, 1875, 2. *New York Herald*, October 11, 1875, 4.

19. *New York Herald*, October 13, 1875, 5.

20. Daniel Denton, *A Brief Description of New York, Formerly Called New Amsterdam* (London: Printed for John Hancock at the First Ship in Popes-Head-Alley in Cornhil at the Three Bibles, 1670). Stephen M. Ostrander, *A History of the City of Brooklyn and Kings County*, vol. 1 (Brooklyn: Published by Subscription, 1894), 4–15. Harrington Putnam, *Origins of Breuckelen* (New York: G. Putnam's, 1898), 17–24.

21. Samuel Purchas, *Henry Hudson's Voyages* (Ann Arbor: University of Michigan Microforms, 1966), 24–43. Henry Cruse Murphy, *Henry Hudson in Holland* (New York: Franklin, 1972), 111–135. James Maurice Scott, *Hudson of Hudson's Bay* (Bath, England: Chivers, 1973), 156–173.

22. Jaspar Dankars and Peter Sluyter, *Journal of Our Voyage to the New Netherland* (London: British Historical Society, 1949; originally 1679), 17–21. Benjamin Thompson, *History of Long Island from Its Discovery and Settlement to the Present Time*, vol. 1 (Port Washington, N.Y.: Friedman, 1962; originally 1839), 23–37. Alice Kenney, *Stubborn for Liberty: The Dutch in New York* (Syracuse, N.Y.: Syracuse University Press, 1975), 34–45.

23. Victor H. Cooper, *A Dangerous Woman* (Bowie, Md.: Heritage Books, 1995), 143–156. Linda Biemer, "Lady Deborah Moody and the Founding of Gravesend," *Journal of Long Island History* 17 (spring 1981), 24–42. Peter R. Christoph, ed., *The Leisler Papers, 1689–1691: Files of the Provincial Secretary of New York Relating to the Administration of Lieutenant-Governor Jacob Leisler* (Syracuse, N.Y.: Syracuse University Press, 1999), 47–63.

24. Clarence Taylor, *The Black Churches of Brooklyn* (New York: Columbia University Press, 1994), 7–10. Daniel Ment, *The Shaping of a City: A Brief History of Brooklyn* (New York: Brooklyn Educational and Cultural Alliance, 1979), 21–22. Jacob Judd, "Brooklyn's Changing Population in the Pre–Civil War Era," *Journal of Long Island History* 4 (spring 1964), 9–18.

25. Henry R. Stiles, *A History of the City of Brooklyn, Including the Old Town and Village of Brooklyn, the Town of Bushwick, and the Village and City of Williamsburgh*, vol. 1 (Brooklyn: Published by Subscription, 1867), 242–273 and 359–376. Ellen M. Snyder-Grenier, *Brooklyn! An Illustrated History* (Philadelphia: Temple University Press, 1996), 25–27.

26. Will Anderson, *The Breweries of Brooklyn: An Informal History of a Great Industry in a Great City* (Croton Falls, N.Y.: Published by the author, 1976), 17–20. Ira Rosenwaike, *Population History of New York City* (Syracuse, N.Y.: Syracuse University Press, 1972), 27–39.

27. Margaret Marsh, *Suburban Lives* (New Brunswick: Rutgers University Press, 1990), 3–8. Robert Fishman, *Bourgeois Utopias: The Rise and Fall of Suburbia* (New York: Basic Books, 1987) 118–125. Henry Binford, *The First Suburbs* (Chicago: University of Chicago Press, 1985), 176–181.

28. Nathaniel Prime, *A History of Long Island from Its Settlement by Europeans to the Year 1845* (New York: Carter, 1845), 377–379. J. T. Bailey, *An Historical Sketch of the City Brooklyn* (Brooklyn: Published by the Author, 1840), 31–35. Marc Linder and Lawrence S. Zacharias, *Of Cabbages and Kings County: Agriculture and the Formation of Modern Brooklyn* (Iowa City: University of Iowa Press, 1999), 112–115.

29. *Kings County Rural Gazette*, June 15, 1872, 1; February 22, 1873, 1; and July 26, 1873, 1. *Brooklyn Daily Eagle, Consolidation No. 22* (Brooklyn: Brooklyn Daily Eagle, 1898), 45–48.

30. James Fenimore Cooper, *Notions of the Americans Picked Up by a Traveling Bachelor*, vol. 1 (Philadelphia: Carey, Lea and Carey, 1828), 124–125. Charles Dickens, *American Notes* (London: Nelson, 1842), 128–129.

31. Whitman's work as town booster can be seen in his editorial "The Future of Brooklyn," *Brooklyn Daily Times*, July 14, 1858, which appears in Emory Holloway and Vernolian Schwarz, eds., *I Sit and Look Out: Editorials from the Brooklyn Daily Times* (New York: Columbia University Press, 1932), 146–147. Gertrude Lefferts Vanderbilt, *The Social History of Flatbush, and Manners and Customs of the Dutch Settlers in Kings County* (Brooklyn: Loeser, 1909; originally 1880), 269–272 and 301–303.

32. John K. Sharp, *History of the Diocese of Brooklyn, 1853–1953*, vol. 1 (New York: Fordham University Press, 1953), 89–90. Golda G. Strander, "Jesuit Educational Institutions in the City of New York, 1683–1860," *Historical Records and Studies* 24 (1934), 215–216.

33. George A. Little, *Brendan the Navigator* (Dublin: Gill, 1946), 12–25. Sandy Dengler, *The Emerald Sea: The Quest of Brendan the Navigator* (Chicago: Moody Press, 1994), 15–18. John H. Kennedy, *Thomas Dongan, Governor of New York, 1682–1688* (New York: AMS Press, 1974; originally 1930), 111–122.

34. David Bent, Anthony Robins, and David Framberger, *Building Blocks of Brooklyn: A Study of Urban Growth* (Brooklyn: Brooklyn Educational and Cultural Alliance, 1979), 33–36. Harold Coffin Syrett, *The City of Brooklyn, 1865–1898: A Political History* (New York: AMS Press, 1968; originally 1944), 9–14.

35. Henry W. B. Howard, ed., *The Eagle and Brooklyn* (Brooklyn: Brooklyn Daily Eagle, 1893), 97–98. *Brooklyn Daily Eagle*, October 25, 1875, 2. Henry R. Stiles, *A History of the City of Brooklyn*, vol. 3 (Brooklyn: Published by Subscription, 1870), 584–586. J. H. and C. M. Goodsell, *The City of Brooklyn* (Brooklyn: J. H. and C. M. Goodsell, 1871), 27–31.

36. Raymond A. Schroth, *The Eagle and Brooklyn: A Community Newspaper, 1841–1855* (Westport, Conn.: Greenwood Press, 1974), 103–105. *New York Sun*, September 3, 1835, 1. Ulf Jonas Bjork, "The Moon Hoax, The *New York Sun* Stuns Readers with Discovery of Lunar Life," in William David Sloan and James D. Startt, eds., *The Media in America: A History* (Northport, Ala.: Vision Press, 1999), 126–127.

37. Martin H. Weyrauch, ed., *The Pictorial History of Brooklyn Issued by the Brooklyn Daily Eagle on Its Seventy-Fifth Anniversary, October 26, 1916* (Brooklyn: Brooklyn Daily Eagle, 1916), 16–17. William E. Robinson, "The History of the Press of Brooklyn and Kings County," in Henry R. Stiles, ed., *The Civil, Political, Professional History and Commercial and Industrial Record of the County of Kings and the City of Brooklyn, New York, from 1683 to 1884*, vol. 2 (New York: W. W. Munsell, 1884), 1181–1183.

38. Thomas L. Brasher, *Whitman as Editor of the Brooklyn Daily Eagle* (Detroit: Wayne State University Press, 1970), 17–20. *Brooklyn Daily Eagle*, February 27, 1846, 1, and January 6, 1848, 2.

39. *Brooklyn Daily Eagle*, June 1, 1846, 2; September 29, 1846, 2; and May 10, 1847, 1.

40. *Brooklyn Daily Eagle*, April 27, 1846, 2, and November 22, 1846, 2. Brasher,

Whitman as Editor, 11–14. Justin Kaplan, *Walt Whitman: A Life* (New York: Simon and Schuster, 1980), 74–89.

41. *Brooklyn Daily Eagle,* July 19, 1848, 2. Schroth, *The Eagle and Brooklyn,* 92–95. Regina Morantz-Sanchez, *Conduct Unbecoming a Woman: Medicine on Trial in Turn-of-the-Century Brooklyn* (New York: Oxford University Press, 1999), 13–16. Brasher, *Whitman as Editor,* 18–19.

42. *Brooklyn Daily Eagle,* August 1, 1846, 3; September 30, 1846, 2, and May 3, 1847, 4. Weyrauch, *Pictorial History of Brooklyn,* 18–19.

43. Schroth, *The Eagle and Brooklyn,* 104–107. Howard, *The Eagle and Brooklyn,* 92–94. Stiles, *History and Record,* vol. 2, 218–219. Syrett, *City of Brooklyn,* 18–19.

44. *Brooklyn Daily Union,* November 10, 1869, 1; October 23, 1871, 1; October 4, 1873, 2; and July 1, 1875, 1. *Brooklyn Daily Eagle,* November 11, 1871, 2; March 5, 1872, 2, and September 15, 1873, 1. *Brooklyn Daily Times,* October 5, 1873, 1. Syrett, *City of Brooklyn,* 71–76.

45. *Brooklyn Daily Union,* October 12, 1875, 2, and October 27, 1875, 2

46. Stiles, *History and Record,* 1177–1178. See also "Family Tree" of Brooklyn newspapers and their histories, Newspapers Section, Brooklyn Public Library.

47. *Brooklyn Daily Times,* May 10, 1869, 2; January 6, 1870, 1; October 23, 1871, 2. Syrett, *City of Brooklyn,* 22–23.

48. *Brooklyn Daily Times,* March 21, 1875, 1; October 18, 1875, 3; and October 23, 1875, 1.

49. Stephen M. Griswold, *Sixty Years with Plymouth Church* (New York: Revell, 1907), 25–29. Brooklyn Trust Co., *Historic Brooklyn* (Brooklyn: Brooklyn Trust Co., 1941), 49–50. David W. McCullough, *Brooklyn and How It Got That Way* (New York: Dial Press, 1983), 247–249.

50. Paxton Hibben, *Henry Ward Beecher: An American Portrait* (New York: Doran, 1927), 12–34. James H. Callender, *Yesterdays on Brooklyn Heights* (New York: Dorland Press, 1927), 145–150. Richard Dwight Hillis, "Henry Ward Beecher," in *A Church in History* (Brooklyn: Plymouth Church of the Pilgrims, 1949), 41–58.

51. Altina L. Walter, *Reverend Beecher and Mrs. Tilton: Sex and Class in Victorian America* (Amherst: University of Massachusetts Press, 1982), 7–11. Clifford E. Clark, Jr., *Henry Ward Beecher: Spokesman for Middle-Class America* (Urbana: University of Illinois Press, 1978), 221–225. Robert Shaplen, *Free Love and Heavenly Sinners* (New York: Knopf, 1954), 35–41.

52. *Brooklyn Daily Eagle,* November 6, 1875, 2. *Brooklyn Daily Times,* October 13, 1875, 1, and October 26, 1875, 2. Charles F. Marshall, *The True History of the Brooklyn Scandal* (Philadelphia: National, 1874), 23–32. Richard Wightman Fox, *Trials of Intimacy: Love and Loss in the Beecher-Tilton Scandal* (Chicago: University of Chicago Press, 1999), 3–10.

53. J.E.P. Doyle, *Plymouth Church and Its Pastor* (St. Louis: Bryan, Brand, 1875), 53–70 and 275–279. Marshall, *True History,* 42–43 and 93–100. John Henry Barrows, *Henry Ward Beecher: The Shakespeare of the Pulpit* (New York: Funk and Wagnalls, 1893), 127–135. A. McElroy Wylie, "Mr. Beecher as a Social Force," *Scribner's* 4 (October 1872), 754.

54. *Brooklyn Daily Eagle,* August 1, 1874, 1. *Brooklyn Daily Times,* August 16, 1875, 2. Henry Bowen, *The Great Brooklyn Romance* (New York: J. H. Paxon, 1874), 94–99. *Chicago Tribune,* October 1, 1874, 1. *Nation,* September 24, 1874, 201.

55. Richard S. Storrs, *The Church of the Pilgrims, Brooklyn, New York* (New York: A. S. Barnes, 1886), 123–145. Richard S. Storrs, *The Divine Origin of Christianity Indicated by Its Historical Effects* (New York: A.D.F. Randolph, 1884), 42–53. William C. Beecher and Samuel Scoville, *A Biography of Rev. Henry Ward Beecher* (New York: Charles Webster, 1888), 543–546. William G. McLoughlin, *The Meaning of Henry Ward Beecher* (New York: Knopf, 1970), 24–27.

56. *Brooklyn Daily* Eagle, January 9, 1871, 1. Henry Ward Beecher, *Autobiographical Reminiscences* (New York: Frederick A. Stokes, 1898), 23–28. Joseph Howard, Jr., *The Life of Henry Ward Beecher* (Philadelphia: Edgewood, 1887), 585–589. Milton Rugoff, *The Beechers: An American Family in the Nineteenth Century* (New York: Harper and Row, 1981), 113–122.

57. *New York Sun*, October 9, 1875, 2. *New York Herald*, October 24, 1875, 1. *New York Tribune*, October 9, 1875, 2, and October 11, 1875, 1.

58. *Brooklyn Daily* Times, October 19, 1875, 1. New York Sun, October 9, 1875, 2. *New York Evening Post*, October 8, 1875, 2.

59. *New York Tribune*, October 23, 1875, 1. *New York Herald*, October 23, 1875, 1.

60. *New York Herald*, October 18, 1875, 3. *Brooklyn Daily Times*, October 15, 1875, 4, and October 16, 1875, 2.

61. *New York Evening Post*, October 8, 1875, 2. *New York Tribune*, October 23, 1875, 2.

62. *New York Herald*, October 25, 1875, 1. *New York Sun*, October 25, 1875, 1.

63. *New York Sun*, October 23, 1875, 1. Letter from G. W. Smith to William R. Moody, 1922, Moody Papers, box 8, folder 96.

64. *New York Herald*, October 25, 1875, 1. *New York Tribune*, October 25, 1875, 2. *New York Sun*, October 25, 1875, 1.

65. *New York Evening Post*, October 25, 1875, 2. *New York Herald*, October 25, 1875, 2. *Brooklyn Daily Eagle*, October 23, 1875, 2. *Brooklyn Daily Times*, October 23, 1875, 1.

66. *New York Daily Graphic*, October 25, 1875, 1. *Brooklyn Daily Times*, October 25, 1875, 1. *Brooklyn Sunday Sun*, October 24, 1875, 4.

67. *New York Tribune*, October 25, 1875, 1. *New York Herald*, October 25, 1875, 1. *New York Evening Mail*, October 25, 1875, 1.

68. *New York Herald*, October 25, 1875, 1. *Brooklyn Daily Times*, October 25, 1875, 1. *New York Sun*, October 25, 1875, 1 and 2.

69. *Brooklyn Daily Times*, October 25, 1875, 1 and 2. *New York Daily Graphic*, October 25, 1875, 1. *New York Herald*. October 25, 1875, 1 and 2.

70. *Brooklyn Daily Eagle*, October 25, 1875, 2. *Brooklyn Daily Times*, October 25, 1875, 2, and October 26, 1875, 1.

71. *Brooklyn Daily Eagle*, October 27, 1875, 2 *Brooklyn Daily Times*, October 28, 1875, 2, and October 30, 1875, 2.

72. *Long Island Democrat*, November 2, 1875, 1. *Long-Islander* (Huntington, L.I.), November 5, 1875, 2. *Kings County Rural Gazette* (Flatbush), November 6, 1875, 1.

73. *Brooklyn Daily Eagle*, October 11, 1875, 1. *New York Herald*, October 30, 1875, 1. *Brooklyn Daily Times*, October 29, 1875, 1.

74. *New York Sun*, October 30, 1875, 1, and November 2, 1875, 1. *New York Evening Post*, November 4, 1875, 1. *Brooklyn Daily Times,* November 4, 1875, 1.

New York Tribune, November 6, 1875, 1. *Brooklyn Daily Eagle*, November 6, 1875, 1.

75. *Brooklyn Daily Eagle*, November 12, 1875, 3. *Brooklyn Daily Times*, November 12, 1875, 1. *New York Graphic*, November 12, 1875, 2. *New York Evening Post*, November 11, 1875, 2.

76. *Brooklyn Daily Eagle*, October 28, 1875, 1, and November 18, 1875, 1. *Brooklyn Daily Times*, November 13, 1875, 1. *New York Herald*, November 13, 1875, 1.

77. *New York Sun*, November 20, 1875, 1. *New York Herald*, November 20, 1875, 3.

78. *Brooklyn Daily Eagle*, November 17, 1875, 1, and November 18, 1875, 1. *Brooklyn Daily Times*, November 17, 1875, 1, and November 20, 1875, 2.

79. *Brooklyn Daily Eagle*, November 11, 1875, 1. *Brooklyn Sunday Sun*, November 14, 1875, 1. *New York Tribune*, November 23, 1875, 2.

80. *Brooklyn Daily Eagle*, November 18, 1875, 1. *New York Herald*, November 15, 1875, 2.

81. *Brooklyn Sunday Sun*, November 21, 1875, 2.

4. "IT'S HARDER GETTING INTO THE DEPOT THAN HEAVEN"

1. *Philadelphia Times*, January 12, 1876, 4.

2. Carey Kinsolving, "The Preacher and the Printer: An Evaluation of Benjamin Franklin's Coverage of George Whitefield," paper presented at the annual meeting of the Association for Education in Journalism and Mass Communication, Kansas City, Missouri, August 12, 1993.

3. Thomas Scharf and Thompson Westcott, *History of Philadelphia, 1609–1884* (Philadelphia: L. H. Evarts, 1884), vol. 1, 840, and vol. 3, 1961. *Philadelphia Inquirer*, November 22, 1875, 4. *Philadelphia Evening Bulletin*, November 20, 1875, 4. *Philadelphia Daily Press*, November 24, 1875, 6.

4. *North American and U.S. Gazette*, November 29, 1875, 1. *Philadelphia Sunday Dispatch*, December 19, 1875, 1.

5. Henry Adams Gibbons, *John Wanamaker*, vol. 1 (New York: Harper, 1926), 133–140. See also "Rules for the Ushers of the Religious Meetings at Thirteenth and Market Streets, Philadelphia, Commencing Nov. 21st, 1875," in History, Moody, Evangelism, Revivals Philadelphia Revival, Moody Papers, East Northfield, file 14.

6. *Philadelphia Times*, November 26, 1875, 1.

7. *Philadelphia Inquirer*, February 26, 1916, 4. *Philadelphia Public Ledger*, February 27, 1916, 3, and February 28, 1916, 4. *Philadelphia Record*, February 28, 1916, 2.

8. Mark H. Haller, "Recurring Themes," in Allen F. Davis and Mark H. Haller, eds., *The Peoples of Philadelphia: A History of Ethnic Groups and Lower-Class Life, 1790–1940* (Philadelphia: Temple University Press, 1973), 282–283.

9. Charles F. Warwick, *Warwick's Keystone Commonwealth* (Philadelphia: Warwick, 1913), 284–285. Nicholas B. Wainwright, ed., *A Philadelphia Perspective* (Philadelphia: Historical Society of Pennsylvania, 1967), 201–204. Sam Bass Warner, Jr., *The Private City: Philadelphia in Three Periods of Its Growth* (Philadelphia: University of Pennsylvania Press, 1968), 59–62 and 99–109.

10. Thompson Westcott, *The Official Guidebook to Philadelphia* (Philadelphia: Porter and Coates, 1875), 46 and 261. Caroline Golab, "The Immigrant and the City:

Poles, Italians and Jews in Philadelphia, 1870–1920," in Davis and Haller, *Peoples of Philadelphia,* 203–206.

11. Ellis Paxson Oberholtzer, *Philadelphia: A History of the City and Its People,* vol. 3 (Philadelphia: S. J. Clarke, 1911), 303–305, and David R. Johnson, "Crime Patterns in Philadelphia," in Davis and Haller, *Peoples of Philadelphia,* 89–101.

12. Nicholas B. Wainwright, *History of the Philadelphia National Bank: A Century and a Half of Philadelphia Banking, 1803–1953* (Philadelphia: Philadelphia National Bank, 1953), 128–129. *Philadelphia Public Ledger,* September 18, 1873, 1. *Philadelphia Sunday Dispatch,* November 21, 1875, 1 and 2. Warner, *Private City,* 65–67.

13. Frank B. Evans, *Pennsylvania Politics, 1872–1877* (Harrisburg: Pennsylvania Historical and Museum Commission, 1966), 13–16 and 234–243. Clinton R. Woodruff, "The Progress of Municipal Reform in Philadelphia," *Harper's* 38 (1894), 1019. J. T. Salter, *Boss Rule: Portraits in City Politics* (New York: McGraw-Hill, 1935), 17–21.

14. George Vickers, *The Fall of Bossism,* vol. 1 (Philadelphia: A. C. Bryson, 1883), 60–70. Edward P. Allison and Boies Penrose, *Philadelphia, 1681–1887* (Philadelphia: Allen, Lane and Scott, 1887), 189–206.

15. A letter from the Office of the Executive Committee for the Gospel Meetings to Philadelphia's Ministers, November 17, 1875, Philadelphia Revival, Moody Papers, East Northfield.

16. "A Revival in Frogtown," *Catholic World* 22 (1876), 699–707.

17. Dennis Clark, *The Irish in Philadelphia* (Philadelphia: Temple University Press, 1973), 65–84. Dorothy Ditter Gandos, "The Cultural Climate of the Centennial City: Philadelphia, 1875–1876," Ph.D. diss., University of Pennsylvania, 1947, 6–12.

18. *North American and U.S. Gazette,* November 29, 1875, 1.

19. Charles Morris, ed., *Makers of Philadelphia* (Philadelphia: L. R. Hamersly, 1894), 166. Harry R. Whitcraft, "Fifty Years of Journalism in Philadelphia," *Beehive* 25 (July 1934), 1 and 4. *North American and U.S. Gazette,* November 23, 1875, 1, and December 9, 1875, 1.

20. Eugene H. Munday, "Collins and M'Leester's Proof Sheet: The Press of Philadelphia, 1870–1871," in "Notes and References Relating to the History of Philadelphia Newspapers," arranged by John M. Heim for the Free Library of Philadelphia in 1937, 65–69, in Scharf and Westcott, *History of Philadelphia,* 3:1970–1972.

21. *North American and U.S. Gazette,* November 22, 1875, 1; December 2, 1875, 1; and December 9, 1875, 1.

22. *Philadelphia Sunday Dispatch,* November 28, 1875, 2.

23. Scharf and Westcott, *History of Philadelphia,* 3:2020. "Report of the State Librarian—Annotated Catalogue of Newspapers in the Pennsylvania State Library, 1927: *Sunday Dispatch,*" 6, Free Library, Philadelphia.

24. Munday, "Collins and M'Leester's Proof Sheet," 37–42.

25. *Philadelphia Sunday Dispatch,* December 5, 1875, 1.

26. *Philadelphia Sunday Dispatch,* December 19, 1875, 1, January 9, 1876, 2, and January 23, 1876, 2.

27. *Philadelphia Public Ledger,* December 18, 1875, 2.

28. George W. Childs, *Recollections* (Philadelphia: J. B. Lippincott, 1890), 9–17, and Morris, *Makers of Philadelphia,* 93.

29. Richard T. Ely, "Mr. Childs and the Workingman," in Childs, *Recollections,* 325–328. Benson J. Lossing, *The American Centenary* (Philadelphia: Porter, 1876), 495–500.

30. *Philadelphia Times,* December 13, 1875, 4, and December 20, 1875, 2. *Philadelphia Public Ledger,* December 20, 1875, 2. *Philadelphia Daily Press,* December 20, 1875, 6.

31. Scharf and Westcott, *History of Philadelphia,* 1:834 and 2:1488. Childs, *Recollections,* 51. George H. Stuart, *The Life of George H. Stuart* (Philadelphia: J. M. Stoddart, 1890), 239–240.

32. *Philadelphia Public Ledger,* November 20, 1875, 1, and January 1, 1876, 2.

33. "Report of the State Librarian—Annotated Catalogue of Newspaper Files in the Pennsylvania State Library, 1900, *The Times,*" Free Library, Philadelphia. See also Morris, *Makers of Philadelphia,* 150.

34. *Philadelphia Times,* November 20, 1875, 1 and 2, and November 22, 1875, 1 and 2.

35. *Philadelphia Times,* November 23, 1875, 2; December 4, 1875, 2; and January 17, 1876, 2.

36. Davis's novel *A Stranded Ship: A Story of Sea and Shore* (New York: G. P. Putnam, 1869) would go through several editions. He would also write for *Harper's,* the *Atlantic,* the *Century, Scribner's, Lippincott's,* and *Putnam's.* His son, Richard Harding Davis, would be the mostly highly paid and widely read journalist of the Gilded Age. See Morris, *Makers of Philadelphia,* 170, and Richard J. Beamish, "Brief History of the *Philadelphia Inquirer,*" supplement to the *Philadelphia Inquirer,* June 1, 1929.

37. *Philadelphia Inquirer,* November 22, 1875, 4.

38. Scharf and Westcott, *History of Philadelphia,* 3:2016–2018. "*Daily Evening Bulletin,*" entry in the Newspaper Files, State Historical Society of Wisconsin, compiled by Ada Tyng Griswold, Madison, Wisconsin.

39. "Report of the State Librarian—Annotated Catalogue of Newspaper Files in the Pennsylvania State Library, 1900, *Evening Bulletin.*" See also Munday, "Collins and M'Leester's Proof Sheet," 21–24.

40. *Philadelphia Evening Bulletin,* November 20, 1875, 4 and 6, and December 11, 1875, 4.

41. See Scharf and Westcott, *History of Philadelphia,* 3:2026, and Morris, *Makers of Philadelphia,* 162.

42. Munday, "Collins and M'Leester's Proof Sheet," 74.

43. *Philadelphia Daily Press,* December 27, 1875, 8.

44. *Forney's Weekly Press,* December 11, 1875, 6.

45. *Philadelphia Evening Telegraph,* November 20, 1875, 4, and November 22, 1875, 1.

46. *Philadelphia Public Record,* October 14, 1872, 2, and November 22, 1875, 2.

47. John Hall and George H. Stuart, *The American Evangelists D. L. Moody and Ira D. Sankey in Great Britain and Ireland* (New York: Dodd and Mead, 1875), 8.

48. *Philadelphia Sunday Dispatch,* November 21, 1875, 2, November 28, 1875, 2 and December 5, 1875, 1.

49. Stuart, *Life of George H. Stuart,* 272.

50. Letter from George H. Stuart, chairman of the Christian Commission, September 15, 1862, to commission members, Papers of the U.S. Christian Commission,

YMCA Archives, University of Minnesota Library, St. Paul, Minnesota, box 1, folder 13. See also Centennial Brochure of the U.S. Christian Commission, Army and Navy File Copy, YMCA Archives, box 1, folder 4.

51. Stuart, *Life of George H. Stuart,* 19–22 and 73–82.

52. *The Verdict of Time* (Philadelphia: Association Press, 1905), 11–22. Laurence L. Doggett, *History of the Young Men's Christian Organization* (New York: Association Press, 1922), 16–25. C. Howard Hopkins, *History of the Y.M.C.A. in North America* (New York: Association Press, 1951), 4–8 and 42–43.

53. Marion L. Bell, *Crusade in the City: Revivalism in Nineteenth-Century Philadelphia* (Lewisburg, Penn.: Bucknell University Press, 1977), 178–184. Hopkins, *History of the Y.M.C.A. in North America,* 44–45. Morris, *Makers of Philadelphia,* 119.

54. *Proceedings of the Fifth Annual Convention of the YMCAs of the United States and British Provinces* (New York: Executive Committee, 1860), 9–15, YMCA Archives, University of Minnesota.

55. John H. Appel, *The Business Biography of John Wanamaker* (New York: Macmillan, 1930), 22–24, and John Wanamaker, *Maxims of Life and Business* (New York: Harper, 1923), 108–109.

56. Bell, *Crusade in the City,* 187–188. Stuart, *Life of George H. Stuart,* 105–113. Talbot W. Chambers, *The Noon Prayer Meeting of the North Dutch Church, Fulton Street, New York* (New York: Board of Publication of the Reformed Protestant Dutch Church, 1858), 45–52 and 83–91. Richard C. Morse, *History of the North American YMCAs* (New York: Association Press, 1918), 16–23.

57. Victor Rosewater, *History of Cooperative News-Gathering in the United States* (New York: Appleton-Century-Crofts, 1930), 67–73. Oliver Gramling, *A.P.: The Story of News* (New York: Holt, Rinehart and Winston, 1940), 33–44.

58. The advertisement, the first for a Wanamaker store, appears in *Philadelphia Public Ledger,* April 27, 1861, 3. Stuart urged Wanamaker to reconsider. See Appel, *Biography of John Wanamaker,* 39–42.

59. "United States Christian Commission for the Army and Navy for the Year 1862," first annual report, Philadelphia, April 1863, 7–22, YMCA Archives, University of Minnesota. Lemuel Moss, *Annals of the United States Christian Commission* (Philadelphia: J. B. Lippincott, 1868), 94–113.

60. Stuart, *Life of George H. Stuart,* 134 and 272. See also "United States Christian Commission for the Army and Navy for the Year 1865," fourth annual report, Philadelphia, March 1866, 38–40, and Rev. W. E. Boardman, "Christ in the Army: A Selection of Sketches of the Work of the U.S. Christian Commission, Produced for the Ladies Christian Commission, 1865," 33–39, YMCA Archives, University of Minnesota.

61. Stuart assured Wanamaker: "I care nothing about his grammar, so long as he brings sinners to Christ." See Stuart, *Life of George H. Stuart,* 272–273. Gibbons, *John Wanamaker,* 2:133–134.

62. Moody's financial plight is described in letters he wrote on November 24, 1871, and March 20, 1872, in Moody Letters, Moody Papers, Chicago.

63. See letter from Moody to his Chicago church, July 12, 1875, advising that Stuart would be distributing $20,000 from the sale of hymnals to pay off the remaining debt of Moody's Chicago church. Moody Letters, Moody Papers, Chicago.

64. Thomas K. Cree, "Mr. Moody as an Evangelist," Biographical Papers of Thomas K. Cree, YMCA Archives, University of Minnesota, 6–7. See also Stuart, *Life of George H. Stuart,* 275–277, and Appel, *Biography of John Wanamaker,* 74–77.

65. Gibbons, *John Wanamaker,* 135. Cree, "Mr. Moody as an Evangelist," 8–9.

66. Letter from the Committee on Music to Philadelphia area ministers, November 4, 1875, Philadelphia Revival, Moody Papers, East Northfield.

67. "Circular," undated, to "the members of Messrs. Moody and Sankey's Choir," Philadelphia Revival, Moody Papers, East Northfield. See also Gibbons, *John Wanamaker,* 136–137.

68. Cree, "Mr. Moody as an Evangelist," 8.

69. *Philadelphia Times,* November 22, 1875, 1–2.

70. Letter from the Ministerial Committee for the Gospel Meetings to Philadelphia Area Ministers, November 17, 1875, Philadelphia Revival, Moody Papers, East Northfield.

71. Cree, "Mr. Moody as an Evangelist," 9–10.

72. Dwight L. Moody, *To All People: Comprising Sermons, Bible Readings, Temperance Addresses, and Prayer-meeting Talks, Delivered in the Boston Tabernacle* (New York: E. B. Treat, 1877), 181. D. L. Moody, *Thou Fool: And Eleven Other Sermons Never Before Published* (New York: Christian Herald, 1911), 78.

73. Wanamaker's comment appears in *Advertising World,* September 15, 1897, 1. See also Gibbons, *John Wanamaker,* 2:14–16, and Henry R. Boss, *A Brief History of Advertising* (Chicago: Frederick Weston, 1888), 22–26.

74. Morris, *Makers of Philadelphia,* 55 and 78. Childs, *Recollections,* 15–16.

75. The anecdote appears in Gibbons, *John Wanamaker,* 135–136. See also Appel, *Biography of John Wanamaker,* 39–55, and Wanamaker, *Maxims of Life and Business,* 55–57.

76. See Moody's letters to Wanamaker, November 5, 1877, and January 9, 1878, in Moody Papers, Chicago. See also Gibbons, *John Wanamaker,* 133.

77. *Philadelphia North American and U.S. Gazette,* November 27, 1875, 1.

78. *Philadelphia Inquirer,* November 27, 1875, 2.

79. *Philadelphia Evening Bulletin,* November 29, 1875, 8.

80. *Philadelphia Daily Press,* November 25, 1875, 8.

81. *Philadelphia Daily Press,* November 26, 1875, 8.

82. *Philadelphia Evening Bulletin,* November 24, 1875, 4 and 8, and November 29, 1875, 8.

83. Letters from Thomas K. Cree, secretary of the executive committee, December 1, 1875, and January 19, 1876, to members of the press, Philadelphia Revival, Moody Papers, East Northfield.

84. Letter from Cree to Philadelphia newspaper editors, January 3, 1876, Philadelphia Revival, Moody Papers, East Northfield.

85. Cree, "Mr. Moody as an Evangelist," 12–13.

86. *Forney's Weekly Press,* December 4, 1875, 4, and December 11, 1875, 6.

87. *Philadelphia Public Ledger,* December 18, 1875, 2.

88. Childs, *Recollections,* 90–109.

89. Stuart's account also contains the claim that one justice of the Supreme Court was "converted" to Christ that night through the earnest prayer of a faithful wife. See Stuart, *Life of George H. Stuart,* 279–280.

90. *Philadelphia Evening Bulletin*, December 20, 1875, 8. *Philadelphia Daily Press*, December 20, 1875, 6. *Philadelphia Times*, December 20, 1875, 4.

91. *Philadelphia Public Ledger*, December 15, 1875, 1, and January 12, 1875, 1. *Philadelphia Inquirer*, December 2, 1875, 2, and December 3, 1875, 3. *Philadelphia Evening Bulletin*, December 10, 1875, 1.

92. *Philadelphia Daily* Press, November 29, 1875, 6. *Philadelphia Evening Bulletin*, December 15, 1875, 8.

93. *Philadelphia Sunday Dispatch*, December 19, 1875, 1; January 9, 1876, 1; and January 23, 1876, 2.

94. *North American and U.S. Gazette*, November 29, 1875, 1.

95. *Philadelphia Evening Telegraph,* December 1, 1875, 5. *Philadelphia Public Record,* December 25, 1875, 2. *Frank Leslie's Illustrated Newspaper*, February 19, 1876, 390.

96. *Philadelphia Sunday Dispatch*, December 19, 1875, 1 and 2; December 26, 1875, 1 and 2; and January 9, 1876, 1.

97. Cree, "Mr. Moody as an Evangelist," 12–13. *Philadelphia Evening Bulletin*, November 22, 1875, 1, and December 7, 1875, 1. *Philadelphia Daily Press*, January 7, 1876, 5. *Philadelphia Times*, December 5, 1875, 2.

98. William E. B. DuBois, *The Philadelphia Negro* (New York: Benjamin Bloom, 1899), 41–45. E. Franklin Frazier, *The Negro Church in America* (New York: Schocken, 1964), 24–39 and 133–147. Bell, *Crusade in the City*, 126–136.

99. "The Church and the Poor," *Nation*, November 18, 1875, 321–322.

100. "A Revival in Frogtown," 707.

101. *North American and U.S. Gazette*, January 17, 1876, 1.

102. *Philadelphia Inquirer*, January 18, 1876, 2, and January 21, 1876, 3.

103. *Philadelphia Daily Press*, January 11, 1876, 6.

104. *Philadelphia Daily Press*, January 5, 1876, 5.

105. *Philadelphia Evening Telegraph*, January 14, 1876, 8.

106. *Philadelphia Times*, January 21, 1876, 1.

107. Cree, "Mr. Moody as an Evangelist," 17–18 and 27–29.

108. Lefferts A. Loetscher, "Presbyterianism and Revivals in Philadelphia," *Pennsylvania Magazine of History and Biography* 69 (1944), 63–66.

109. Stuart, *Life of George H. Stuart,* 286–287.

110. Cree, "Mr. Moody as an Evangelist," 11–12 and 19–20.

111. Letter from D. L. Moody to John Wanamaker, November 5, 1877, Moody Papers, Chicago.

112. Appel, *Biography of John Wanamaker,* 92–95. Gibbons, *John Wanamaker,* 141–143.

113. Wanamaker, "Bringing Business Efficiency into Christian Service," is an undated article that first appeared in the *Sunday School Times*, John Wanamaker File, Moodyanna Collection, Moody Bible Institute, Chicago.

114. *Philadelphia Press*, January 2, 1900, 1.

115. Wanamaker's letter to the Moody Bible Institute, January 7, 1920, details Moody's plans to evangelize America's great cities, starting with Philadelphia, in the new century; Wanamaker File, Moodyanna Collection, Moody Bible Institute, Chicago.

116. *Philadelphia Public Ledger*, January 9, 1900, 1.

117. *Philadelphia Public Ledger*, January 12, 1900, 1.

118. Loetscher, "Presbyterianism and Revivals in Philadelphia," 67–69. Dorothy

Gondos Beers, "The Centennial City, 1865–1876," in Russell F. Weigley, ed., *Philadelphia: A Three-Hundred-Year History* (New York: Norton, 1982), 444–446. Bell, *Crusade in the City,* 242–245.

119. *Philadelphia Evening Bulletin,* November 23, 1875, 8.

120. *Philadelphia Inquirer,* December 27, 1875, 3.

121. *Philadelphia Public Ledger,* January 1, 1876, 2.

122. *Philadelphia Evening Bulletin,* December 24, 1875, 4.

123. *Philadelphia Daily Press,* November 22, 1875, 1.

124. *North American and U.S. Gazette,* December 31, 1875, 1, and January 17, 1876, 1.

125. *Forney's Weekly Press,* January 22, 1876, 1.

5. "THE GREATEST SHOW ON EARTH"

1. Compare the cover plate of the March 11, 1876, *Harper's* to the advertisement *Harper's* carried in its March 29, 1873, issue featuring Barnum rising from the ocean waters to lead his "animal curiosities" to safety and celebration. See also P. T. Barnum, *Barnum's Own Story: The Autobiography of P. T. Barnum* (Gloucester, Mass.: Smith, 1972), 445.

2. Phineas T. Barnum, *The Life of P. T. Barnum, Written by Himself* (Urbana: University of Illinois Press, 2000; originally 1855), 13–16, 44–49, 179–180, and 214–215. Phineas T. Barnum, *Here Comes Barnum* (New York: Harcourt, Brace, 1932), 22–32. Catherine M. Andronik, *Prince of Humbug: A Life of P. T. Barnum* (New York: Atheneum, 1994), 19–24.

3. Neil Harris, *Humbug: The Art of P. T. Barnum* (Boston: Little, Brown, 1973), 23–25. Barnum, *Life of P. T. Barnum,* 394–395. Felix Sutton, *Master of Ballyhoo: The Story of P. T. Barnum* (New York: Putnam, 1968), 69–71 and 159–161.

4. See letter from William E. Dodge to Farmer Hall, January 9, 1876, Moody Papers, box 8, folder 97.

5. Barnum, *Life of P. T. Barnum,* 129 and 396. George W. Haines, *Players and Playgoers* (New York: Bruce, Haines, 1874), 80–83. Bluford Adams, *E. Pluribus Barnum: The Great Showman and the Making of U.S. Popular Culture* (Minneapolis: University of Minnesota Press, 1997), 164–168.

6. *New York Sun,* February 25, 1836, 1. *New York Herald,* February 27, 1836, 1 and 2. Barnum, *Barnum's Own Story,* 148–154. Irving Wallace, *The Fabulous Showman: The Life and Times of P. T. Barnum* (New York: Knopf, 1959), 112–125.

7. Robert Boyd, *The Lives and Labors of Moody and Sankey* (Toronto: A. H. Hovey, 1876), 244–246.

8. *New York Times,* April 25, 1874, 7; April 28, 1874, 5; and July 8, 1874, 4.

9. *P. T. Barnum's Roman Hippodrome Advance Courier* (Buffalo: Courier, 1875), 1–3. *New York Times,* November 24, 1874, 4, and December 24, 1874, 4.

10. *New York Herald,* April 28, 1874, 9. *New York Tribune,* November 2, 1874, 12. *New York Times,* July 8, 1874, 4, and November 5, 1874, 4. Adams, *E. Pluribus Barnum,* 184–192.

11. *New York Times,* December 2, 1875, 4. Harris, *Humbug,* 256–258.

12. A. H. Saxon, *P. T. Barnum: The Legend and the Man* (New York: Columbia University Press, 1989), 359–371. Philip B. Kunhardt, *P. T. Barnum: America's Greatest Showman* (New York: Knopf, 1995), 288–302. Joseph G. Vitale, *There's a Customer*

Born Every Minute: Barnum's Secrets to Business Success (New York: AMACOM, 1998), 183–188.

13. *New York Tribune*, February 5, 1876, 1 and 2. *New York Evening Mail*, February 6, 1876, 1. *New York Sun*, February 8, 1876, 1 and 2.

14. *Frank Leslie's Illustrated Newspaper*, January 20, 1877, 329. *Harper's January*, 20, 1877, 41. Wheaton Joshua Lane, *Commodore Vanderbilt: An Epic of the Steam Age* (New York: Knopf, 1942), 321–336. *Woodhull and Claflin's Weekly*, November 2, 1872, 1 and 2. Arlene Kisner, *Woodhull and Claflin's Weekly: The Lives and Writings of the Notorious Victoria Woodhull and Her Sister Tennessee Claflin* (Washington, N.J.: Time Change Press, 1972). 11–21. Emanie Sachs Arling, *The Terrible Siren* (New York: Arno Press, 1972; originally 1928), 143–161.

15. Nast's caricature of Woodhull urging supporters to "be saved by free love" appears in *Harper's,* February 17, 1872, 140. See also Lois Beachy Underhill, *The Woman Who Ran for President: The Many Lives of Victoria Woodhull* (New York: Penguin Books, 1996), 273–288, and Barbara Goldsmith, *Other Powers: The Age of Suffrage, Spiritualism and the Scandalous Victoria Woodhull* (New York: Knopf, 1998), 323–339.

16. Bouck White, *The Book of Daniel Drew* (New York: Doubleday, Page, 1910), 323–327. Clifford Browder, *The Money Game in Old New York* (Lexington: University of Kentucky Press, 1986), 115–129. Jones Willoughby, *James Fiske, Jr.: The Life of a Green Mountain Boy* (Philadelphia: W. Flint, 1872), 33–39. *New York Times*, January 8, 1872, 1. *New York Tribune*, January 11, 1872, 1.

17. Matthew Josephson, *The Robber Barons: The Great American Capitalists, 1861–1901* (New York: Harcourt, Brace, 1934), 167–173. Allan Nevins, *The Emergence of Modern America, 1865–1878* (New York: Macmillan, 1927), 291–301. *New York Herald*, September 19, 1873, 1. *New York Tribune*, September 22, 1873, 1.

18. Horace White, "The Financial Crisis in America," *Fortnightly Review* 25 (1876), 810–820. Dumas Malone and Basil Rauch, *The New Nation, 1865–1917* (New York: Appleton-Century-Crofts, 1960), 29–40.

19. Washington Irving, *A History of New York from the Beginning of the World to the End of the Dutch Dynasty* (New York: AMS Press, 1973; originally 1809), 53–67. Maud W. Goodwin, *Dutch and English on the Hudson* (New Haven: Yale University Press, 1919), 116–123. William Smith, Jr., *The History of the Province of New-York* (Cambridge: Belknap Press, 1972), vol. 1, 165–177.

20. Hendrick Van Loon, *Life and Times of Peter Stuyvesant* (New York: Holt, 1928), 134–156. David M. Ellis, *A Short History of New York State* (Ithaca, N.Y.: Cornell University Press, 1957), 13–25. Shaun O'Connell, *Remarkable, Unspeakable New York: A Literary History* (Boston: Beacon Press, 1995), 12–16.

21. Michael Kammen, *Colonial New York: A History* (New York: Oxford University Press, 1975), 32–35. Oliver A. Rink, *Holland on the Hudson* (Ithaca, N.Y.: Cornell University Press, 1986), 139–152. Ellis H. Roberts, *New York: The Planting and Growth of the Empire State* (Boston: Houghton Mifflin, 1915; originally 1887), vol. 1, 36–51.

22. Bayrd Still, *Mirror for Gotham* (New York: New York University Press, 1956), 15–25. Joyce D. Goodfriend, *Before the Melting Pot: Society and Culture in Colonial New York City, 1664–1730* (Princeton: Princeton University Press, 1992), 46–60.

23. Edwin G. Burrows and Mike Wallace, *Gotham: A History of New York City to 1898* (New York: Oxford University Press, 1999), 157–158. Frank Lambert,

" 'Pedlar in Divinity': George Whitefield and the Great Awakening, 1737–1745," *Journal of American History* 77 (1990), 815–828.

24. Joel Tyler Headley, *The Great Riots of New York, 1712 to 1873* (New York: Dover, 1971; originally 1873), 27–45, Daniel Horsmanden, *A Journal of the Proceedings in the Detection of the Conspiracy Formed by Some White People, in Conjunction with Negro and Other Slaves for Burning the City of New-York in America, and Murdering the Inhabitants* (Boston: Beacon Press, 1971; originally 1744), 323–355.

25. Milton Klein, "The Cultural Tyros of Colonial New York," *South Atlantic Quarterly* 66 (1967), 218–232. T. H. Breen, "An Empire of Goods: The Anglicization of Colonial America, 1690–1776," *Journal of British Studies* 25 (1986), 476–489. Gary B. Nash, "Urban Wealth and Poverty in Pre-Revolutionary America," *Journal of Interdisciplinary History* 6 (1976), 554–570.

26. John E. Crowley, *The Privileges of Independence: Neomercantilism and the American Revolution* (Baltimore: Johns Hopkins University Press, 1993), 167–188. Bernard Mason, "Adjustment to a War Economy: Entrepreneurial Activity in New York during the Revolution," *Business History Review* 40 (1966), 190–212.

27. Evan Cornog, *The Birth of Empire: De Witt Clinton and the American Experience, 1769–1828* (New York: Oxford University Press, 1998), 158–172. Paul Gilje, *The Road to Mobocracy: Popular Disorder in New York City, 1763–1834* (Chapel Hill: University of North Carolina Press, 1987), 254–267. Charles H. Livermore, "The Rise of Metropolitan Journalism, 1800–1840," *American Historical Review* 6 (1900–1901), 446–454.

28. Talbot W. Chambers, *The Noon Prayer Meeting of the North Dutch Church, Fulton Street, New York* (New York: Board of Publication of the Reformed Protestant Dutch Church, 1858), 39–45. Samuel Irenaeus Prime, *The Power of Prayer, Illustrated in the Wonderful Display of Divine Grace at Fulton Street and Other Meetings* (New York: n.p., 1859), 32–43. *New York Herald*, February 27, 1857, 1, and March 3, 1857, 1. *New York Tribune*, April 7, 1857, 1, and April 12, 1857, 1.

29. William C. Conant, *Narratives of Remarkable Conversions and Revival Incidents, Including a Review of Revivals* (New York: Derby and Jackson, 1858), 357–367 and 440–441. James Waddell Alexander, *The Revival and Its Lessons* (New York: A.D.F. Randolph, 1858), 6–9.

30. Edwin G. Burrows and Mike Wallace, *Gotham: A History of New York City to 1898* (New York: Oxford University Press, 1999), 860–868. Philip S. Foner, *Business and Slavery: The New York Merchants and the Irrepressible Conflict* (Chapel Hill: University of North Carolina Press, 1941), 77–93.

31. Joseph George, Jr., " 'A Catholic Family Newspaper' Views the Lincoln Administration: John Mullaly's Copperhead Weekly," *Civil War History* 24 (spring 1978), 112–121. Howard R. Marraro, "Lincoln Italian Volunteers from New York," *New York History* 24 (winter 1943), 56–65.

32. Adrian Cook, *The Armies of the Streets: The New York City Draft Riots of 1863* (Lexington: University Press of Kentucky, 1974), 115–136. Iver Bernstein, *The New York City Draft Riots* (New York: Oxford University Press, 1990), 259–264. Ernest A. McKay, *The Civil War and New York City* (Syracuse, N.Y.: Syracuse University Press, 1990), 195–215. *New York Tribune*, July 17, 1863, 1. *New York Times*, July 17, 1863, 1.

33. *New York Times*, March 8, 1876, 1. Denis Tilden Lynch, *"Boss" Tweed: The Story of a Grim Generation* (New York: Arno Press, 1974; originally 1927), 337–353.

James K. McGuire, *The Democratic Party of the State of New York* (New York: United States History, 1905), 177–201.

34. Gustavus Myers, *The History of Tammany Hall* (New York: Boni and Liveright, 1917), 233–241. Morris Robert Werner, *Tammany Hall* (New York: Greenwood Press, 1928), 176–189. Jerome Mushkat, *The Reconstruction of the New York Democracy, 1861–1874* (Rutherford, N.J.: Fairleigh Dickinson University Press, 1981), 222–245.

35. Glyndon G. Van Deusen, *Thurlow Weed: Wizard of the Lobby* (New York: Da Capo Press, 1969; originally 1947), 112–128. Nevins, *Emergence of Modern America,* 182–183. Alexander C. Flick, *Samuel Jones Tilden* (New York: Dodd, Mead, 1939), 204–210.

36. *New York Times,* March 8, 1876, 1, and March 9, 1876, 2. Ellis P. Oberholtzer, *History of the United States,* vol. 2 (New York: Macmillan, 1918), 585–589. Frank Michael O'Brien, *The Story of the Sun* (New York: Doran, 1918), 270–275.

37. James Parton, "Falsehood in the Daily Press," *Harper's* (July 1874), 274–275. Ted Curtis Smythe, "The Press and Industrial America, 1865–1883," in William David Sloan and James D. Startt, eds., *The Media in America: A History* (Northport, Ala.: Vision Press, 1999), 211–212.

38. Francis Brown, *Raymond of the Times* (New York: Norton, 1951), 321–335. Augustus Maverick, *Henry J. Raymond and the New York Press* (New York: Arno Press, 1970; originally 1870), 455–478.

39. *New York Times,* September 20, 1870, 4; July 8, 1871, 4; July 12, 1871, 4; and July 13, 1871, 4. Elmer Davis, *The History of the New York Times* (New York: New York Times, 1921), 23–41. Meyer Berger, *The Story of the New York Times, 1851–1951* (New York: Simon and Schuster, 1951), 35–53.

40. Syd Hoff, *Boss Tweed and the Man Who Drew Him* (New York: Coward, McCann and Geohegan, 1978), 22–33. Albert B. Paine, *Thomas Nast: His Period and His Pictures* (Gloucester, Mass.: Smith, 1967; originally New York: 1904), 15–23. *Harper's,* September 23, 1871, 889, and October 7, 1871, 940.

41. Charles Wingate, "Episode in Municipal Government," *North American Review* (July 1875), 150. John Foord, *The Life and Public Service of Andrew Haswell Green* (Garden City, N.J.: Doubleday, 1913), 91–96.

42. *New York Tribune,* February 19, 1876, 1. *New York Herald,* March 3, 1876, 1. *New York Times,* March 4, 1876, 1 and 4, and March 9, 1876, 5. *New York Sun,* March 5, 1876, 1, and March 6, 1876, 1. See also William S. McFeely, *Grant: A Biography* (New York: Norton, 1981), 400–418. William B. Hesseltine, *Ulysses S. Grant, Politician* (New York: Dodd, Mead, 1935), 351–357.

43. *New York Times,* April 2, 1876, 6. *New York Sun,* February 9, 1876, 2, and February 10, 1876, 2.

44. *New York Tribune,* January 14, 1874, 1. *New York Sun,* January 15, 1874, 1. *New York Evening Mail,* January 15, 1874, 1.

45. O'Connell, *Remarkable, Unspeakable New York,* 34–37. Ann L. Buttenwieser, *Manhattan Water-Bound* (Syracuse, N.Y.: Syracuse University Press, 1999), 66–71. Anthony Jackson, *A Place Called Home: A History of Low-Income Housing in Manhattan* (Cambridge: MIT Press, 1976), 16–21.

46. Charles E. Rosenberg, *The Cholera Years: The United States in 1832, 1849 and 1866* (Chicago: University of Chicago Press, 1952), 47–63. Robert W. DeForest and Lawrence Veiller, eds., *The Tenement House Problem* (New York: Arno Press, 1970: originally 1923), 88–93. Buttenwieser, *Manhattan Water-Bound,* 67–69.

47. The letter from Alvah Wiswall, Master of St. John's Guild, appears in *New York Times*, March 4, 1876, 8. See also Louise L. Stevenson, *The Victorian Homefront: American Thought and Culture, 1860–1880* (New York: Twayne, 1991), xxiii–xxvi, and Arthur Meier Schlesinger, *The Rise of the City, 1878–1898* (New York: Macmillan, 1933), 83–84.

48. *New York Times*, April 1, 1876, 4. *New York Sun*, February 20, 1876, 2.

49. *New York Times*, March 15, 1876, 4, and March 27, 1876, 8. *New York Evening Post*, February 7, 1876, 2. *New York Tribune*, March 20, 1876, 2.

50. *New York Times*, March 6, 1876, 1. *New York Herald*, February 25, 1876, 1. *New York Evening Mail*, April 1, 1876, 1.

51. *New York Tribune*, February 8, 1876, 1. *New York Evening Mail*, February 8, 1876, 1. *New York Herald*, February 8, 1876, 1.

52. John Bigelow, *The Life of Samuel J. Tilden* (New York: Harper, 1895), 153–174. *Harper's*, February 17, 1877, 132. Paul L. Haworth, *The Hayes-Tilden Disputed Presidential Election of 1876* (Indianapolis: Bobbs-Merrill, 1927; originally 1906), 283–303. Thurlow Weed, *Life of Thurlow Weed* (New York: Da Capo Press, 1970; originally 1884), 227–235 and 278–291.

53. Moody's relationship to Weed is described in William R. Moody, *The Life of Dwight L. Moody* (New York: Fleming H. Revell, 1900), 283–284. See also *New York Tribune*, March 8, 1876, 1; *New York Times*, March 11, 1876, 2, and March 14, 1876, 4; and *New York Sun*, April 20, 1876, 2.

54. *New York Tribune*, February 8, 1876, 1. *New York Evening Mail*, February 8, 1876, 1.

55. *New York Herald*, February 6, 1876, 1. *New York Sun*, February 8, 1876, 2.

56. *New York Tribune*, February 8, 1876, 1 and 5. *New York Times*, February 8, 1876, 1. *New York Evening Post*, February 8, 1876, 3, and February 9, 1876, 2.

57. *New York Times*, February 8, 1876, 5. *New York Herald*, February 8, 1876, 1.

58. *New York Sun*, February 8, 1876, 3. *New York Evening Post*, February 8, 1876, 1.

59. Boyd, *Moody and Sankey*, 245. *Independent*, February 10, 1876, 16.

60. *New York Evening Mail*, February 8, 1876, 3. For auction details, see Miscellaneous Revival Memorabilia, Moody Papers, East Northfield, folder 1.

61. *New York Tribune*, February 9, 1876, 1 and 2. See also the paper's preface to *Glad Tidings, Comprising Sermons and Prayer-Meeting Talks, Delivered at the N.Y. Hippodrome* (New York: E. B. Treat, 1876).

62. *Christian Advocate* (Methodist), April 27, 1876, 133. See also William E. Dodge's letter to Farmer Hall, March 3, 1876, Moody Papers, box 8, folder 97. *New York Witness Extra*, February 14, 1876, 1. Boyd, *Moody and Sankey*, 245.

63. Whitelaw Reid, *Horace Greeley* (New York: Scribner's, 1879), 16–24. Whitelaw Reid, *The Cipher Dispatches* (New York: New York Tribune, 1879), 33–44. John R. Commons, "Horace Greeley and the Working-Class Origins of the Republican Party," *Political Science Quarterly* 24 (September 1909), 472–473.

64. Royal Cortissoz, *The Life of Whitelaw Reid* (New York: Scribner's, 1921), 131–147. Bingham Duncan, *Whitelaw Reid: Journalist, Politician, Diplomat* (Athens: University of Georgia Press, 1975), 265–283. Reid's anticipation of New York's religious revival can be found in the *New York Tribune's* prospectus for 1876, Newspaper Collections, New York Public Library.

65. *New York Tribune*, February 7, 1876, 1; February 8, 1876, 1, and February

10, 1876, 1. Whitelaw Reid, *Some Newspaper Tendencies* (New York: Holt, 1879), 66–74.

66. Charles J. Rosebault, *When Dana Was the Sun* (Freeport, N.Y.: Books for Libraries, 1931), 157–161. Frank M. O'Brien, *The Story of the Sun* (New York: Appleton-Century-Crofts, 1928; originally 1918), 145–151. Candace Stone, *Dana and the Sun* (New York: Dodd, Mead, 1938), 163–169.

67. Charles Dana, *The Art of Newspaper Making* (New York: D. Appleton, 1900), 83–88; Janet E. Steele, *The Sun Shines for All* (Syracuse, N.Y.: Syracuse University Press, 1993), 91–111; and Edward P. Mitchell, "The Newspaperman's Newspaper," *Scribner's* 76 (August 1924), 149–150. See also *New York Sun*, February 8, 1876, 2; February 10, 1876, 2; and February 13, 1876, 2.

68. *New York Sun*, February 20, 1876, 4.

69. Don C. Seitz, *The James Gordon Bennetts: Father and Son* (New York: Bobbs-Merrill, 1928), 348–356. Richard O'Connor, *The Scandalous Mr. Bennett* (New York: Doubleday, 1962), 179–194. The *Herald's* high opinion of its own significance is found in *New York Herald*, February 20, 1876, 6.

70. *New York Herald*, February 6, 1876, 4 and 6.

71. *New York Times* prospectus for 1876, Newspaper Section, New York Public Library. See also Davis, *History of the New York Times,* 232–254, and Berger, *Story of the New York Times,* 137–154. *New York Times*, February 12, 1876, 4, and April 2, 1876, 6.

72. Thurlow Weed Barnes and Harriet Weed, eds., *Life of Thurlow Weed*, vol. 2 (Boston: Houghton Mifflin, 1884), 276–282. Glyndon G. Van Deusen, *Thurlow Weed* (Boston: Little, Brown, 1947), 102–110 and 355–365. The movement toward independent, unaffiliated newspapers is analyzed in Rutenbeck, 361–375; Jana Hyde, "The Industrial Press, 1865–1883: Professional Journalism or Pawn of Urbanism?" in William David Sloan, ed., *Perspectives on Mass Communication History* (Hillsdale, N.J.: Erlbaum, 1991), 186–198; Gerald J. Baldasty, "The Media and the National Economy, 1880–1900," in James D. Startt and William David Sloan, eds., *The Significance of the Media in American History* (Northport, Ala.: Vision Press, 1994), 165–181; Ted Curtis Smythe, "The Advertisers' War to Verify Newspaper Circulation, 1870–1914," *American Journalism* 3 (1986), 167–180; and Emily Erickson Hoff, "The Press and a New America, 1865–1900," in William David Sloan, ed., *The Age of Mass Communication* (Northport, Ala.: Vision Press, 1998), 233–250..

73. *New York Sun*, March 10, 1876, 3.

74. Moody, *Life of Dwight L. Moody,* 284. *New York Sun*, February 28, 1876, 1. *New York Times,* March 11, 1876, 8.

75. *New York Evening Post*, February 16, 1876, 1. *New York Sun*, February 10, 1876, 1; February 28, 1876, 1; and March 26, 1876, 1. *New York Tribune*, February 10, 1876, 1. *New York Times*, March 14, 1876, 6. *New York Herald*, February 9, 1876, 6.

76. *New York Tribune*, March 9, 1876, 2, and March 11, 1876, 1. *New York Times*, March 11, 1876, 8. *New York Sun*, March 12, 1876, 1.

77. *New York Tribune*, February 18, 1876, 2; March 11, 1876, 1; and March 16, 1876, 4.

78. *New York Tribune*, March 11, 1876, 1, and April 13, 1876, 2. *New York Times*, March 14, 1876, 6.

79. *New York Tribune*, March 11, 1876, 1. *New York Times*, March 11, 1876, 8.

80. *New York Tribune*, March 11, 1876, 2, and March 13, 1876, 2. *New York Herald*, March 10, 1876, 8.

81. *New York Herald*, March 10, 1876, 8. *New York Times*, March 11, 1876, 8. *New York Tribune*, March 11, 1876, 2. *New York Sun*, March 12, 1876, 1.

82. *New York Sun*, April 19, 1876, 2.

83. *New York Herald*, April 20, 1876, 4. *New York Times*, March 14, 1876, 6, and March 25, 1876, 4.

84. *New York Herald*, March 12, 1876, 7; March 16, 1876, 3 and 4; and April 23, 1876, 10.

85. *New York Tribune*, February 7, 1876, 1; February 8, 1876, 1; and February 11, 1876, 2.

86. *New York Tribune*, February 19, 1876, 2; February 28, 1876, 2; and March 3, 1876, 2.

87. *New York Tribune*, March 27, 1876, 2; April 14, 1876, 2; and April 19, 1876, 3.

88. *New York Sun*, April 19, 1876, 2. *Sunday School Times*, April 8, 1876, 235. *Frank Leslie's Illustrated Newspaper*, March 4, 1876, 5. *Harper's*, March 11, 1876, 12–13. *New York Witness Extra*, February 28, 1876, 1. *New York Evening Post*, April 19, 1876, 2.

6. "FROM THE CURBSTONE TO THE ASHPIT, THE FIX IS IN"

1. *Chicago Tribune*, January 13, 1869, 4, and January 14, 1869, 4.

2. *Chicago Tribune*, January 8, 1869, 1, and October 2, 1876, 1 and 2. Frederick Francis Cook, *Bygone Days in Chicago* (Chicago: Clurg, 1910), 305–311.

3. Melville E. Stone, *Fifty Years a Journalist* (New York: Greenwood, 1968; originally 1921), 71–72. *Chicago Tribune*, October 20, 1876, 3. Elias Nason, *The Lives of the Eminent American Evangelists Dwight L. Moody and Ira D. Sankey* (Boston: B. B. Russell, 1877), 183–184.

4. Letter from John V. Farwell to Dwight L. Moody, April 24, 1876, in John V. Farwell, *Early Recollections of Dwight L. Moody* (Chicago: Winona, 1907), 158–159.

5. *Chicago Times*, November 26, 1876, 8. *Chicago Tribune*, January 12, 1869, 4, and June 27, 1870, 1.

6. *Chicago Times*, October 1, 1876, 1, and December 17, 1876, 8.

7. *Chicago Tribune*, October 24, 1876, 7. The *Chicago Inter-Ocean's* bound volume of Moody's sermons in Chicago appeared under the title *Great Joy, Comprising Sermons and Prayer-Meeting Talks, Delivered at the Chicago Tabernacle by D. L. Moody* (New York: E. B. Treat, 1877).

8. Lloyd Wendt, *Chicago Tribune: The Rise of a Great American Newspaper* (Chicago: Rand McNally, 1979), 39–42; John Moses and Maj. Joseph Kirkland, *The History of Chicago* (Chicago: Munsell, 1895), 196; and A. N. Waterman, *Historical Review of Chicago and Cook County*, vol. 1 (Chicago: Lewis, 1908), 123–126.

9. William Bross, "History of the Chicago Tribune," in Rufus Blanchard, *Discovery and Conquests of the North-west, with the History of Chicago* (Wheaton, Ill.: R. Blanchard, 1881), 452–54; Henry H. Hurlbut, *Chicago Antiquities* (Chicago: Fergus, 1881), 601–611; and James McCague, *When Chicago Was Young* (Champaign, Ill.: Garrard, 1971), 17–22.

10. Philip Kinsley, *The Chicago Tribune: Its First Hundred Years*, vol. 2 (Chicago: Chicago Tribune, 1945), 97–111, and Paul Gilbert and Charles Lee Bryson, *Chicago and Its Makers* (Chicago: Mendelsohn, 1929), 857.

11. *Christ in the Army* (New York: Ladies Christian Commission, 1865), 33–39 and 125–126. YMCA Archives, YMCA. See also Frank Smith, *Facts and Figures* (Toledo: Spear, Johnson, 1884), 92–101; *U.S. Christian Commission for the Army and Navy for the Year 1865, Fourth Annual Report* (Philadelphia: YMCA, 1866), 18–23 and 38–40; and "The Army Christian Commission during the Civil War, 1861–1865," undated document, 1–6.

12. Thomas K. Cree, "Mr. Moody as an Evangelist," YMCA Archives, undated document, 1–5; *Proceedings of the Thirteenth Annual Convention of the YMCA of the U.S. and British Provinces* (New York: Executive Committee, 1868), 70 and 84, YMCA Archives; *Proceedings of the Fourteenth Annual Convention of the YMCA of the U.S. and British Provinces* (New York: Executive Committee, 1869), 32, 44, and 70; *Proceedings of the Fifteenth Annual Convention of the YMCA of the United States and British Provinces* (New York: Executive Committee, 1870), 107–108; Emmett Dedmon, *Great Enterprises: One Hundred Years of the YMCA in Metropolitan Chicago* (New York: Rand McNally, 1957), 82–84; C. Howard Hopkins, *History of the Y.M.C.A. in North America* (New York: Association Press, 1951), 137–141; and *Chicago Tribune*, March 2, 1873, 4.

13. *Everybody's Paper* 9, 2 (1877), 6; *Advance* (Chicago), September 7, 1876, 8; and Richard K. Curtis, *They Called Him Mister Moody* (Garden City, N.Y.: Doubleday, 1962), 309–311.

14. John V. Farwell, *Some Recollections of John V. Farwell* (Chicago: Donnelley, 1911), 6–11 and 101–103, and Farwell, *Early Recollections*, 7–10 and 43–44.

15. *YMCA Proceedings* (1868), 87–88 and 122–123. *YMCA Proceedings* (1869), 59 and 61. *Chicago Tribune*, October 1, 1867, 4; October 4, 1867, 3; and October 5, 1867, 4.

16. *Chicago Tribune*, March 28, 1869, 2 and 4.

17. *Chicago Tribune*, November 2, 1867, 4.

18. *Chicago Tribune*, April 4, 1869, 2; April 12, 1869, 4; April 13, 1869, 1; and April 25, 1869, 3.

19. Farwell, *Some Recollections*, 114–118.

20. *Tenth Census of the United States* (1880), vol. 19, *Report on the Social Statistics of Cities,* compiled by George E. Wanng, Jr. (Washington, D.C.: Government Printing Office, 1881), 491–92; Herman Kogan and Lloyd Wendt, *Chicago: A Pictorial History* (New York: Dutton, 1958), 115–30.

21. Letter from M. K. Jessup to John V. Farwell, January 17, 1872, Moody Papers, box 8, folder 95. See also in the same folder Moody's letters to Farwell, June 30, 1873, and May 7, 1874.

22. Finis Farr, *Chicago: A Personal History of America's Most American City* (New Rochelle, N.Y.: Arlington House, 1973), 110–125; and Bessie Louise Pierce, *A History of Chicago*, vol. 3, *The Rise of a Modern City, 1871–1893* (Chicago: University of Chicago Press, 1957), 23–41.

23. *Chicago Times*, October 7, 1876, 6; Justin E. Walsh, *To Print the News and Raise Hell* (Chapel Hill: University of North Carolina, 1968), 11–16; *Chicago Tribune*, October 18, 1876, 4; and Wendt, *Chicago Tribune*, 256–258.

24. Wilbur Storey, "The History of the *Chicago Times*," in Blanchard, *Discovery and Conquests of the North-west,* 476–477; *Chicago Times,* October 29, 1876, 6; and Mary Ronan, "Wilbur Fiske Storey and the *Chicago Times, 1861–1884*," master's thesis, Northwestern University, 1935, 3–5.

25. Stone, *Fifty Years a Journalist,* 21 and 65, and *Chicago Times,* January 21, 1877, 8.

26. Ronan, "Wilbur Fiske Storey," 25–27, and Walsh, *To Print the News,* 23–30.

27. *Chicago Times,* September 24, 1876, 1 and 2; September 28, 1876, 5; and September 29, 1876, 3.

28. *Chicago Post,* February 28, 1877, 2. Franc B. Wilkie, *Personal Reminiscences of Thirty-five Years of Journalism* (Chicago: F. J. Schulte, 1891), 97–99. *Chicago and Its Resources, Twenty Years After, 1871–1891* (Chicago: Chicago Times, 1892), 4–7.

29. *Chicago Tribune,* August 31, 1875, 4. Medill's June 1875 letter is cited by Wendt, *Chicago Tribune,* 253–254. By late summer Medill and William Bross, the president of the Tribune Company, abandoned their page one experiment.

30. *Chicago Tribune,* May 16, 1874, 1 and 2; August 31, 1875, 2 and 4; and November 6, 1875, 1. Kinsley, *Chicago Tribune,* 223–225.

31. *Chicago Tribune,* April 22, 1876, 1 and 4, and May 1, 1876, 4. Wendt, *Chicago Tribune,* 253–256. James O'Donnell Bennett, *Joseph Medill: A Brief Biography and an Appreciation* (Chicago: Chicago Tribune, 1947), 37–43.

32. Walter E. Ewert, "The History of the *Chicago Inter Ocean, 1872–1914*," master's thesis, Northwestern University, 1940, 24–26. A. T. Andreas, *History of Chicago,* vol. 3 (Chicago: A. T. Andreas, 1886), 699–700. Gilbert and Bryson, *Chicago and Its Makers,* 858.

33. *Chicago Inter-Ocean,* March 25, 1872, 2, and March 27, 1873, 2. Ewert, "History of the *Chicago Inter Ocean,"* 27–28. Willis J. Abbot, "Chicago Newspapers and Their Makers," *Review of Reviews* 11 (June 1895), 342–43.

34. James L. Regan, *Story of Chicago, In Connection with the Printing Business* (Chicago: Regan, 1912), 73–81. *A History of the City of Chicago* (Chicago: Inter-Ocean Publishing, 1900), 113–130. Thomas C. MacMillan, *The Inter-Ocean Curiosity Shop* (Chicago: Inter-Ocean Publishing, 1886), 18–27.

35. Ewert, "History of the *Chicago Inter Ocean,"* 29–31. Farwell, *Early Recollections,* 158 and 167.

36. *Chicago Inter-Ocean,* June 10, 1876, 9, and June 12, 1876, 2.

37. Stone, *Fifty Years a Journalist,* 38–43. David Paul Nord, "The Urbanization of Journalism in Chicago," *Journal of Urban History* 11 (August 1985), 411–41. Edwin Emery, *The Press And America: An Interpretive History of the Mass Media,* 3rd ed. (Englewood Cliffs, N.J.: Prentice-Hall, 1972), 298–300.

38. *Chicago Daily News,* December 20, 1876, 2. Stone, *Fifty Years a Journalist,* 52–54. David Paul Nord, "The Business Values of American Newspapers: The Nineteenth-Century Watershed in Chicago," *Journalism Quarterly* 61 (1984), 265–273.

39. Stone, *Fifty Years a Journalist,* 12–17 and 27. J. M. Buckley, *A History of Methodists in the United States* (New York: Scribner's, 1903), 281–300. Samuel B. Halliday and D. S. Gregory, *The Church in America and Its Baptisms of Fire* (New York: Funk and Wagnalls, 1896), 98–112.

40. Charles H. Dennis, *Victor Lawson: His Time and His Work* (New York: Green-

wood, 1968; originally 1935), 12 and 19. *Chicago Daily News*, November 1, 1876, 2. Letter from Victor Lawson to J. C. Bergstresser, February 28, 1878, Outgoing Letters, Personal Series, Victor Lawson Papers, Newberry Library, Chicago.

41. Letter from Lawson to John D. Nattles, publisher of the *Sunday School Times*, October 16, 1878, Lawson Papers. Dennis, *Victor Lawson*, 23–29, 56, and 67.

42. Letter from Lawson to George Stinson, October 25, 1878, Lawson Papers. Dennis, *Victor Lawson*, 39, 45, and 62–64.

43. Lawsons's letters to advertisers, February 28, 1878; March 8, 1878; June 18, 1878; and February 11, 1879, Victor Lawson Papers. His letter of February 7, 1879, to the U.S. Mint urges that pennies be shipped to Chicago.

44. *Chicago Daily News*, September 16, 1876, 1, and October 11, 1876, 2.

45. *Chicago Daily News*, June 2, 1876, 2; June 3, 1876, 2, and September 29, 1876, 1 and 2.

46. Moody's letters to McCormick, April 15, 1868; November 24, 1871; February 24, 1873; and May 1, 1873, Letters of D. L. Moody, vol. 1, Moodyanna Collection, Moody Bible Institute, Chicago. See also William T. Hutchinson, *Cyrus Hall McCormick, Harvest, 1856–1884* (New York: Appleton, 1935), 301–305.

47. *Chicago Daily News*, September 20, 1876, 2.

48. *Chicago Daily Journal*, June 19, 1876, 2.

49. Andrew Shuman, "History of the *Chicago Evening Journal*," in Blanchard, *Discovery and Conquests of the North-west*, 470–4. *Chicago Evening Journal*, June 5, 1876, 1.

50. Letter from Farwell to Moody, February 8, 1876, cited in Farwell, *Early Recollections*, 148–149. See also letter from Farwell to J. W. Dean, February 15, 1876, cited at 153–54, and letters from Farwell to Moody, July 25, 1876, and July 26, 1876, cited at 159–161.

51. Letter from Farwell to E. W. Blatchford, September 6, 1876, cited in Farwell, *Early Recollections*, 163–164. See also his letter to Major Cole, July 27, 1876, cited at 161–162.

52. *Chicago Evening Journal*, June 3, 1876, 6, and September 30, 1876, 2.

53. *Chicago Inter-Ocean*, May 30, 1876, 2.

54. *Chicago Inter-Ocean*, June 1, 1876, 1 and 8.

55. Sunderland's remarks of June 11 were widely quoted in Chicago's press. For background, see Jabez Thomas Sunderland, *Orthodoxy and Revivalism* (New York: James Miller, 1877), 42–58.

56. *Chicago Inter-Ocean*, June 13, 1876, 3, and July 1, 1876, 3. *Chicago Daily News*, June 10, 1876, 1. *Chicago Evening Journal*, June 12, 1876, 5.

57. *Chicago Tribune*, June 11, 1876, 9; August 6, 1876, 13; August 13, 1876, 13; and September 23, 1876, 9. W. H. Daniels, *D. L. Moody and His Work* (Hartford, Conn.: American, 1876) became a basic reference work on Moody's early evangelistic campaigns. He would follow it the next year with *Moody: His Words, Work, and Workers* (New York: Nelson and Phillips, 1877).

58. *Chicago Inter- Ocean*, July 7, 1876, 8. *Chicago Daily News*, June 6, 1876, 2, and June 20, 1876, 1.

59. *Chicago Daily Journal*, July 15, 1876, 5, and August 11, 1876, 4. *Chicago Inter-Ocean*, August 12, 1876, 6. The story of the church panic appeared in the *Springfield Republican*, August 23, 1876, 1, and was repeated in the *Chicago Tribune*, September 3, 1876, 13.

60. Letter from Farwell to E. W. Blatchford, head of the executive committee, September 6, 1876, cited in Farwell, *Early Recollections*, 163–164.

61. Cree, "Mr. Moody as an Evangelist," 22–23. For Cree's involvement in publicizing Moody's big-city campaigns, see D. L. Moody Papers, YMCA Archives, University of Minnesota, St. Paul, folder 2.

62. *Chicago Inter-Ocean*, September 23, 1876, 10. *Chicago Evening Journal*, September 29, 1876, 4. Cree, "Mr. Moody as an Evangelist," 23–24.

63. *Chicago Times*, December 7, 1876, 5. *Chicago Tribune*, October 12, 1876, 1. *Chicago Inter-Ocean*, September 25, 1876, 4.

64. *Chicago* Times, September 24, 1876, 1. *Chicago Tribune*, October 20, 1876, 3.

65. *Chicago Inter-Ocean*, September 30, 1876, 2. *Chicago Times*, September 26, 1876, 3, and September 28, 1876, 5. *Chicago Daily News*, September 26, 1876, 2, and September 29, 1876, 2.

66. *Chicago Tribune*, September 25, 1876, 3. *Chicago Daily News*, September 30, 1876, 1.

67. *Advance*, September 21, 1876, 40. *Standard*, September 21, 1876, 2. *Chicago Times,* September 24, 1876, 2. *Everybody's Paper* 9, 2 (1877), 6.

68. *Chicago Tribune*, September 30, 1876, 1, and October 2, 1876, 1. *Chicago Inter-Ocean*, September 30, 1876, 1. *Chicago Daily News*, September 30, 1876, 1, and October 2, 1876, 1.

69. *Chicago Times*, September 29, 1876, 3; October 1, 1876, 1; and October 2, 1876, 4.

70. *Chicago Inter-Ocean*, October 2, 1876, 1 and 2. *Chicago Evening Journal*, October 2, 1876, 1. *Chicago Daily News*, October 2, 1876, 1 and 2.

71. *Chicago Inter-Ocean*, October 2, 1876, 2. *Chicago Tribune*, October 2, 1876, 2. *Chicago Times*, October 2, 1876, 1.

72. *Chicago Times*, October 2, 1876, 2. *Chicago Evening* Journal, October 2, 1876, 2. Chicago *Tribune*, October 2, 1876, 2 and 4.

73. *Chicago Times*, October 2, 1876, 4; October 16, 1876, 4; and December 31, 1876, 8.

74. *Chicago Tribune*, October 3, 1876, 5; October 4, 1876, 5; and October 7, 1876, 7. *Chicago Inter-Ocean*, October 3, 1876, 4. Ewert, "History of the *Chicago Inter Ocean,"* 165–166.

75. *Chicago Inter-Ocean*, October 3, 1876, 4; October 21, 1876, 2; and November 6, 1876, 4

76. *Chicago Inter-Ocean*, October 21, 1876, 1 and 2; November 1, 1876, 2; and December 9, 1876, 2.

77. *Chicago Inter-Ocean*, October 2, 1876, 1 and 4; December 8, 1876, 1; and December 9, 1876, 1.

78. *Chicago Daily News*, September 26, 1876, 2; October 3, 1876, 1; and October 4, 1876, 1. Letter from Lawson to Storey, February 8, 1879, Lawson Papers, Dennis, *Victor Lawson,* 24–25 and 36–37.

79. *Chicago Daily News*, October 14, 1876, 1; November 4, 1876, 1; and December 18, 1876, 2.

80. *Chicago Evening Journal*, September 30, 1876, 2; October 2, 1876, 4; and October 5, 1876, 4.

81. *Chicago Evening Journal*, November 25, 1876, 2 and 6. Cree, "Mr. Moody as an Evangelist," 27–28.

82. Cree, "Mr. Moody as an Evangelist," 29. *Chicago Tribune,* October 24, 1876, 7, and October 25, 1876, 2. *Chicago Inter*-Ocean, October 26, 1876, 2. Chicago *Daily News,* November 24, 1876, 2.

83. *Chicago Tribune,* October 18, 1876, 5; October 27, 1876, 8; and October 28, 1876, 7.

84. *Chicago Tribune,* October 24, 1876, 1, and November 15, 1876, 2. *Chicago Inter-Ocean,* October 27, 1876, 2. *Chicago Evening Journal,* November 14, 1876, 2.

85. *Chicago Tribune,* October 15, 1876, 3; October 19, 1876, 5; and November 7, 1876, 5.

86. *Chicago Times,* November 26, 1876, 8; December 18, 1876, 4; and December 27, 1876, 4.

87. *Chicago Tribune,* October 18, 1876, 4.

88. D. L. Moody, letter to his mother, October 12, 1876, D. L. Moody letters, vol. 1, Moodyanna Collection, Moody Bible Institute, Chicago. The *Inter-Ocean's* dramatic rendering of the event appeared on October 7, 1876, 2.

89. *Chicago Inter-Ocean,* October 7, 1876, 2, and *Chicago Tribune,* October 7, 1876, 7.

90. *Chicago Tribune,* October 8, 1876, 4, and October 9, 1876, 8. *Chicago Inter-Ocean,* October 11, 1876, 2, and October 13, 1876, 1. *Chicago Times,* October 13, 1876, 5.

91. *Chicago Tribune,* October 8, 1876, 4. Dedmon, *Great Enterprises,* 39–40. *Chicago Evening* Journal, October 28, 1876, 5. (Congregational) *Advance,* October 26, 1876, 123 and 126–127. *Chicago Times,* October 30, 1876, 1.

92. *Chicago Times,* October 16, 1876, 4, and October 31, 1876, 5. *Chicago Inter-Ocean,* October 25, 1876, 1. *Chicago Tribune,* October 20, 1876, 3, and October 31, 1876, 5.

93. *Chicago Times,* November 14, 1876, 8. Cree, "Mr. Moody as an Evangelist," 29. *Tabernacle News,* November 18, 1876, 1 and 3–4, available in the Moodyanna collection, Moody Bible Institute, Chicago.

94. *Chicago Inter-Ocean,* November 22, 1876, 1 and 2. *Chicago Tribune,* November 22, 1876, 1.

95. *Chicago Times,* November 24, 1876, 5. *Chicago Tribune,* November 24, 1876, 2.

96. *Chicago Evening Journal,* December 13, 1876, 4. *Chicago Times,* December 14, 1876, 4. *Chicago Tribune,* December 14, 1876, 7.

97. *Chicago Times,* December 15, 1876, 4 and 5. *Chicago Tribune,* December 15, 1876, 7. *Chicago Inter-Ocean,* December 15, 1876, 2.

98. *Chicago Evening Journal,* December 15, 1876, 4. *Chicago Daily News,* December 14, 1876, 2. *Chicago Inter-Ocean,* December 15, 1876, 2. *Chicago Times,* December 15, 1876, 5.

99. (Congregational) *Advance,* December 14, 1876, 256. *Chicago Tribune,* December 17, 1876, 4. *Chicago Inter-Ocean,* December 18, 1876, 2.

100. *Chicago Times,* December 17, 1876, 5. The newspaper's numbers reflect three daily services led by Moody over 10 weeks.

101. *Chicago Evening Journal,* December 23, 1876, 2. *Chicago Tribune,* December 25, 1876, 2.

102. D. W. Whittle, ed., *Memoirs of Philip P. Bliss* (New York: A. S. Barnes, 1877),

15–35. Daniels, *Moody: His Words, Work, and Workers,* 489–490. Nason, *Lives of the Eminent American Evangelists,* 263–278.

103. (Congregational) *Advance,* December 21, 1876, 277–278. *Chicago Tribune,* December 18, 1876, 2. *Chicago Times,* December 18, 1876, 3.

104. M. Laird Simons, *Holding the Fort* (Philadelphia: Porter and Coates, 1877), xvi–xiviii. Whittle, *Memoirs,* 75–90. (Congregational) *Advance,* December 7, 1876, 239 and 242–243.

105. P. P. Bliss and Ira D. Sankey, *Gospel Hymns and Sacred Songs* (New York: Biglow and Main, 1875). Letter from Bliss to Ira Sankey, August 11, 1876, Letters from 1876, Moody Papers, box 8, folder 97.

106. Letter from J. H. Vincent, conductor of the Chautauqua Assembly, to Whittle, January 4, 1877, in Whittle, *Memoirs,* 72–75. Letters of Bliss to Whittle, May 11, 1876; August 22, 1876; and September 18, 1876, in Whittle, *Memoirs,* 75, 270, and 271.

107. Ira D. Sankey, *My Life and the Story of the Gospel Hymns* (Philadelphia: Sunday School Times, 1906), 79–81 and 124–126. Whittle, *Memoirs,* 75–76.

108. *Chicago Tribune,* October 18, 1876, 5. *Chicago Daily News,* October 26, 1876, 4, and October 28, 1876, 4. *Chicago Inter-Ocean,* November 4, 1876, 2. Whittle, *Memoirs,* 81–82.

109. George E. Morgan, *R. C. Morgan: His Life and Times* (London: Pickering and Inglies, 1908), 169–171. William Moody, *The Life of Dwight L. Moody* (New York: Fleming H. Revell, 1900), 131–143.

110. Whittle's diary entries for December 1876, in Whittle, *Memoirs,* 86–87. Bliss, letter to Whittle, December 17, in Whittle, *Memoirs,* 272. See also Cree, "Mr. Moody as an Evangelist," 30.

111. Whittle, *Memoirs,* 91–93. *Chicago Evening Telegraph,* December 27, 1876, 2. *Chicago Inter-Ocean,* December 27, 1876, 3.

112. *Chicago Times,* December 30, 1876, 3, and January 6, 1877, 1. Whittle, *Memoirs,* 94.

113. *Chicago Inter-Ocean,* December 30, 1876, 6. Nason, *Lives of the Eminent American Evangelists,* 277–279. Cree, "Mr. Moody as an Evangelist," 30–31.

114. *Chicago Inter-Ocean,* January 1, 1877, 1. *Chicago Times,* January 3, 1877, 1. *Chicago Tribune,* January 1, 1877, 1.

115. *Cleveland Leader,* December 30, 1876, 1 and 2. *Erie Dispatch,* December 31, 1876, 1. *Chicago Inter-Ocean,* January 1, 1877, 1. *Chicago Times,* December 31, 1876, 1. *New York Herald,* January 1, 1877, 1.

116. Stephen D. Peet, *The Ashtabula Disaster* (Chicago: J. S. Goodman and Louis Lloyd, 1877), 183–196. Whittle, *Memoirs,* 94. *Chicago Times,* December 31, 1876, 1. *New York Herald,* December 31, 1876, 1.

117. *Chicago Times,* December 31, 1876, 3, and January 1, 1877, 1. *Chicago Daily News,* January 1, 1877, 1. *Chicago Evening Journal,* January 2, 1877, 1. *Chicago Tribune,* January 1, 1877, 1. *Chicago Inter-Ocean,* January 1, 1877, 1.

118. *Chicago Tribune,* January 1, 1877, 1, and January 3, 1877, 5. *Chicago Inter-Ocean,* January 1, 1877, and January 2, 1877, 1. *Chicago Daily News,* January 2, 1877, 2. *Chicago Times,* January 2, 1877, 1.

119. *Chicago Times,* January 1, 1877, 2. *Chicago Daily News,* January 2, 1877, 1. *Chicago Inter-Ocean,* January 1, 1877, 5.

120. *Chicago Tribune*, January 1, 1877, 4. *Chicago Evening Journal*, January 2, 1877, 4. Whittle, *Memoirs*, 94–95.

121. (Baptist) *Standard*, December 28, 1876, 1, and cited in *Chicago Times*, December 31, 1876, 5. (Congregational) *Advance*, December 7, 1876, 237–238; December 28, 1876, 302–303; and January 18, 1877, 357–358.

122. *Chicago Inter-Ocean*, January 2, 1877, 3; January 15, 1877, 2; and January 17, 1877, 4.

123. *Chicago Tribune*, January 6, 1877, 7. *Chicago Times*, January 4, 1877, 3, and January 6, 1877, 9. *Chicago Inter-Ocean*, January 6, 1877, 7. Whittle, *Memoirs*, 366–367.

124. *Chicago Times*, January 1, 1877, 4, and January 13, 1877, 2. *Chicago Evening Journal*, January 13, 1877, 2, and January 15, 1877, 4. *Chicago Daily News*, January 15, 1877, 2.

125. *Chicago Times*, January 16, 1877, 1 and 5. *Chicago Inter-Ocean*, January 16, 1877, 8, and January 17, 1877, 2.

126. *Chicago Tribune*, January 18, 1877, 4. *Chicago Evening Journal*, January 17, 1877, 4. *Chicago Daily News*, January 15, 1877, 2.

127. *Chicago Evening Journal*, January 18, 1877, 4. *Chicago Inter-Ocean*, January 17, 1877, 4.

128. *Chicago Times*, December 31, 1876, 5; January 1, 1877, 4; and January 21, 1877, 2.

129. Farwell, *Early Recollections*, 148–149. *Chicago Tribune*, December 16, 1876, 6; December 21, 1876, 3; and December 24, 1876, 13.

130. *Chicago Times*, January 21, 1877, 8.

131. *Chicago Tribune*, November 15, 1876, 7.

132. (Congregational) *Advance*, November 16, 1876, 178.

133. Elizabeth L. Eisenstein, *The Printing Press as an Agent of Change: Communications and Cultural Transformation in Early Modern Europe* (Cambridge, England: Cambridge University Press, 1979), 12–25.

134. *Chicago Tribune*, January 17, 1877, 7. *Chicago Times*, January 17, 1877, 5. *Chicago Inter-Ocean*, January 17, 1877, 2.

135. Farwell, *Early Recollections*, 167–168.

136. The *Inter-Ocean* of November 9, 1876, 4, is "thrilled" at the sight of "epidemic religion." The *Times* of October 2, 1876, 1, saw the harvest and the harvesters very differently.

137. McLaren's criticism of the revival appears in a December 1876 issue of the *Diocese* and is cited in *Chicago Times*, December 24, 1876, 5.

138. *Chicago Tribune*, December 23, 1899, 1 and 2. *Chicago Daily News*, December 23, 1899, 4.

139. *Chicago Inter-Ocean*, December 23, 1899, 6. *Chicago Journal*, December 23, 1899, 4. *Chicago Times-Herald*, December 23, 1899, 2.

140. *Chicago Times*, December 3, 1876, 5, and December 24, 1876, 5.

7. "IT IS A MARVEL TO MANY PEOPLE"

1. "*The Boston Daily Globe* Announcement," preface to Dwight L. Moody, *To All People: Comprising Sermons, Bible Readings, Temperance Addresses, and Prayer-meeting Talks, Delivered in the Boston Tabernacle* (New York: E. B. Treat, 1877).

2. Rev. Joseph Cook, "Evangelism in Boston," in *To All People*, 8–9.

3. William R. Moody, *The Life of Dwight L. Moody* (New York: Fleming H. Revell, 1900), 291–294.

4. William R. Moody, *D. L. Moody* (New York: Macmillan, 1930), 280–286.

5. Walter Osborn, archivist of the Moodyanna Collection at the Moody Bible Institute, Chicago, has developed an itinerary of Moody's mission to New England based on notes, letters, sermons, and diaries of Moody in that collection.

6. *Boston Globe*, January 28, 1877, 1.

7. Samuel W. Dike, "A Study of New England Revivals," *American Journal of Sociology* 15 (November 1909), 361–378. Perry Miller, *Errand into the Wilderness* (New York: Harper and Row, 1964), 151–163.

8. George Whitefield, *George Whitefield's Journals* (London: Banner of Truth Trust, 1960); John Gillies, *Historical Collections of Accounts of Revival* (Fairfield, Pa.: Banner of Truth Trust, 1981; originally 1754); Joshua Bradley, *Accounts of Religious Revivals in Many Parts of the United States from 1815 to 1818* (Albany: G. J. Loomis, 1819); Calvin Colton, *History and Character of American Revivals of Religion* (New York: AMS Press, 1973; originally 1832); and Bennet Tyler, *New England Revivals* (Boston: Massachusetts Sabbath School Society, 1846).

9. Jonathan Edwards, *The Works of President Edwards*, vol. 4 (New York: Converse, 1840), 70–72, and Jonathan Edwards, *Discourses on Various Subjects, Nearly Concerning the Great Affair of the Soul's Eternal Salvation* (Boston: S. Kneeland and T. Green, 1738), ii–iii.

10. C. C. Goen, ed., *The Works of Jonathan Edwards*, vol. 4 (New Haven: Yale University Press, 1972), 222–225. Harry S. Stout and Peter S. Onuf, "James Davenport and the Great Awakening in New London," *Journal of American History* 70 (1983), 556–578. Michael J. Crawford, *Seasons of Grace* (New York: Oxford University Press, 1991), 184–185. James West Davidson, *The Logic of Millennial Thought: Eighteenth-Century New England* (New Haven: Yale University Press, 1977), 123–138.

11. J. William T. Youngs, *God's Messengers: Religious Leadership in Colonial New England, 1700–1750* (Baltimore: Johns Hopkins University Pres, 1976), 163–185. Marilyn J. Westerkamp, *Triumph of the Laity: Scots-Irish Piety and the Great Awakening* (New York: Oxford University Press, 1988), 138–157. James Walsh, "The Great Awakening in the First Congregational Church of Woodbury, Connecticut," *William and Mary Quarterly* 28 (1971), 543–562.

12. Arnold A. Dallimore, *George Whitefield: The Life and Times of the Great Evangelist of the Eighteenth-Century Revival*, vol. 1 (London: Banner of Truth Trust, 1971), 149–163. Frank Lambert, *"Pedlar in Divinity": George Whitefield and the Transatlantic Revivals, 1737–1770* (Princeton: Princeton University Press, 1994), 6–9. Harry S. Stout, *The Divine Dramatist: George Whitefield and the Rise of Modern Evangelicalism* (Grand Rapids, Mich.: Eerdman, 1991), 173–191. Carey Kinsolving, "The Preacher and the Printer: An Evaluation of Benjamin Franklin's Coverage of George Whitefield," paper presented at the annual meeting of the Association for Education in Journalism and Mass Communication, Kansas City, Missouri, August 12, 1993.

13. Robert Currie, "A Micro-theory of Methodist Growth," *Proceedings of the Wesley Historical Society* 36 (1967), 65–73. Susan Durden, "A Study of the First Evangelical Magazines, 1740–1748," *Journal of Ecclesiastical History* 27 (1976), 255–275. Susan O'Brien, "A Transatlantic Community of Saints: The Great Awakening and the First Evangelical Network, 1735–1755," *American Historical Review* 91 (December

1986), 811–832. Umphrey Lee, *John Wesley and Modern Religion* (Nashville: Cokesbury, 1936), 11–26.

14. Moody, *Life of Dwight L. Moody*, 291–292. Moody, *D. L. Moody*, 280–281. Richard K. Curtis, *They Called Him Mister Moody* (Garden City, N.J.: Doubleday, 1962), 263–264.

15. Elias Nason, *The Lives of the Eminent American Evangelists Dwight Lyman Moody and Ira David Sankey* (Boston: B. B. Russell, 1877), 204–206. *Boston Journal*, May 9, 1876, 2. *Boston Evening Traveller*, June 29, 1876, 3.

16. J. C. Pollock, *Moody: A Biographical Portrait of the Pacesetter in Modern Mass Evangelism* (Grand Rapids, Mich.: Zondervan, 1963), 196–198. *Boston Evening Transcript*, September 14, 1876, 2. *Boston Post*, November 7, 1876, 3.

17. *Zion's Herald* (Methodist), January 11, 1877, 11–12. *Congregationalist and Boston Recorder*, January 10, 1877, 12. Henry Drummond, "Mr. Moody: Some Impressions and Facts," *McClure's* 4 (January 1895), 188. Lyman Abbott, *Silhouettes of My Contemporaries* (Garden City, N.J.: Doubleday, Page, 1921), 204–205.

18. Frank Grenville Beardsley, *A History of American Revivals* (New York: American Tract Society, 1912), 271–273. *Boston Transcript*, January 22, 1877, 1.

19. I.A.M. Cumming, *Tabernacle Sketches* (Boston: Times, 1877), 10–11. Nason, *Lives of the Eminent American Evangelists,* 204–205.

20. Moody, *To All People*, 181–182. Cumming, *Tabernacle Sketches,* 14–15. *Boston Globe*, January 22, 1877, 1. *Tabernacle News*, January 29, 1877, 1–2.

21. Edwin Emery, *The Press and America,* 2nd ed. (Englewood Cliffs, N.J.: Prentice-Hall, 1962), 356, 380, and 417. *Boston Sunday Post*, January 7, 1891, 22.

22. Cumming, *Tabernacle Sketches,* 72 and 76.

23. Biographical data on the *Globe*'s staff and working regimen is in a vertical file on the *Boston Globe* and its history maintained at the Boston Public Library.

24. *Boston Sunday Post*, January 7, 1891, 22–23. *Boston Daily Globe*, October 29, 1890, 1–2.

25. "The *Boston Herald*," *Bay State Monthly* 2 (October 1884), 28–30. Biographical data on the *Herald*'s staff, its working relationships, and history is on file at the Boston Public Library.

26. *Boston Sunday Post*, February 4, 1894, 21–22. See also Newspaper File, Boston Public Library.

27. *The Boston Herald and Its History* (Boston: Herald Press, 1878), 55–61. *Boston Herald*, February 9, 1878, 1.

28. *Boston Herald*, February 4, 1877, 4.

29. The words are those of Minot J. Savage, pastor of Boston's Church of the Unity, and reflect the general trend of Unitarian opposition. See *Boston Herald*, February 5, 1877, 1.

30. *Boston Herald,* February 8, 1877, 4; February 12, 1877, 2; and February 25, 1877, 4.

31. Simeon N. D. North, *History and Present Condition of the Newspaper and Periodical Press of the United States* (Washington, D.C.: Government Printing Office, 1884), 3–16. *Boston Herald History*, 56–57.

32. *Boston Journal*, January 25, 1877, 2; January 26, 1877, 1, and January 27, 1877, 2. *Boston Sunday Post*, January 28, 1894, 22–23, and Newspaper File, Boston Public Library.

33. *Boston Daily Advertiser*, January 29, 1877, 2. *Boston Daily Post*, January 21, 1894, 17, and Newspaper File, Boston Public Library.

34. *Boston Daily Post*, semicentennial supplement, November 8, 1881, 1, and January 29, 1877, 3. See also Newspaper File, Boston Public Library.

35. *Boston Evening Traveller*, April 14, 1859, 2. *Springfield* (Massachusetts) *Union*, June 11, 1891, 1.

36. See the paper's account of January 25, 1877, 2.

37. *Boston Evening Traveller,* January 27, 1877, 1.

38. *Boston Transcript*, July 24, 1830, 2, and April 26, 1941, 6. Charles W. Morton, *Boston Evening Transcript: It Has Its Charms* (Philadelphia: Lippincott, 1960), 128–139.

39. *Boston Transcript*, January 27, 1877, 4, and February 3, 1877, 4.

40. *Boston Transcript*, January 27, 1877, 3 and 4. Joseph Edgar Chamberlin, *The Boston Transcript: The First Hundred Years* (Boston: Houghton Mifflin, 1930), 3–13.

41. The *Transcript* targeted women readers. See the retrospective on the *Transcript* in the *Boston Sunday Post,* January 14, 1894, 17.

42. *Boston Transcript*, February 17, 1877, 4.

43. *Congregationalist*, January 17, 1877, 20.

44. *Zion's Herald*, February 1, 1877, 86.

45. Appearing in the *Boston Sunday Times*, March 11, 1877, and cited in Cumming, *Tabernacle Sketches*, 15.

46. *Boston Evening Traveller*, April 30, 1877, 2.

47. *Christian Register*, April 28, 1877, 2.

48. *Christian Register*, February 10, 1877, 2, and March 31, 1877, 2.

49. *Christian Register*, March 3, 1877, 2, and February 3, 1877, 2.

50. *Christian Register*, February 24, 1877, 2 and 3; March 10, 1877, 2 and 3; and March 31, 1877, 2.

51. *Christian Register*, March 31, 1877, 2 and 3, and April 28, 1877, 2.

52. *Boston Transcript*, April 28, 1877, 6.

53. *Boston Transcript*, February 17, 1877, 4; February 19, 1877, 2; March 3, 1877, 5; and March 10, 1877, 6.

54. *Boston Transcript*, February 3, 1877, 4; March 31, 1877, 6; and April 28, 1877, 6.

55. *Boston Transcript*, March 3, 1877, 5; March 26, 1877, 2; and April 28, 1877, 6.

56. *Pilot*, February 17, 1877, 4.

57. *Herald* reporters gained access to the inquiry room by posing as potential converts. See *Boston Herald*, February 4, 1877, 4; February 5, 1877, 1 and 2; and February 8, 1877, 2.

58. *Boston Herald*, February 11, 1877, 2, and February 27, 1877, 2.

59. *Boston Herald*, February 4, 1877, 2; February 8, 1877, 2 and 3; and February 11, 1877, 2.

60. *Boston Herald*, February 12, 1877, 2, and March 25, 1877, 2 and 4.

61. *Boston Herald*, April 22, 1877, 5.

62. Whitman's six-stanza poem "The Revival," dated "February 22, 1877, from Camden," first appears in the *Sunday Times*, February 25, 1877, and is reprinted in Cumming, *Tabernacle Sketches*, 33–34.

63. The argument of the *Examiner and Chronicle* is cited in *Congregationalist*, February 7, 1877, 43.

64. *New Haven Palladium*, February 8, 1877, 2.

65. *Congregationalist*, February 7, 1877, 44.

66. *Vermont Chronicle*, February 14, 1877, 2. *Worcester Gazette*, February 15, 1877, 3.

67. *Zion's Herald*, February 15, 1877, 2, and February 22, 1877, 2. *Independent*, April 18, 1877, 3. *Presbyterian Banner*, February 1, 1877, 3. *Springfield Republican*, May 1, 1877, 2.

68. Cumming, *Tabernacle Sketches*, 72–73.

69. *Boston Journal*, April 2, 1877, 1; April 5, 1877, 1; April 11, 1877, 1; and April 16, 1877, 1.

70. *Boston Evening Traveller*, April 2, 1877, 1; April 5, 1877, 1 and 2; April 6, 1 and 2; and April 7, 1877, 1. *Boston Globe*, April 2, 1877, 2; April 4, 1877, 2; and April 10, 1877, 2.

71. *Boston Evening Traveller*, April 13, 1877, 1, and April 28, 1877, 1. *Boston Journal*, March 27, 1877, 1, and April 19, 1877, 1.

72. *Boston Journal*, April 28, 1877, 2, and *Boston Globe*, April 25, 1877, 2.

73. *Zion's Herald*, April 19, 1877, 126, and May 3, 1877, 140. *Congregationalist*, April 25, 1877, 132.

74. *Zion's Herald*, April 12, 1877, 116; *Congregationalist*, April 11, 1877, 112; *Boston Globe*, April 1, 1877, 2, and April 23, 1877, 2; *Boston Journal*, April 22, 1877, 1 and 2, and April 24, 1877, 1 and 2.

75. *Boston Evening Transcript*, April 28, 1877, 6. *Christian Register*, April 28, 1877, 2.

76. *Christian Register*, March 31, 1877, 2. *Boston Herald*, April 22, 1877, 2.

77. *Congregationalist*, May 2, 1877, 140. Edward Leigh Pell, *D. L. Moody: His Life, His Work, His Words* (Richmond: B. F. Johnson, 1900), 170–172.

78. *Boston Daily Advertiser*, April 26, 1877, 2. *Boston Journal*, April 26, 1877, 1.

79. *Boston Journal*, April 30, 1877, 1. *Boston Evening Traveller*, April 30, 1877, 1. *Boston Post*, April 30, 1877, 1.

80. *Boston Transcript*, February 24, 1877, 4. *Boston Herald*, February 11, 1877, 2.

81. *Congregationalist*, April 11, 1877, 114.

82. *Zion's Herald*, April 12, 1877, 116, and April 19, 1877, 128.

83. Dike, "New England Revivals," 368, 369, and 371.

84. *Boston Globe*, December 22, 1899, 1.

85. *Boston Evening Transcript*, December 22, 1899, 1.

86. *Boston Evening Transcript*, December 23, 1899, 16.

87. *Boston Herald*, December 25, 1899, 4.

88. *Boston Advertiser*, January 9, 1900, 4.

89. *Boston Advertiser*, December 25, 1899, 1.

90. *Boston Herald*, January 1, 1900, 2,

91. These appreciations are in the Moodyanna collection, Moody Bible Institute, Chicago.

92. *Springfield Daily Republican*, December 23, 1899, 6.

93. These appreciations also are in the Moodyanna collection.

94. *Foxboro Reporter*, January 6, 1900, 2. *Quincy Daily Whig*, January 10, 1900, 4.

95. *Haverhill* (Massachusetts) *Gazette*, January 11, 1900, 1. The paper cites an undated editorial of the *Boston Journal* in its summary of church growth.

96. Characteristic of the supplements is the appreciation in the *Boston Journal* on December 23, 1899, that includes long narratives of Moody's life and pictures of his study and his schools for religious training in East Northfield. Many papers urge pastors to draw moral lessons from Moody's life. See the *Natick* (Massachusetts) *Bulletin*, January 12, 1900, 2; *Rockland* (Massachusetts) *Standard*, January 12, 1900, 3; and *Greenfield* (Massachusetts) *Gazette*, January 13, 1900, 1.

97. *Boston Journal*, December 23, 1899, 2.

98. *Boston Transcript*, December 30, 1899, 2.

99. *Boston Transcript*, December 23, 1899, 2.

100. An appreciation from a December 1899 edition of *Zion's Herald* appears in the *Boston Transcript*, December 30, 1899, 2.

101. *Boston Globe*, December 23, 1899, 2.

8. THE BEGINNING

1. *Chicago Tribune*, December 23, 1899, 10.

2. *New York Evening Post*, December 23, 1899, 18. *Chicago Tribune*, December 23, 1899, 10.

3. Billy Graham, *Just As I Am: The Autobiography of Billy Graham* (New York: HarperCollins, 1997), 208–214. Billy Graham, "Crusade Questions," *Moody Monthly* (October 1954), 32–33.

4. Letter from Billy Graham to ministry supporters, September 2000, Billy Graham Evangelistic Association, Minneapolis. *Minneapolis Star-Tribune*, June 16, 1996, section 9, 1–2.

5. David F. Burg, *Chicago's White City of 1893* (Lexington: University of Kentucky, 1976), 37–42. Reid Badger, *The Great American Fair: The World's Columbian Exposition and American Culture* (Chicago: Nelson-Hall, 1979), 111–119. H. M. Higinbotham, *Report of the President to the Board of Directors of the World's Columbian Exposition* (Chicago: Rand McNally, 1898), 33–37. Charles Moore, *Daniel H. Burnham: Architect Planner of Cities* (New York: Da Capo Press, 1968), 23–35.

6. *Springfield* (Massachusetts) *Daily Republican*, December 23, 1899, 6–7. *Daily News* (London), December 23, 1899, 3.

7. *Belfast News-Letter*, December 23, 1899, 5. *Kansas City Star*, December 22, 1899, 1.

8. D. L. Moody, *New Sermons, Addresses and Prayers* (St. Louis: N. D. Thompson, 1877), 33–34.

9. Bruce J. Evensen, " 'Expecting a Blessing of Unusual Magnitude': Moody, Mass Media, and Gilded Age Revival," *Journalism History* 24 (Spring 1998), 27–36.

10. Wilbur Storey, publisher of the *Chicago Times*, defends the "saucepan press" for straining to report news that suited every palate. *Chicago Times*, October 2, 1876, 4; October 16, 1876, 4; and October 31, 1876, 8.

Index